STAR WARS

DARTH VADER AND THE LOST COMMAND

THE RISE OF THE EMPIRE
(1,000–0 YEARS BEFORE THE BATTLE OF YAVIN)

AFTER THE SEEMING final defeat of the Sith, the Republic enters a state of complacency. In the waning years of the Republic, the Senate rife with corruption, the ambitious Senator Palpatine causes himself to be elected Supreme Chancellor. This is the era of the prequel trilogy.

The events in this story take place approximately nineteen years before the Battle of Yavin.

STAR WARS®

DARTH VADER AND THE LOST COMMAND

Script
HADEN BLACKMAN

Pencils
RICK LEONARDI

Inks
DAN GREEN

Colors
WES DZIOBA

Lettering
MICHAEL HEISLER

Front cover art
MICHAEL KUTSCHE

DARK HORSE BOOKS®

president and publisher
MIKE RICHARDSON

editor
RANDY STRADLEY

assistant editor
FREDDYE LINS

collection designer
TINA ALESSI

special thanks to JANN MOORHEAD, DAVID ANDERMAN, TROY ALDERS, LELAND CHEE, SUE ROSTONI, and CAROL ROEDER at LUCAS LICENSING

STAR WARS®: DARTH VADER AND THE LOST COMMAND

This volume collects *Star Wars: Darth Vader and the Lost Command* #1–#5, originally published by Dark Horse Comics.

Published by Dark Horse Books
A division of Dark Horse Comics, Inc.
10956 SE Main Street
Milwaukie, OR 97222

DarkHorse.com | StarWars.com

To find a comics shop in your area, call the Comic Shop Locator Service toll-free at 1-888-266-4226

Library of Congress Cataloging-in-Publication Data

Blackman, W. Haden.
Star Wars : Darth Vader and the lost command / script, Haden Blackman ; pencils, Rick Leonardi ; inks, Dan Green ; colors, Wes Dzioba ; lettering, Michael Heisler ; front cover art, Michael Kutsche ; back cover art, Tsuneo Sanda. -- 1st ed.
     p. cm.
Summary: "Darth Vader is tasked with a mission to locate a lost expeditionary force which is led by the son of Vader's rising nemesis, Moff Tarkin."--Provided by publisher.
ISBN 978-1-59582-778-4 (alk. paper)
1. Graphic novels. 2. Science fiction. I. Kutsche, Michael, ill. II. Sanda, Tsuneo, ill. III. Title.
PZ7.7.B555Ssm 2011
741.5'973--dc23
                         2011020060

First edition: November 2011
ISBN 978-1-59582-778-4

10 9 8 7 6 5 4 3 2 1
Printed at Midas Printing International, Ltd., Huizhou, China

MIKE RICHARDSON President and Publisher NEIL HANKERSON Executive Vice President TOM WEDDLE Chief Financial Officer RANDY STRADLEY Vice President of Publishing MICHAEL MARTENS Vice President of Book Trade Sales ANITA NELSON Vice President of Business Affairs MICHA HERSHMAN Vice President of Marketing DAVID SCROGGY Vice President of Product Development DALE LAFOUNTAIN Vice President of Information Technology DARLENE VOGEL Senior Director of Print, Design, and Production KEN LIZZI General Counsel DAVEY ESTRADA Editorial Director SCOTT ALLIE Senior Managing Editor CHRIS WARNER Senior Books Editor DIANA SCHUTZ Executive Editor CARY GRAZZINI Director of Print and Development LIA RIBACCHI Art Director CARA NIECE Director of Scheduling

Illustration by TSUNEO SANDA

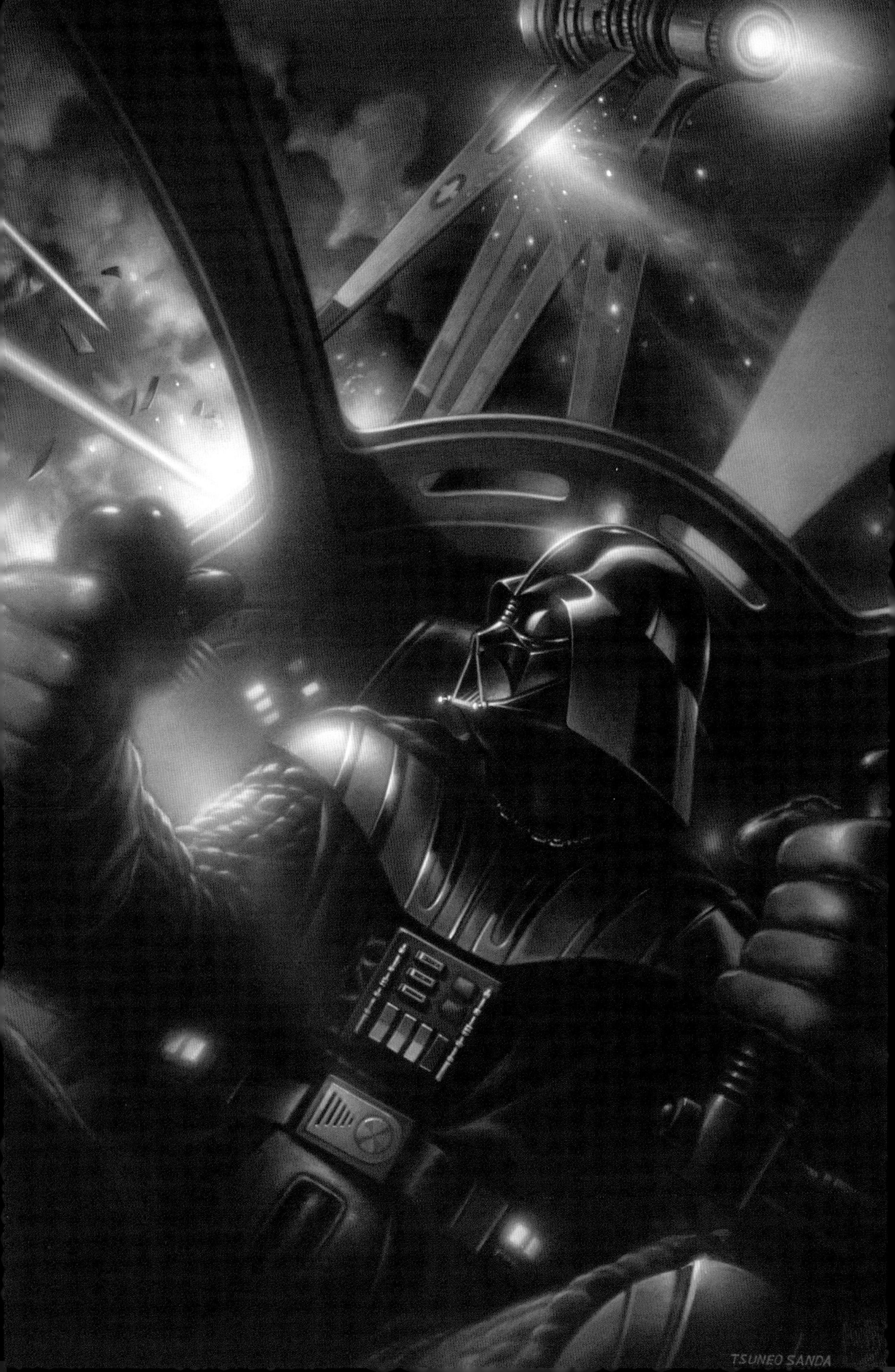
TSUNEO SANDA

THE REPUBLIC has fallen and been replaced by the Empire. Emperor Palpatine consolidates his power, assisted by former Jedi Knight Anakin Skywalker, now known to the galaxy as Darth Vader.

Though Vader has risen to a position of great power, his ascension has not been without sacrifice. He betrayed his Jedi friends, lost his limbs in a battle with his former Master, and inadvertently killed the woman he loved.

Now the galaxy's ostensive second in command is haunted by thoughts of what he gave up, and of what could have been . . .

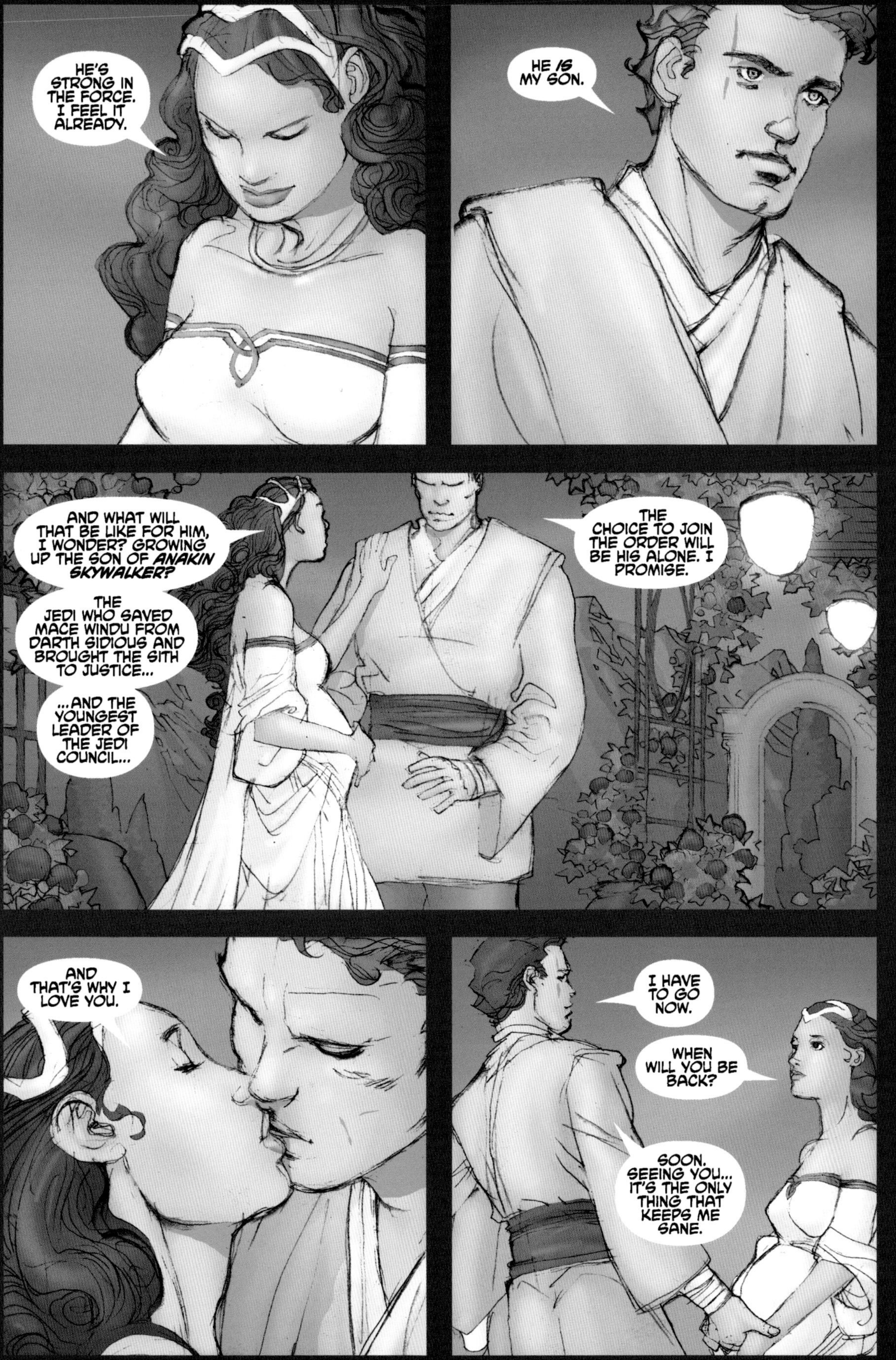
HE'S STRONG IN THE FORCE. I FEEL IT ALREADY.
HE *IS* MY SON.
AND WHAT WILL THAT BE LIKE FOR HIM, I WONDER? GROWING UP THE SON OF *ANAKIN SKYWALKER?*
THE JEDI WHO SAVED MACE WINDU FROM DARTH SIDIOUS AND BROUGHT THE SITH TO JUSTICE...
...AND THE YOUNGEST LEADER OF THE JEDI COUNCIL...
THE CHOICE TO JOIN THE ORDER WILL BE HIS ALONE. I PROMISE.
AND THAT'S WHY I LOVE YOU.
I HAVE TO GO NOW.
WHEN WILL YOU BE BACK?
SOON. SEEING YOU... IT'S THE ONLY THING THAT KEEPS ME SANE.

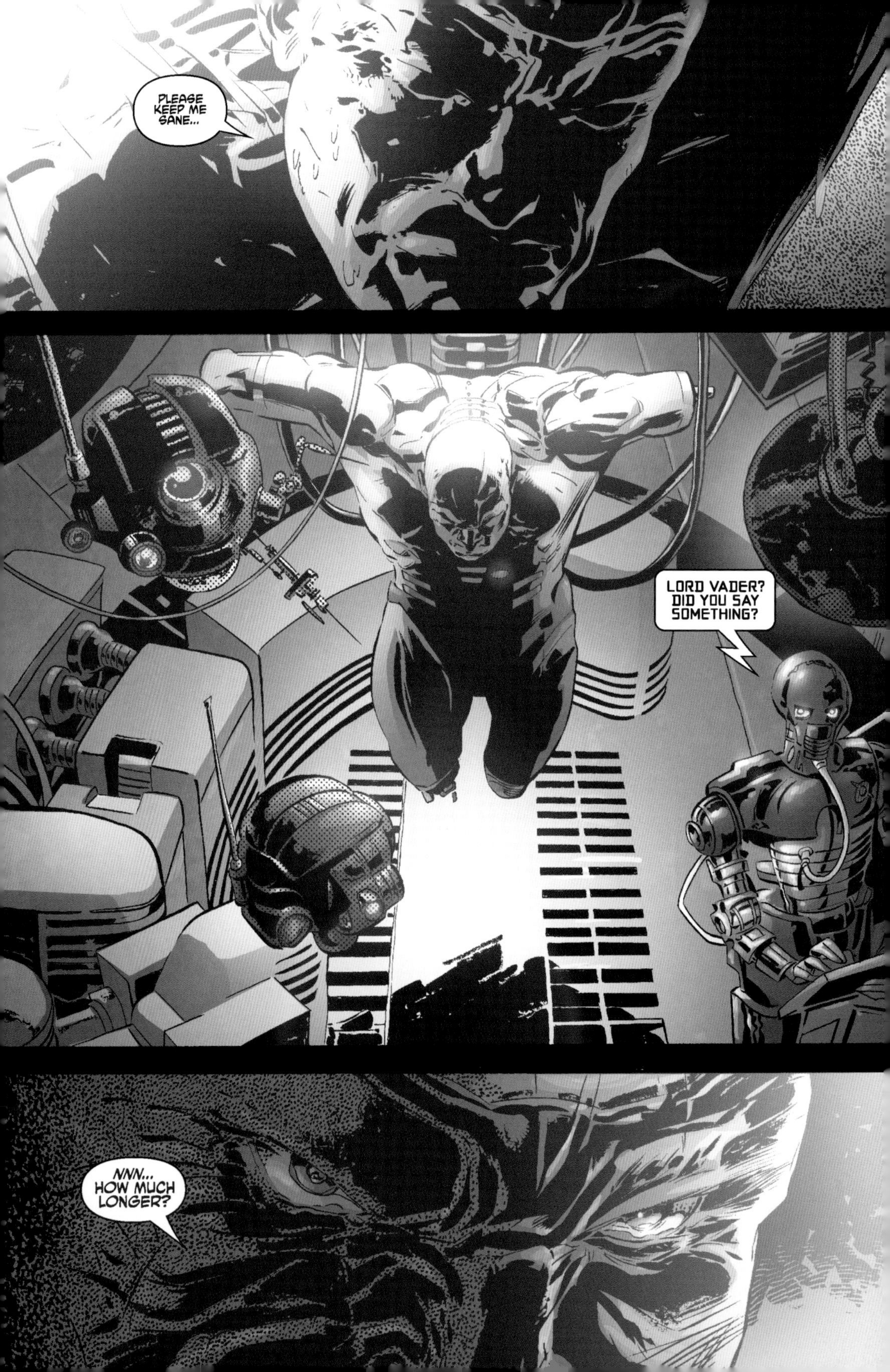
PLEASE KEEP ME SANE...
LORD VADER? DID YOU SAY SOMETHING?
NNN... HOW MUCH LONGER?

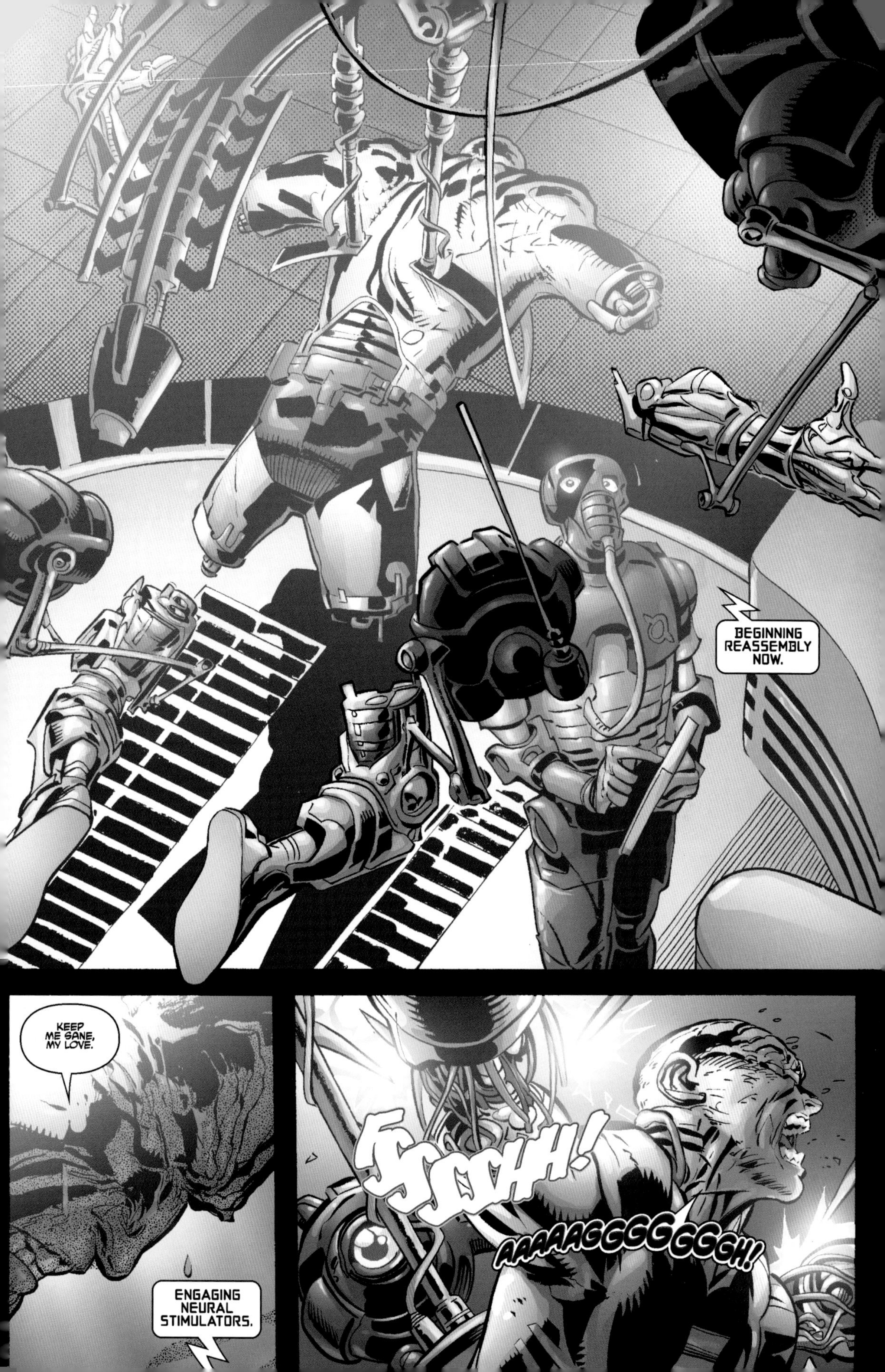
BEGINNING REASSEMBLY NOW.
KEEP ME SANE, MY LOVE.
ENGAGING NEURAL STIMULATORS.
FSSCHH!
AAAAAGGGGGGGH!

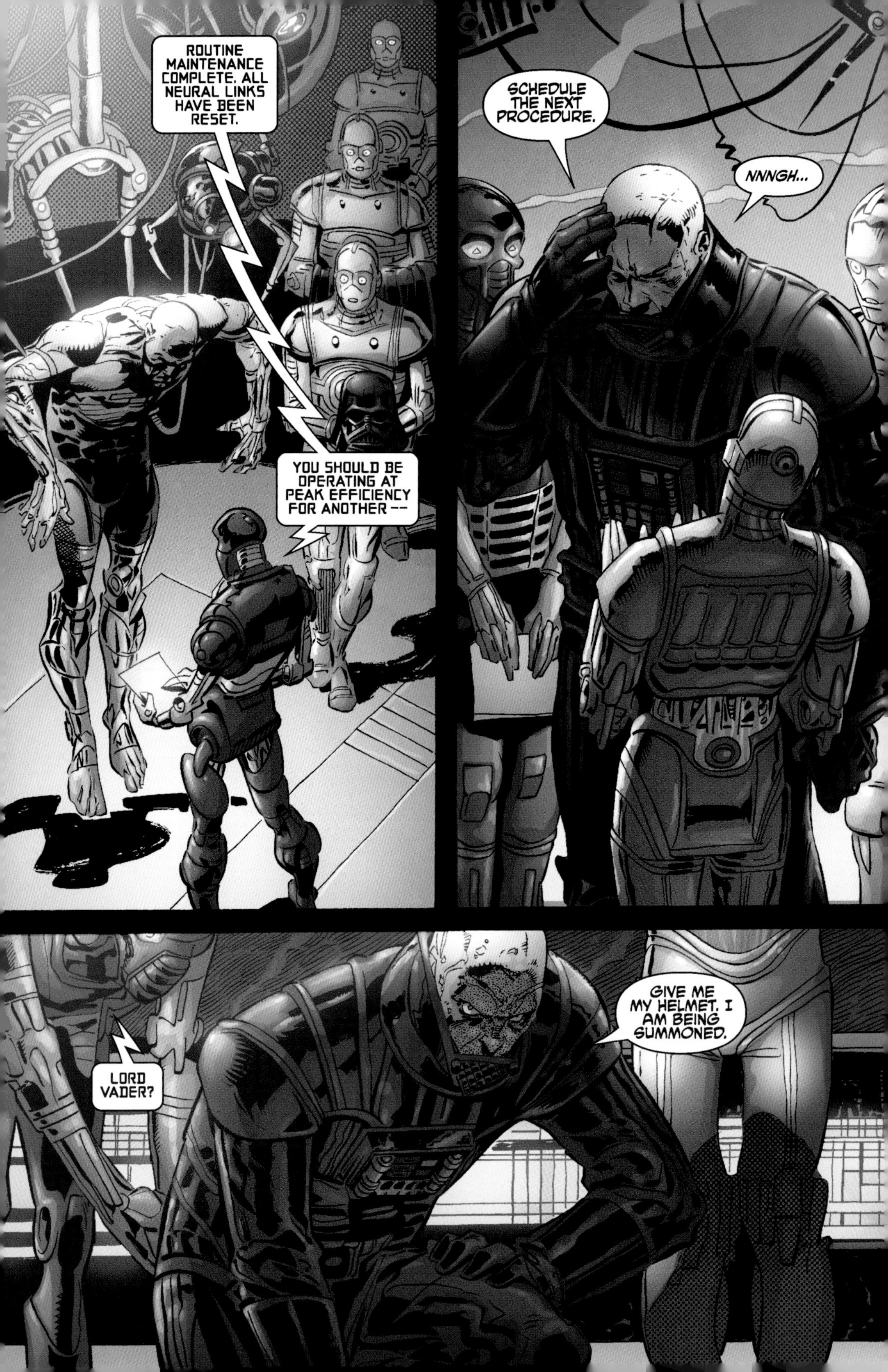
ROUTINE MAINTENANCE COMPLETE. ALL NEURAL LINKS HAVE BEEN RESET.
YOU SHOULD BE OPERATING AT PEAK EFFICIENCY FOR ANOTHER --
SCHEDULE THE NEXT PROCEDURE.
NNNGH...
LORD VADER?
GIVE ME MY HELMET. I AM BEING SUMMONED.

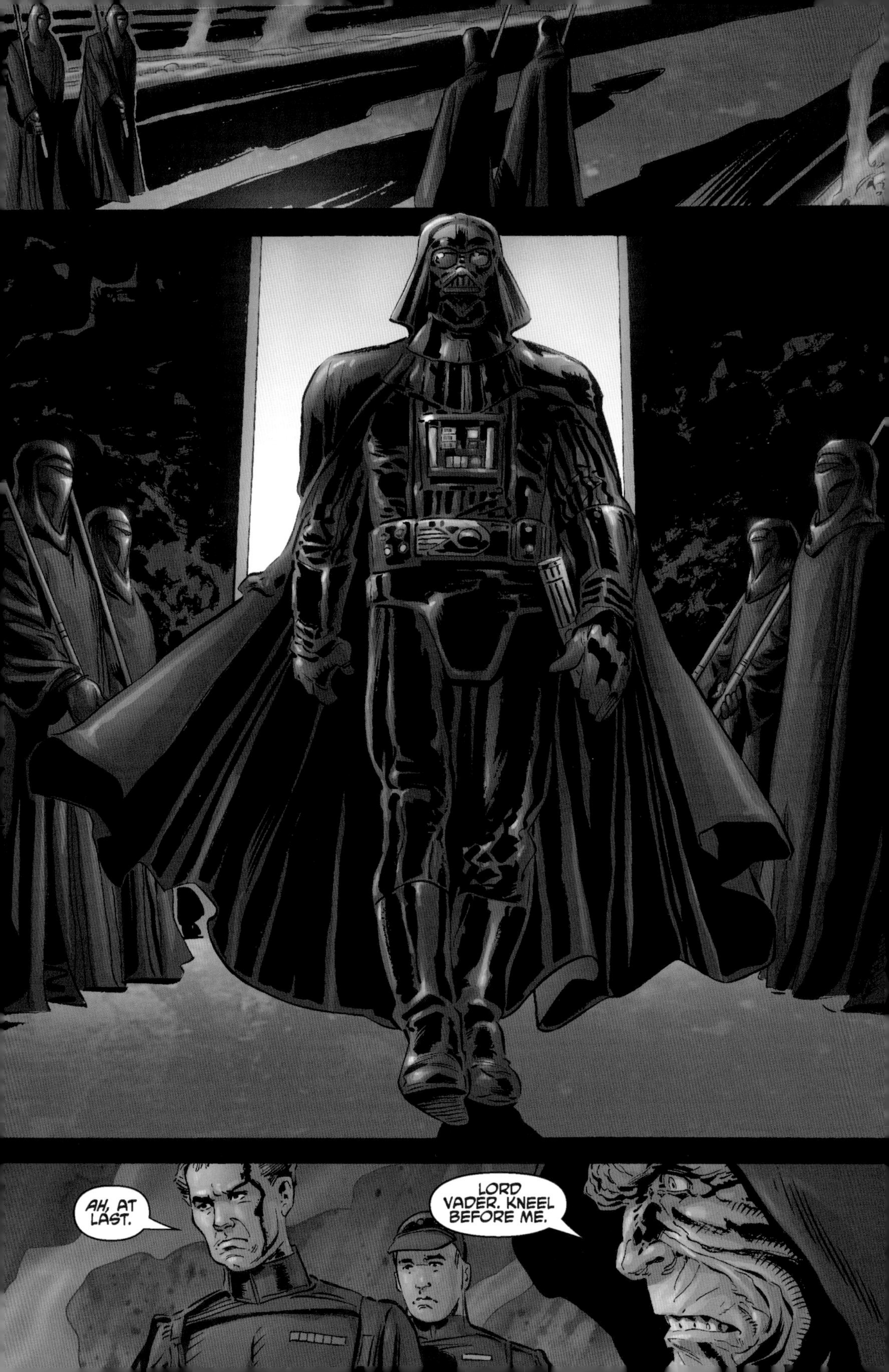
AH, AT LAST.
LORD VADER. KNEEL BEFORE ME.

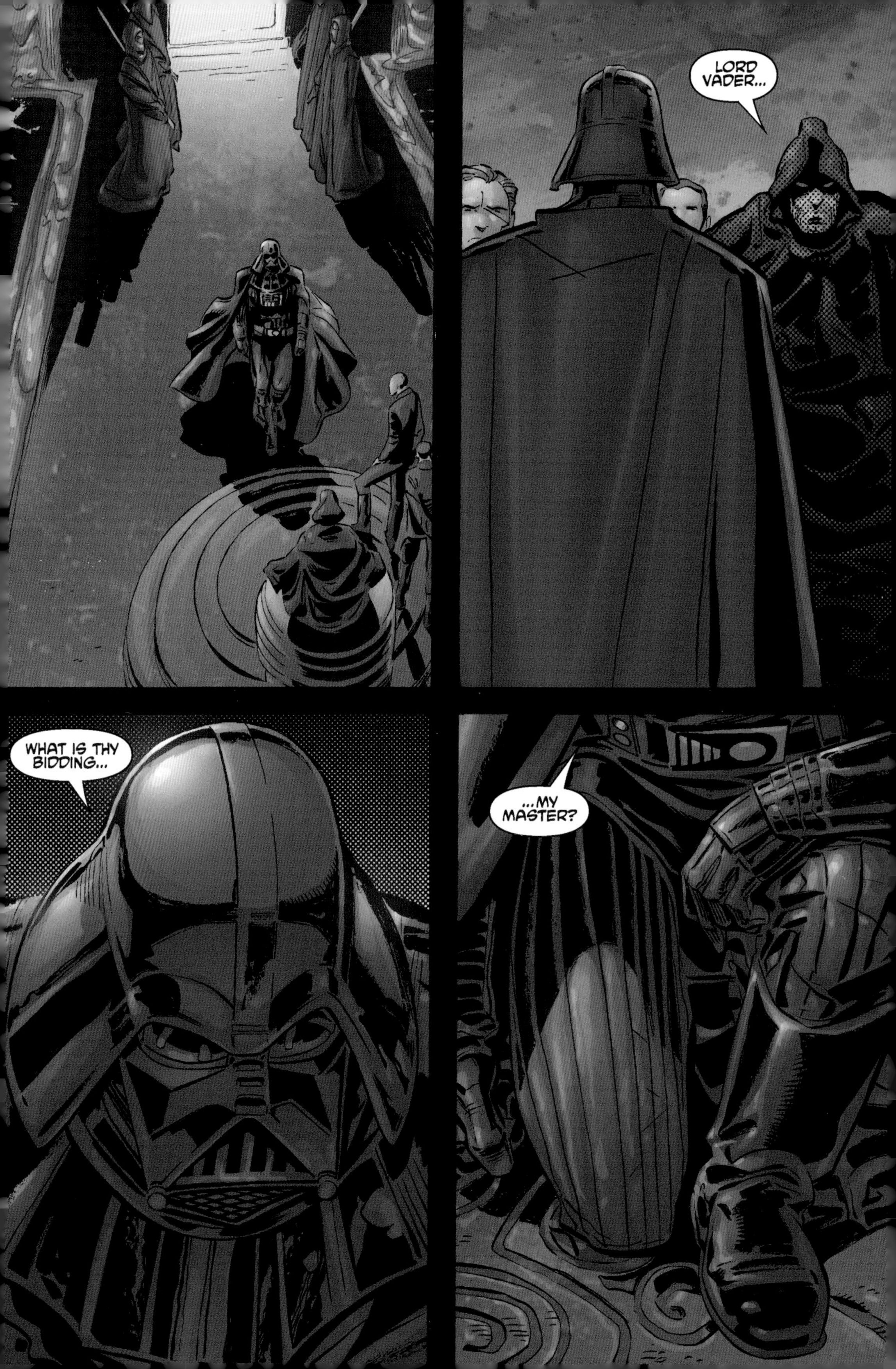
LORD VADER...
WHAT IS THY BIDDING...
...MY MASTER?

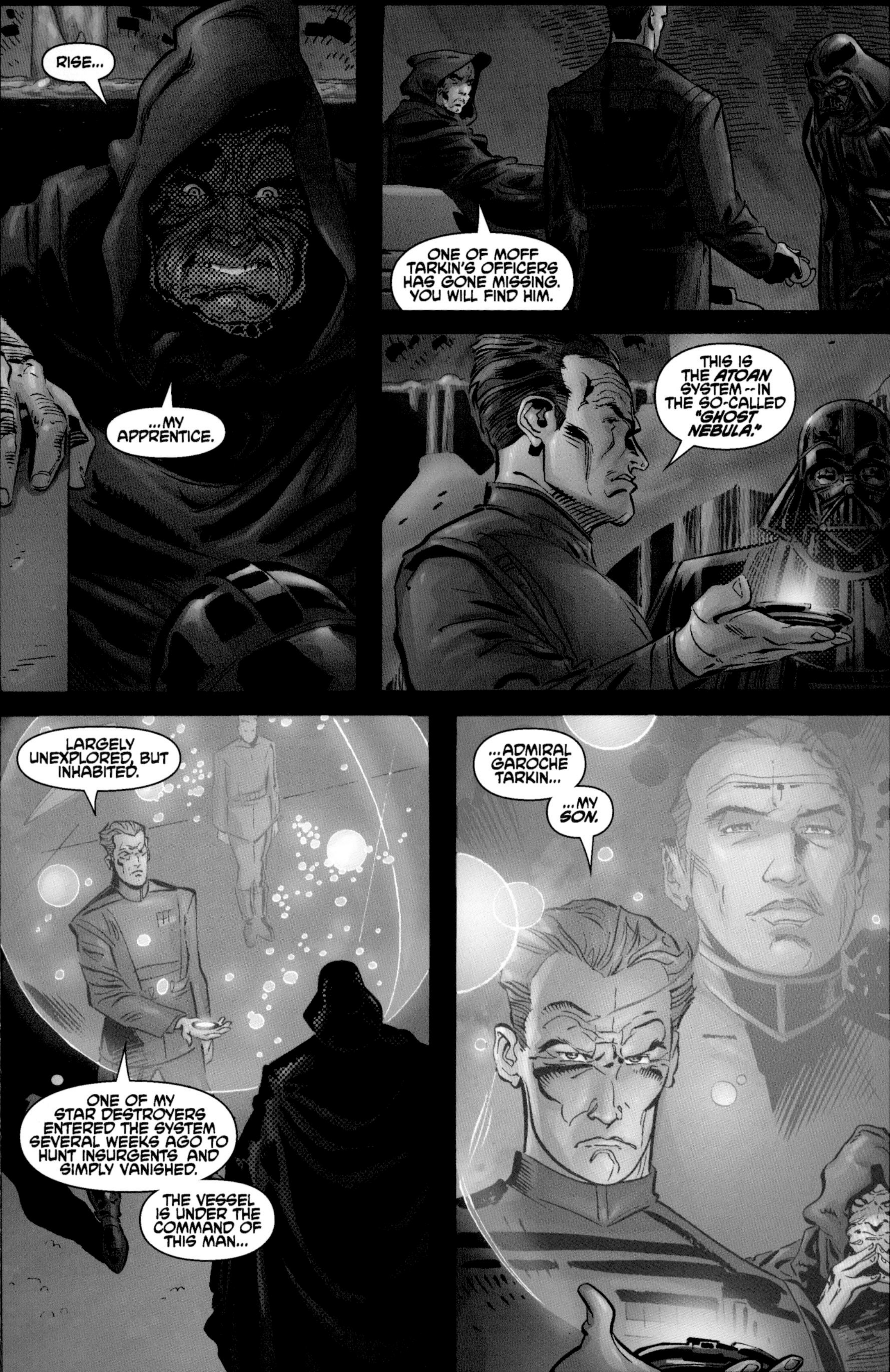
RISE...
...MY APPRENTICE.
ONE OF MOFF TARKIN'S OFFICERS HAS GONE MISSING. YOU WILL FIND HIM.
THIS IS THE ATOAN SYSTEM--IN THE SO-CALLED "GHOST NEBULA."
LARGELY UNEXPLORED, BUT INHABITED.
ONE OF MY STAR DESTROYERS ENTERED THE SYSTEM SEVERAL WEEKS AGO TO HUNT INSURGENTS AND SIMPLY VANISHED.
THE VESSEL IS UNDER THE COMMAND OF THIS MAN...
...ADMIRAL GAROCHE TARKIN...
...MY SON.

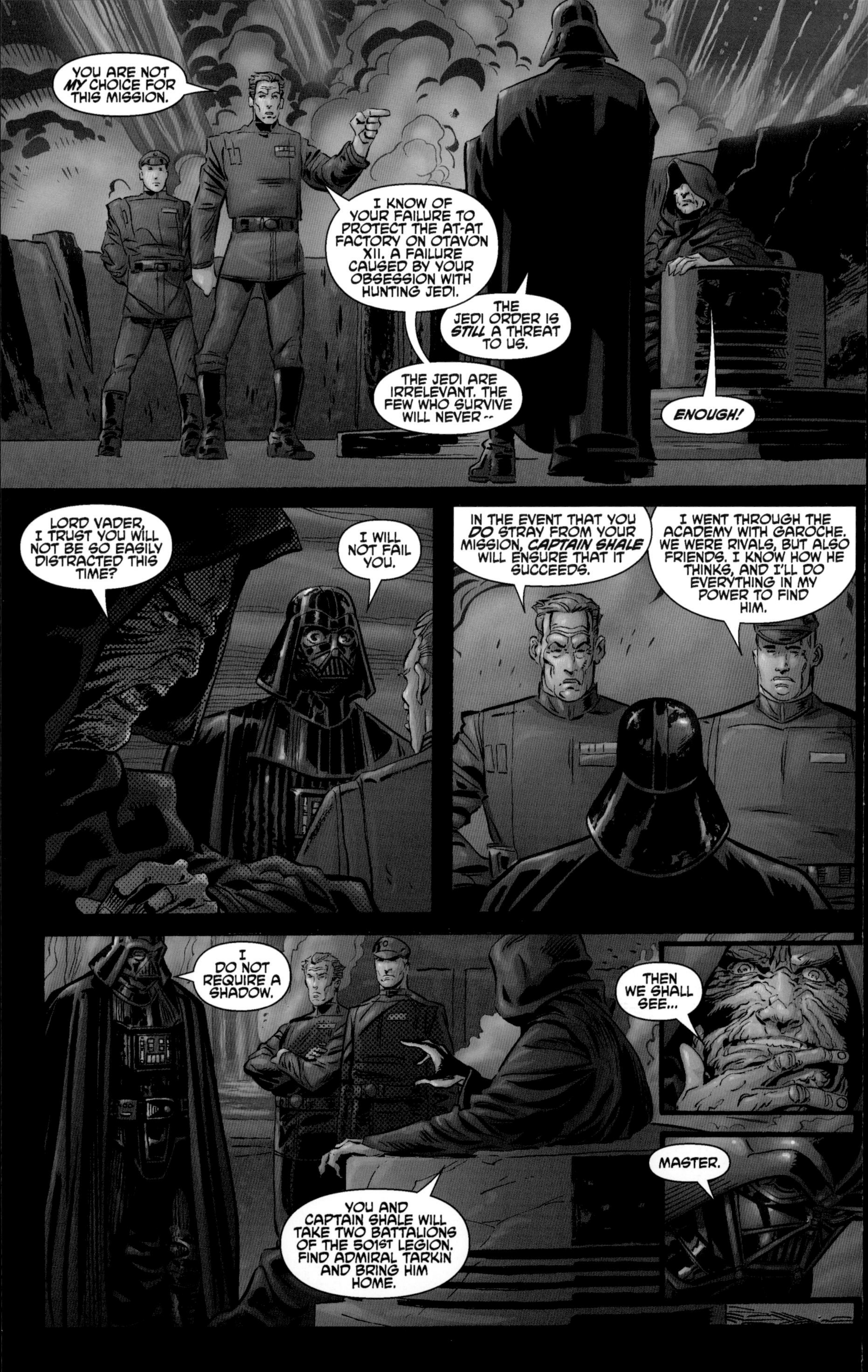
YOU ARE NOT *MY* CHOICE FOR THIS MISSION.
I KNOW OF YOUR FAILURE TO PROTECT THE AT-AT FACTORY ON OTAVON XII. A FAILURE CAUSED BY YOUR OBSESSION WITH HUNTING JEDI.
THE JEDI ORDER IS *STILL* A THREAT TO US.
THE JEDI ARE IRRELEVANT. THE FEW WHO SURVIVE WILL NEVER --
ENOUGH!
LORD VADER, I TRUST YOU WILL NOT BE SO EASILY DISTRACTED THIS TIME?
I WILL NOT FAIL YOU.
IN THE EVENT THAT YOU *DO* STRAY FROM YOUR MISSION, *CAPTAIN SHALE* WILL ENSURE THAT IT SUCCEEDS.
I WENT THROUGH THE ACADEMY WITH GAROCHE. WE WERE RIVALS, BUT ALSO FRIENDS. I KNOW HOW HE THINKS, AND I'LL DO EVERYTHING IN MY POWER TO FIND HIM.
I DO NOT REQUIRE A SHADOW.
THEN WE SHALL SEE...
MASTER.
YOU AND CAPTAIN SHALE WILL TAKE TWO BATTALIONS OF THE 501st LEGION. FIND ADMIRAL TARKIN AND BRING HIM HOME.

THE ATOAN SYSTEM. FOUR DAYS LATER.

OUR INTELLIGENCE ON ATOA IS LIMITED.

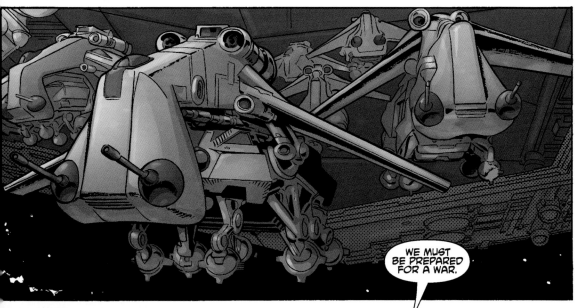

WE MUST BE PREPARED FOR A WAR.

CRUSH ANY RESISTANCE, BUT LEAVE THE OFFICERS ALIVE. FOR INTERROGATION.

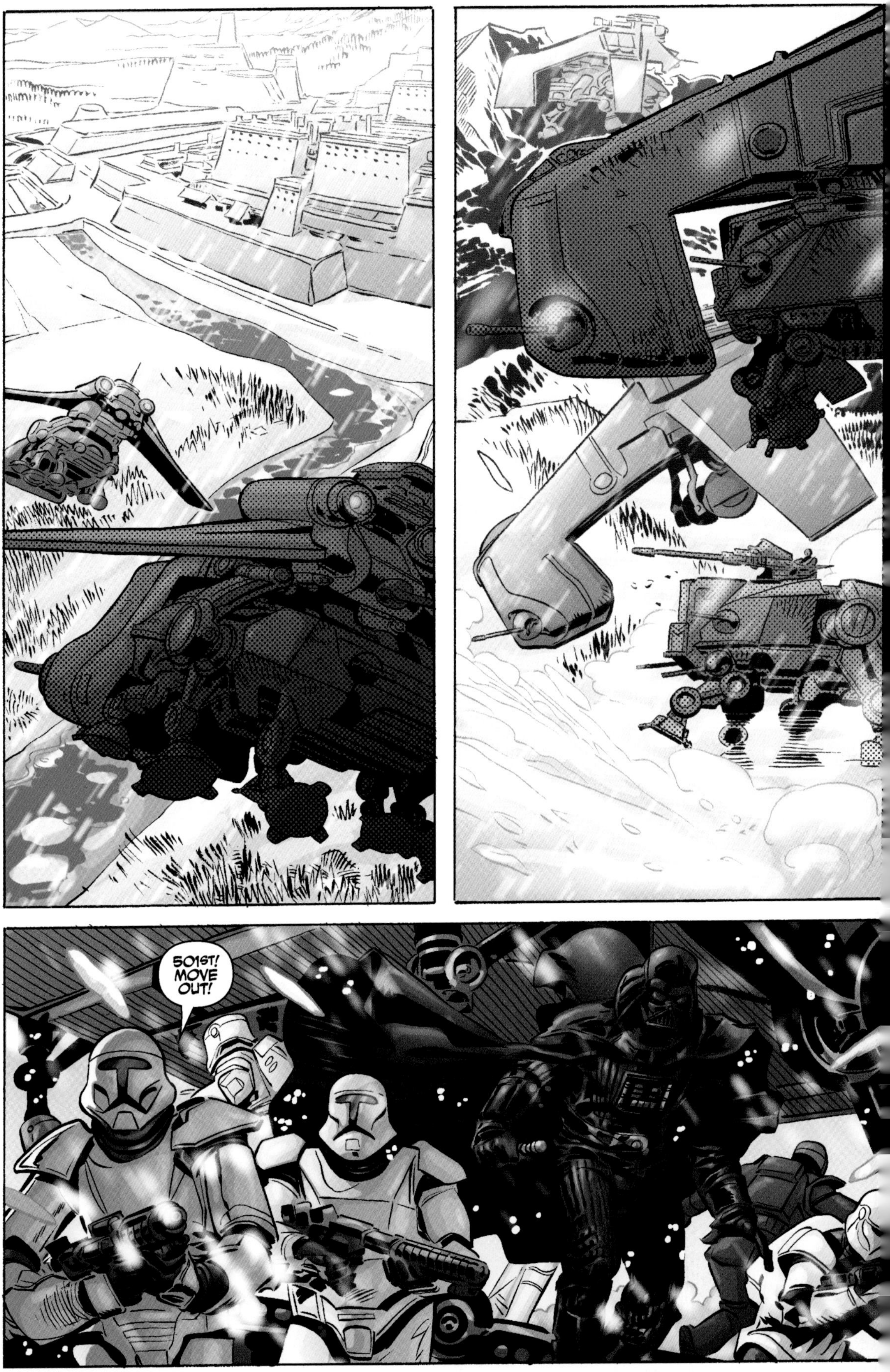
501ST! MOVE OUT!

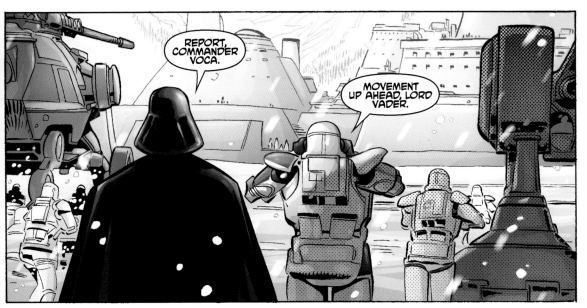

REPORT, COMMANDER VOCA.

MOVEMENT UP AHEAD, LORD VADER.

SCANNING A FEW HUNDRED ARMED SOLDIERS HOLDING THE CITY...

...AND A SCOUTING PARTY HEADED OUR WAY.

CUT THEM DOWN.

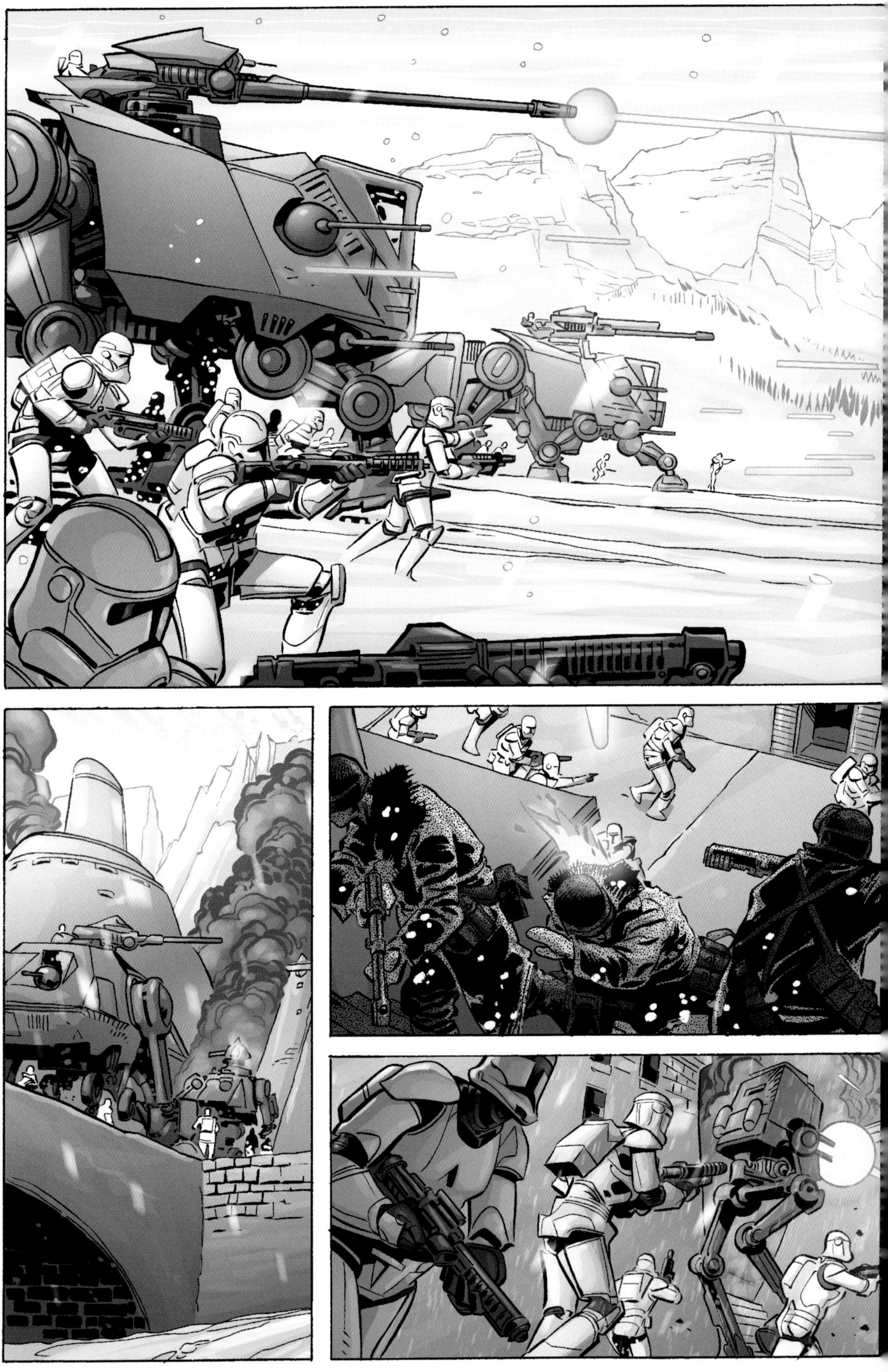

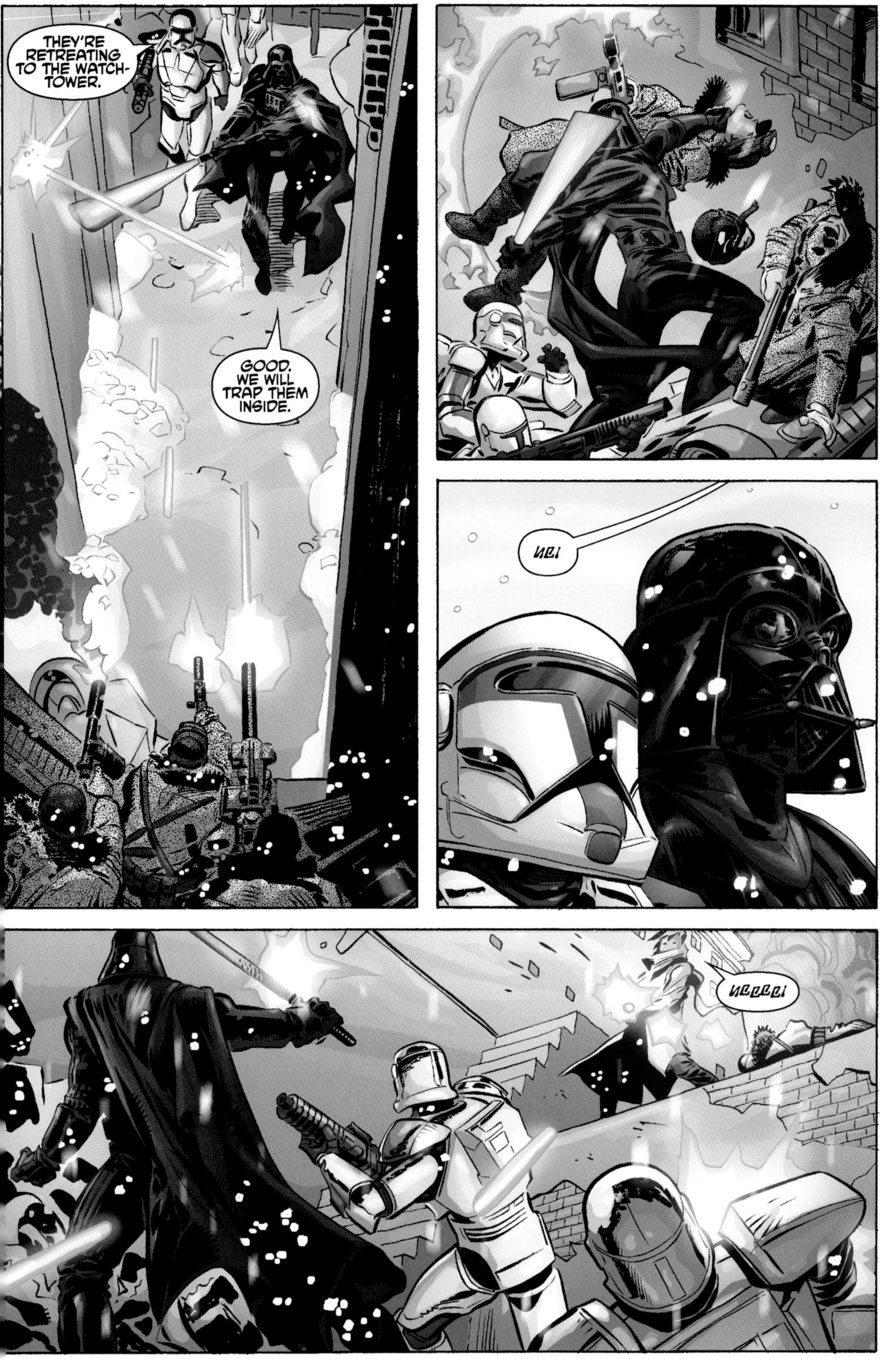
THEY'RE RETREATING TO THE WATCH-TOWER.
GOOD. WE WILL TRAP THEM INSIDE.

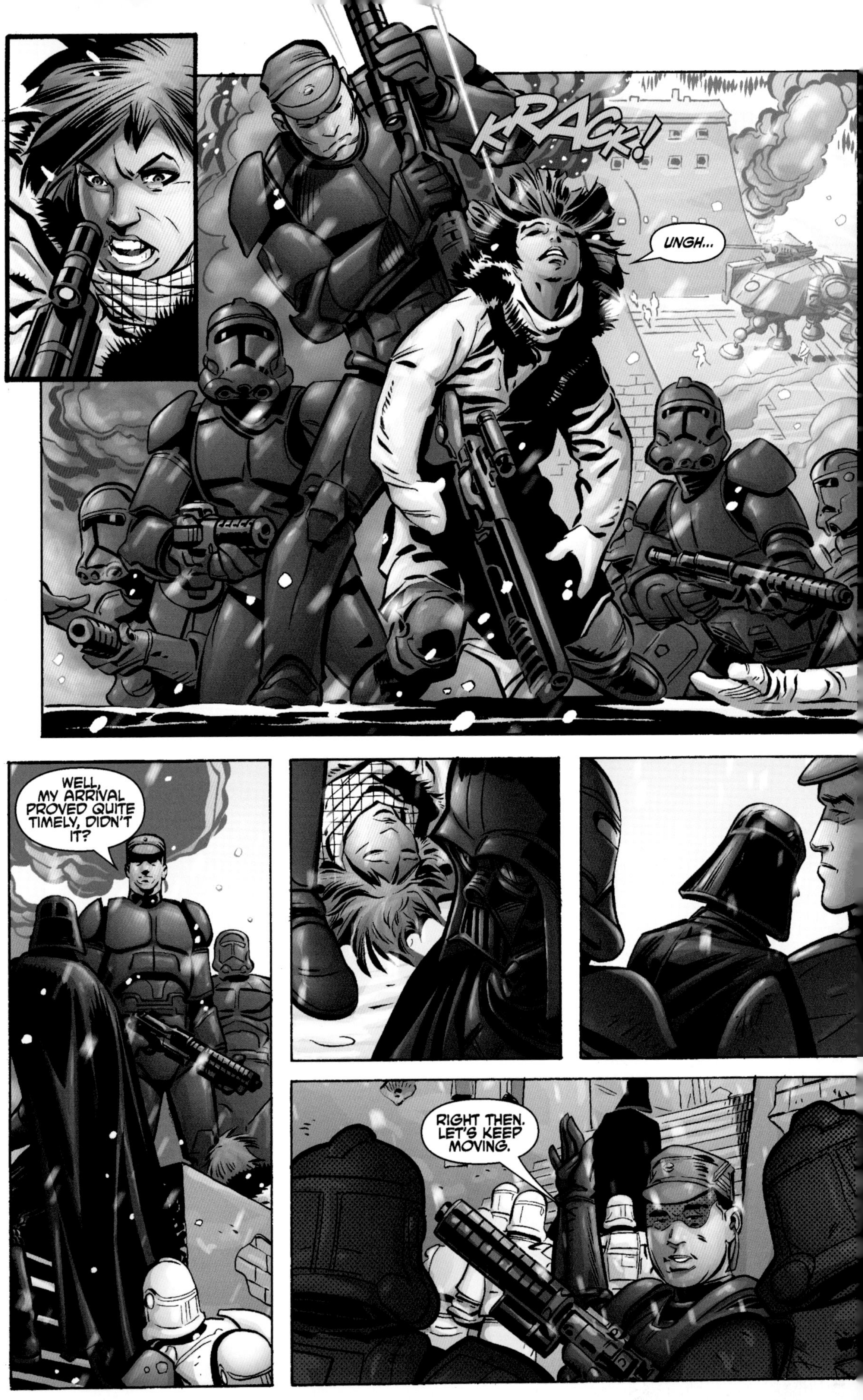
KRACK!
UNGH...
WELL, MY ARRIVAL PROVED QUITE TIMELY, DIDN'T IT?
RIGHT THEN. LET'S KEEP MOVING.

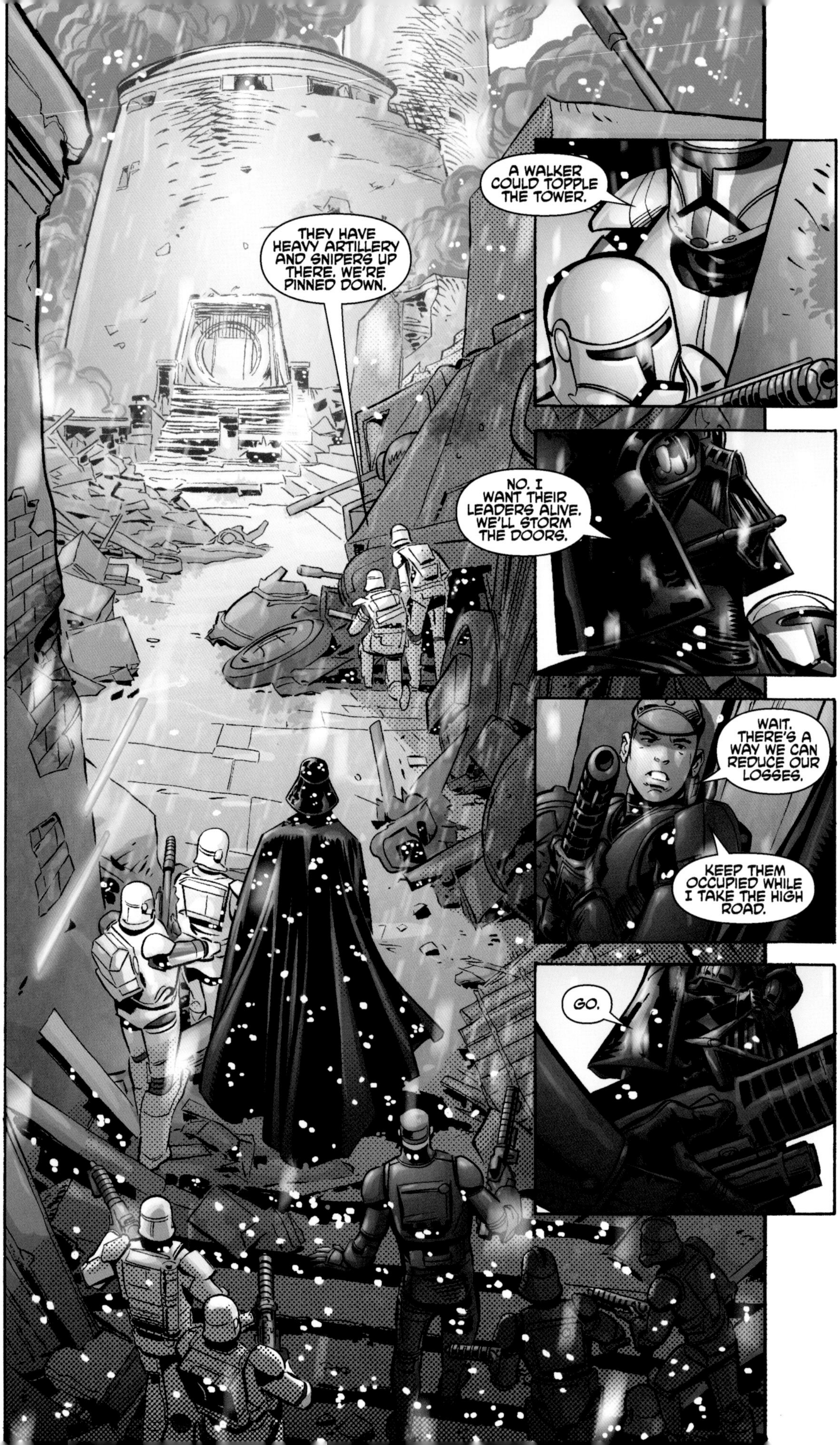
THEY HAVE HEAVY ARTILLERY AND SNIPERS UP THERE. WE'RE PINNED DOWN.
A WALKER COULD TOPPLE THE TOWER.
NO. I WANT THEIR LEADERS ALIVE. WE'LL STORM THE DOORS.
WAIT. THERE'S A WAY WE CAN REDUCE OUR LOSSES.
KEEP THEM OCCUPIED WHILE I TAKE THE HIGH ROAD.
GO.

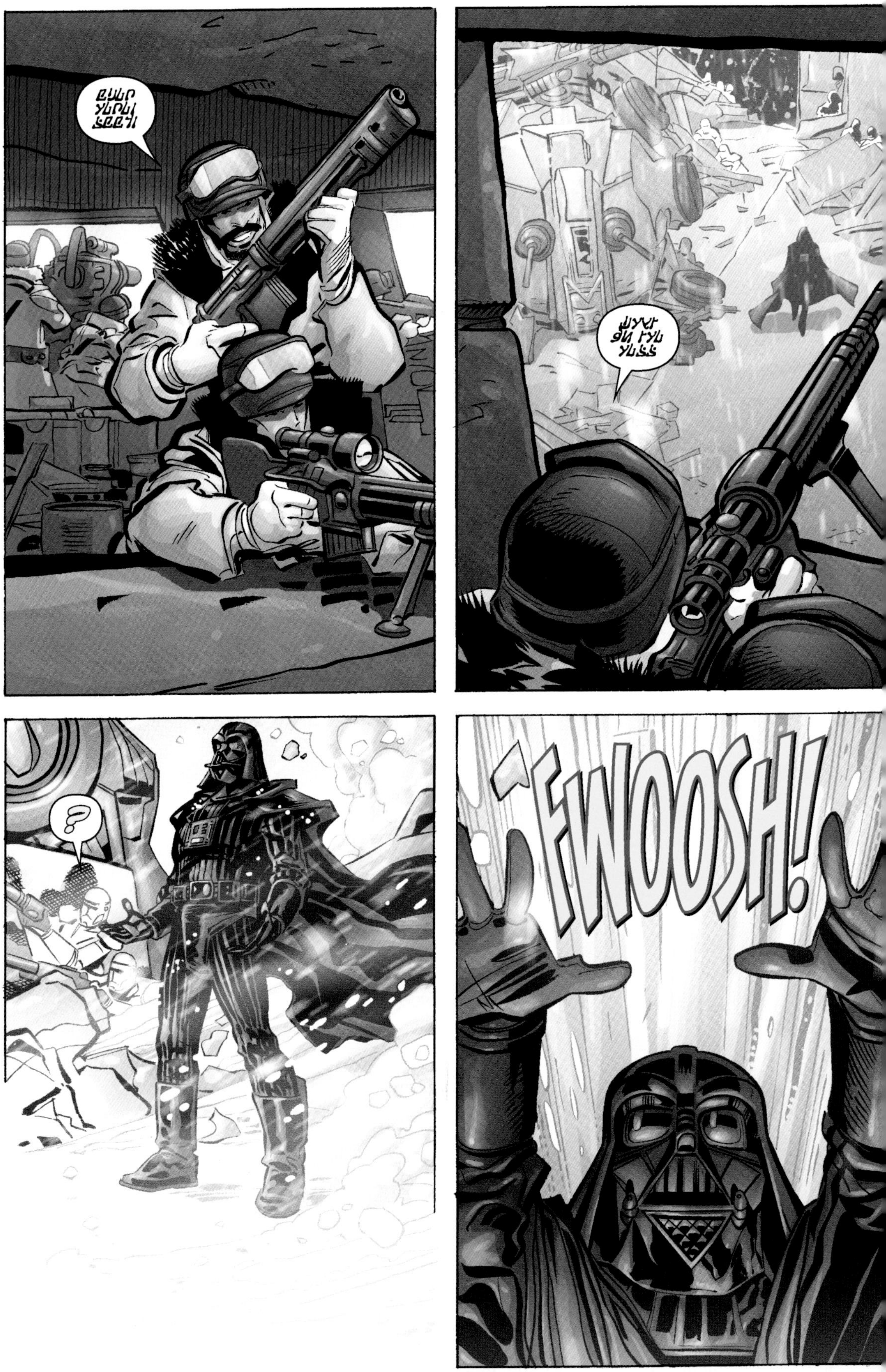
?
FWOOSH!

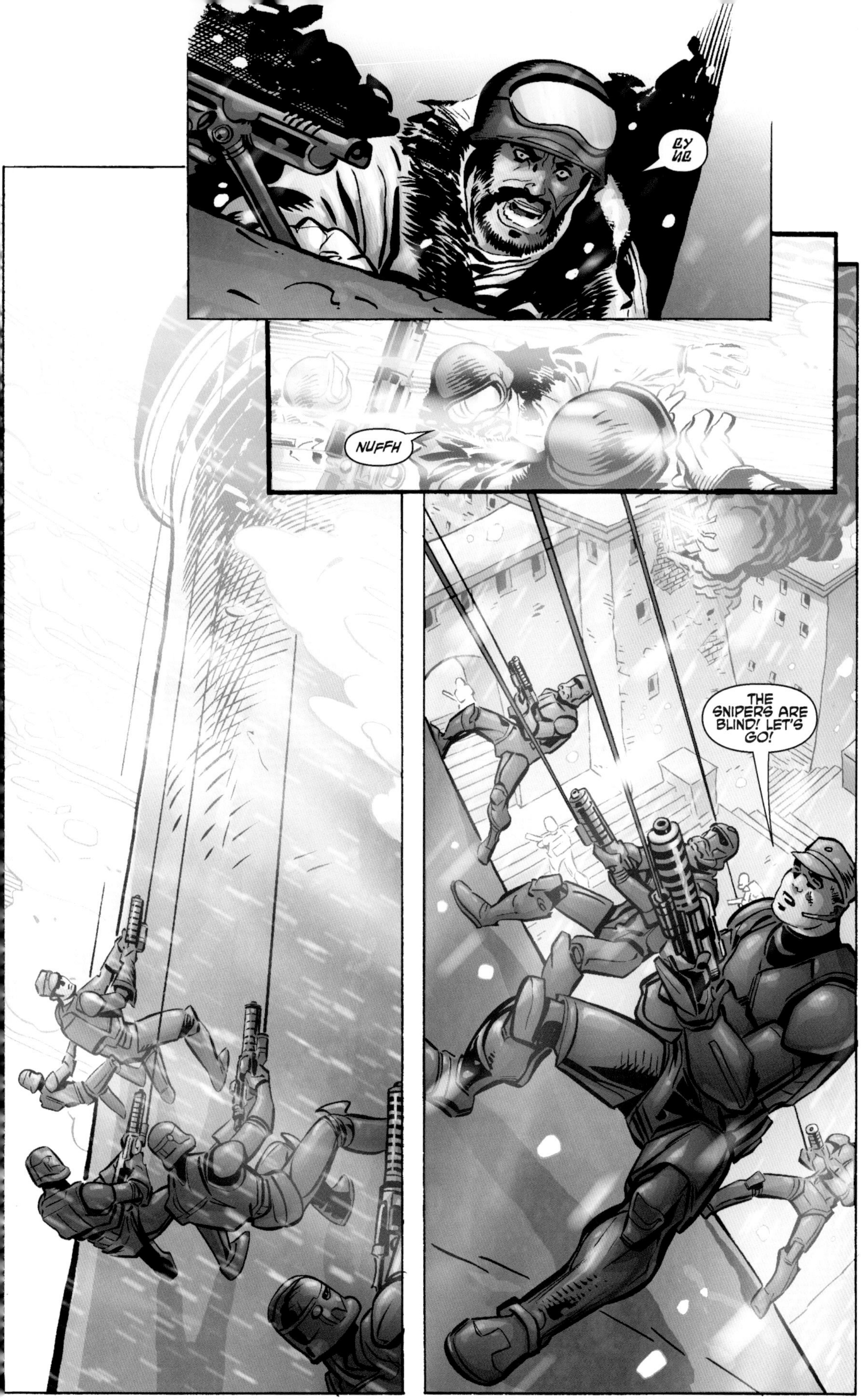
NUFFH
THE SNIPERS ARE BLIND! LET'S GO!

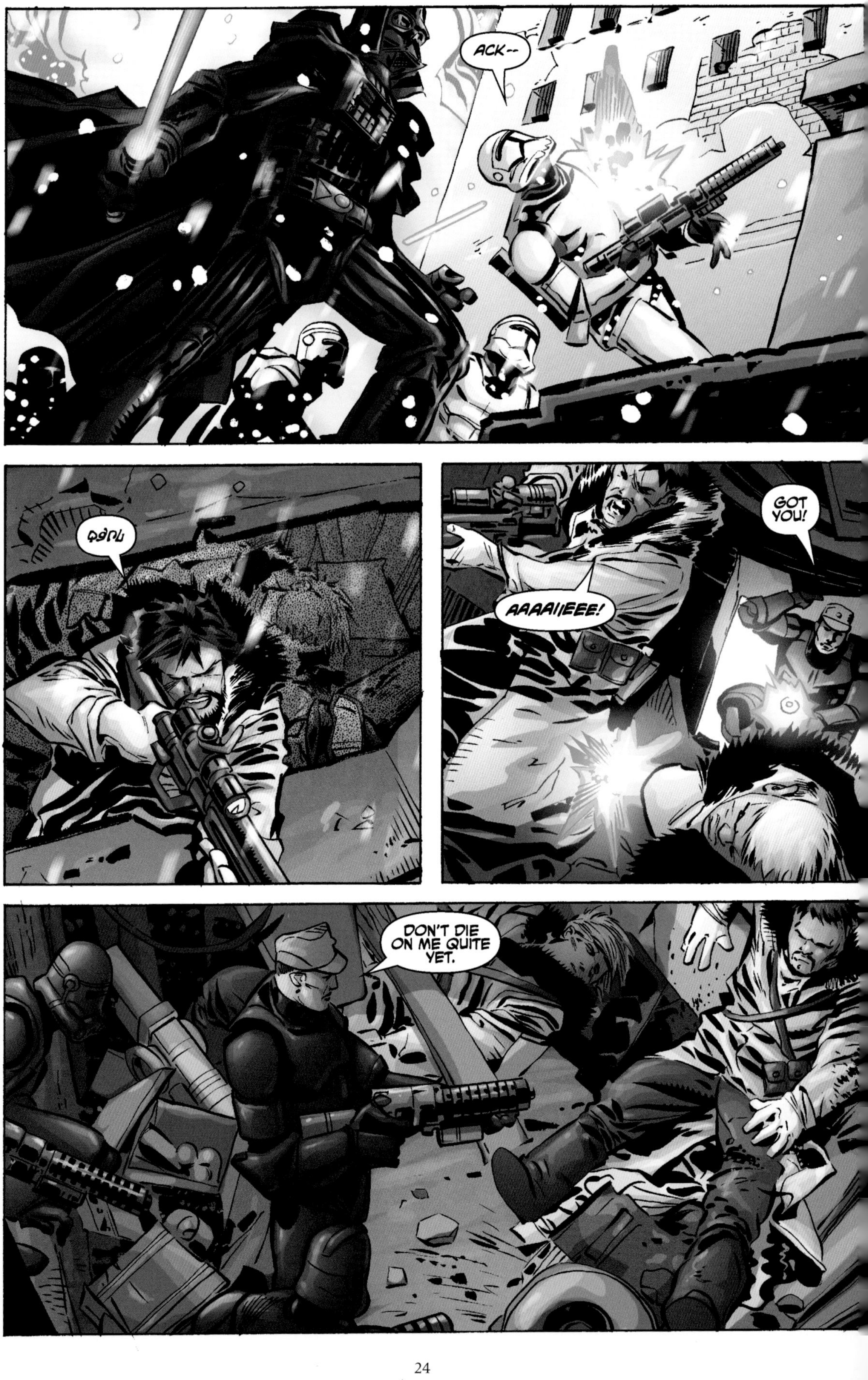
ACK--
GOT YOU!
AAAAIIEEE!
DON'T DIE ON ME QUITE YET.

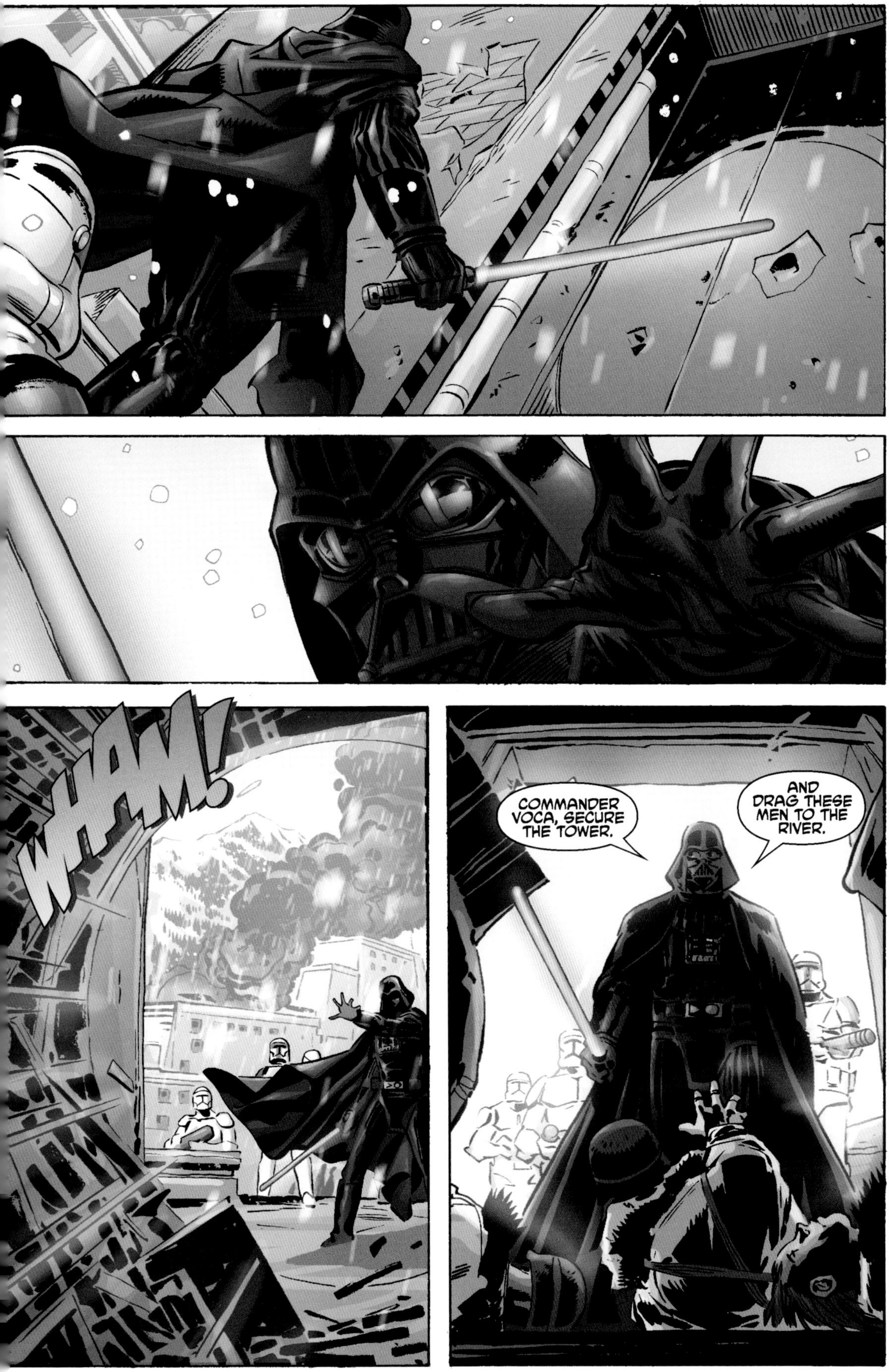
WHAM!
COMMANDER VOCA, SECURE THE TOWER.
AND DRAG THESE MEN TO THE RIVER.

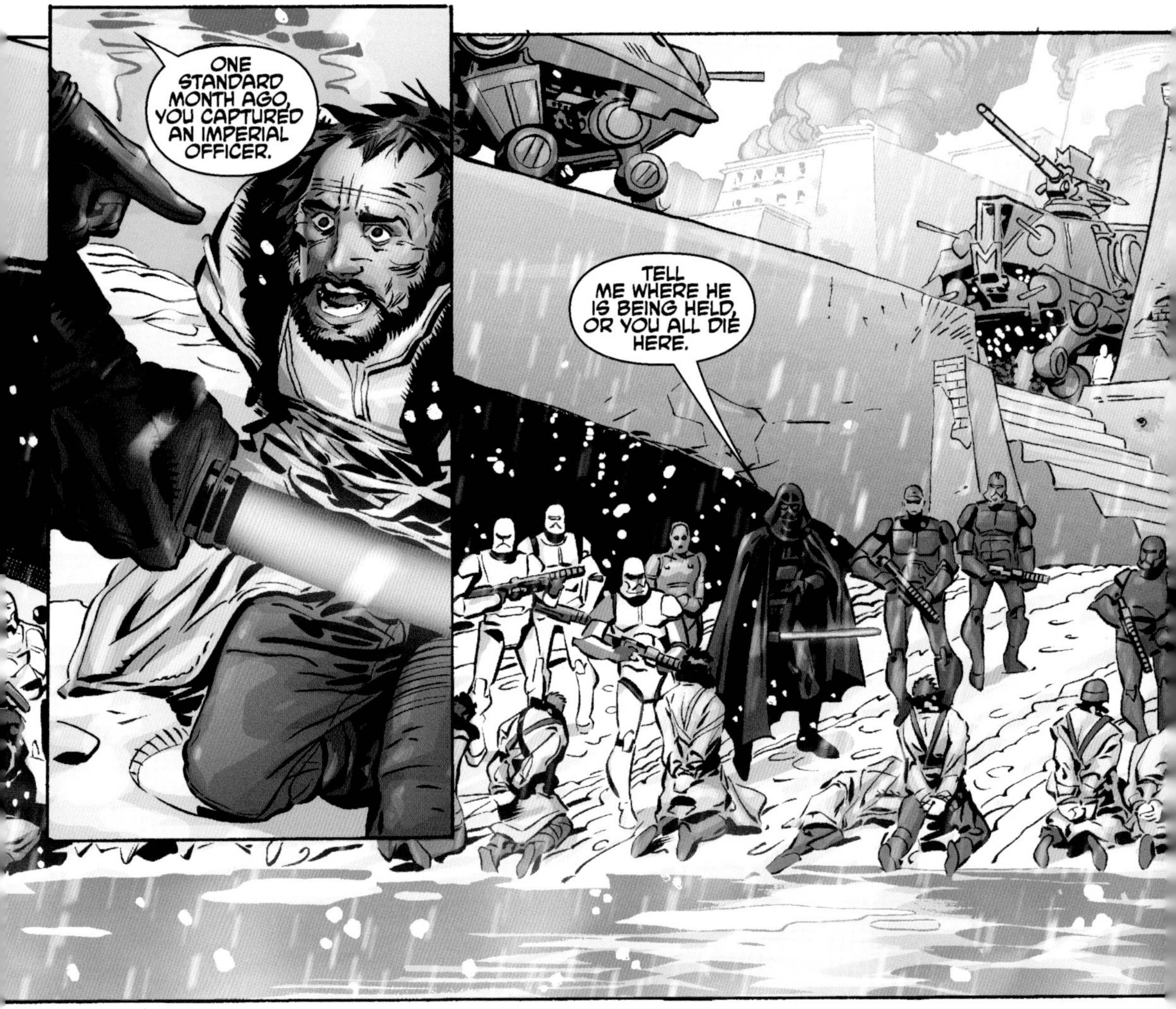
ONE STANDARD MONTH AGO, YOU CAPTURED AN IMPERIAL OFFICER.
TELL ME WHERE HE IS BEING HELD, OR YOU ALL DIE HERE.

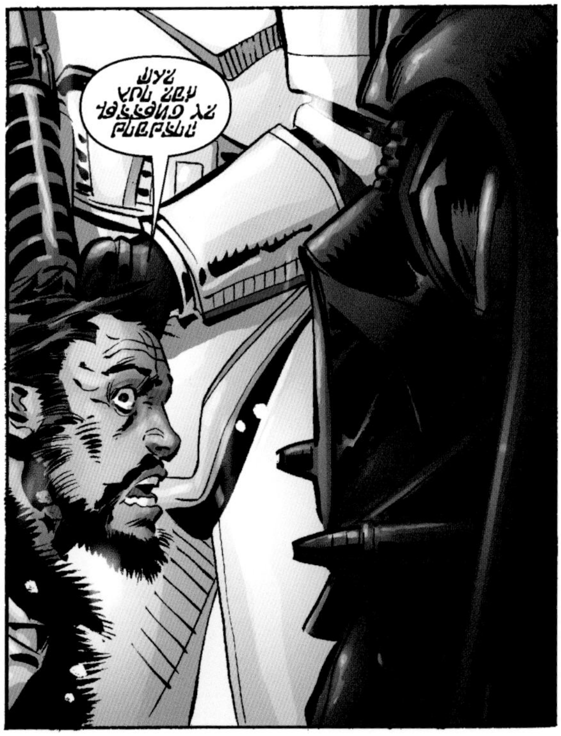

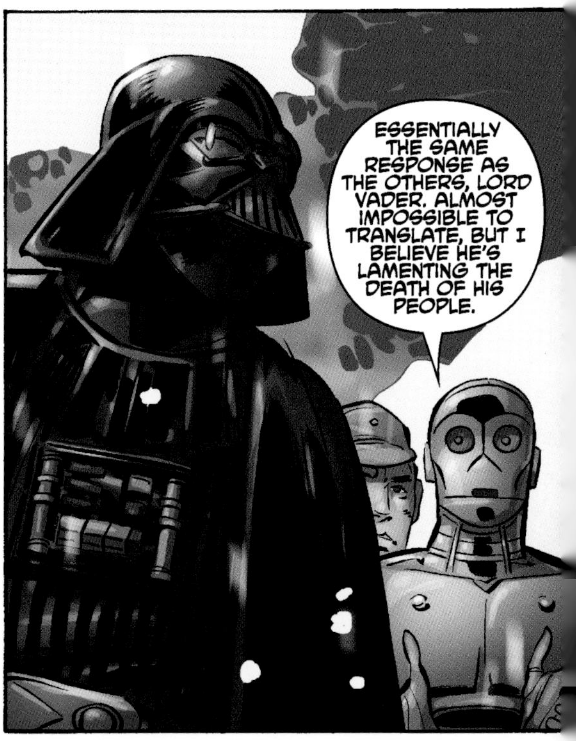
ESSENTIALLY THE SAME RESPONSE AS THE OTHERS, LORD VADER. ALMOST IMPOSSIBLE TO TRANSLATE, BUT I BELIEVE HE'S LAMENTING THE DEATH OF HIS PEOPLE.

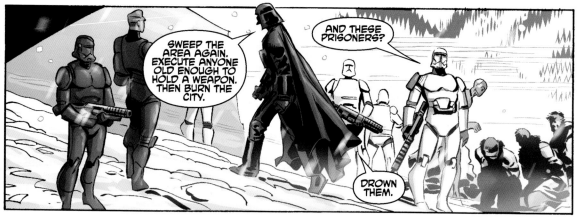

SWEEP THE AREA AGAIN. EXECUTE ANYONE OLD ENOUGH TO HOLD A WEAPON. THEN BURN THE CITY.

AND THESE PRISONERS?

DROWN THEM.

VADER... SOMEONE IS OUT THERE.

HOLD YOUR FIRE.

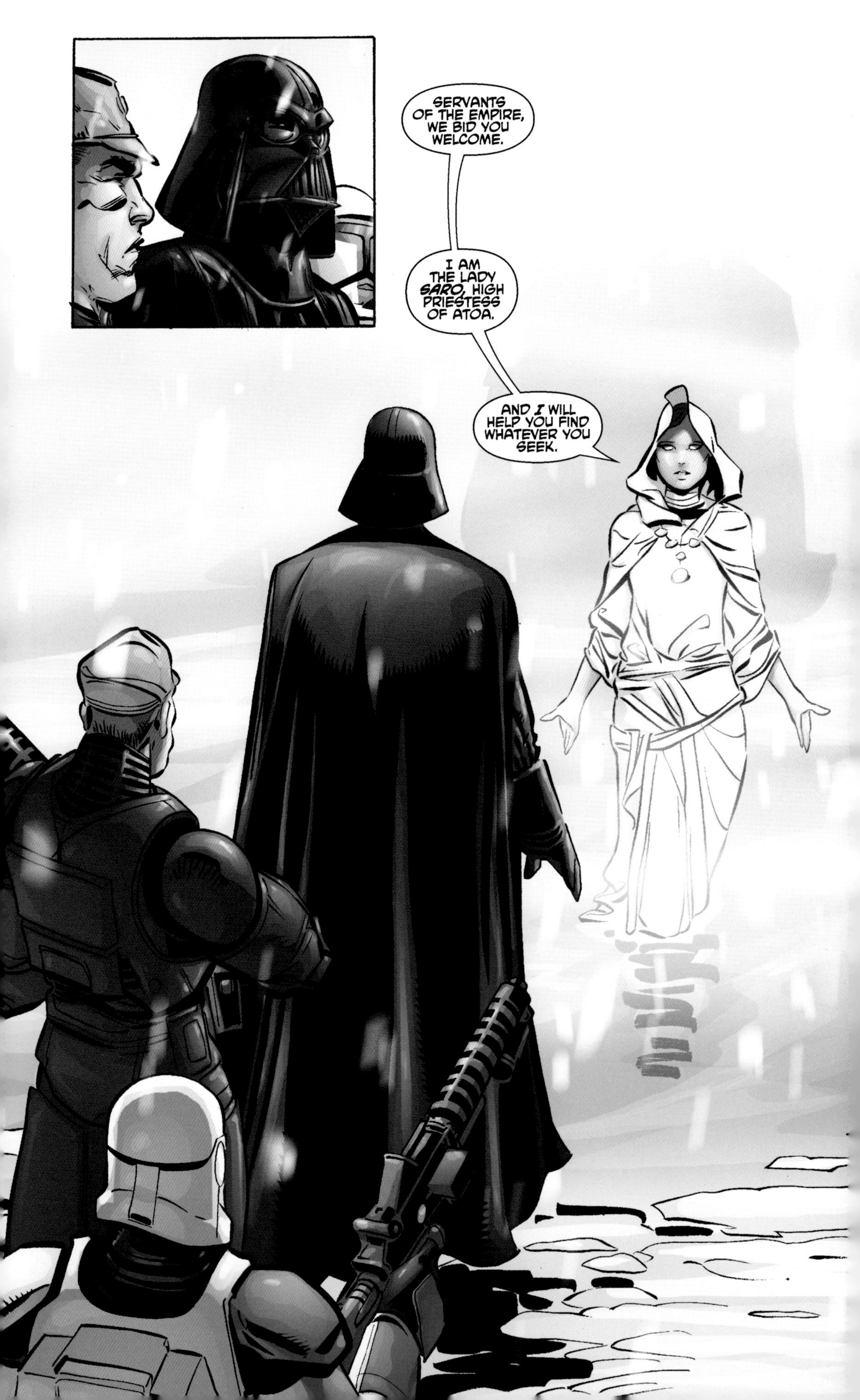
SERVANTS OF THE EMPIRE, WE BID YOU WELCOME.
I AM THE LADY SARO, HIGH PRIESTESS OF ATOA.
AND I WILL HELP YOU FIND WHATEVER YOU SEEK.

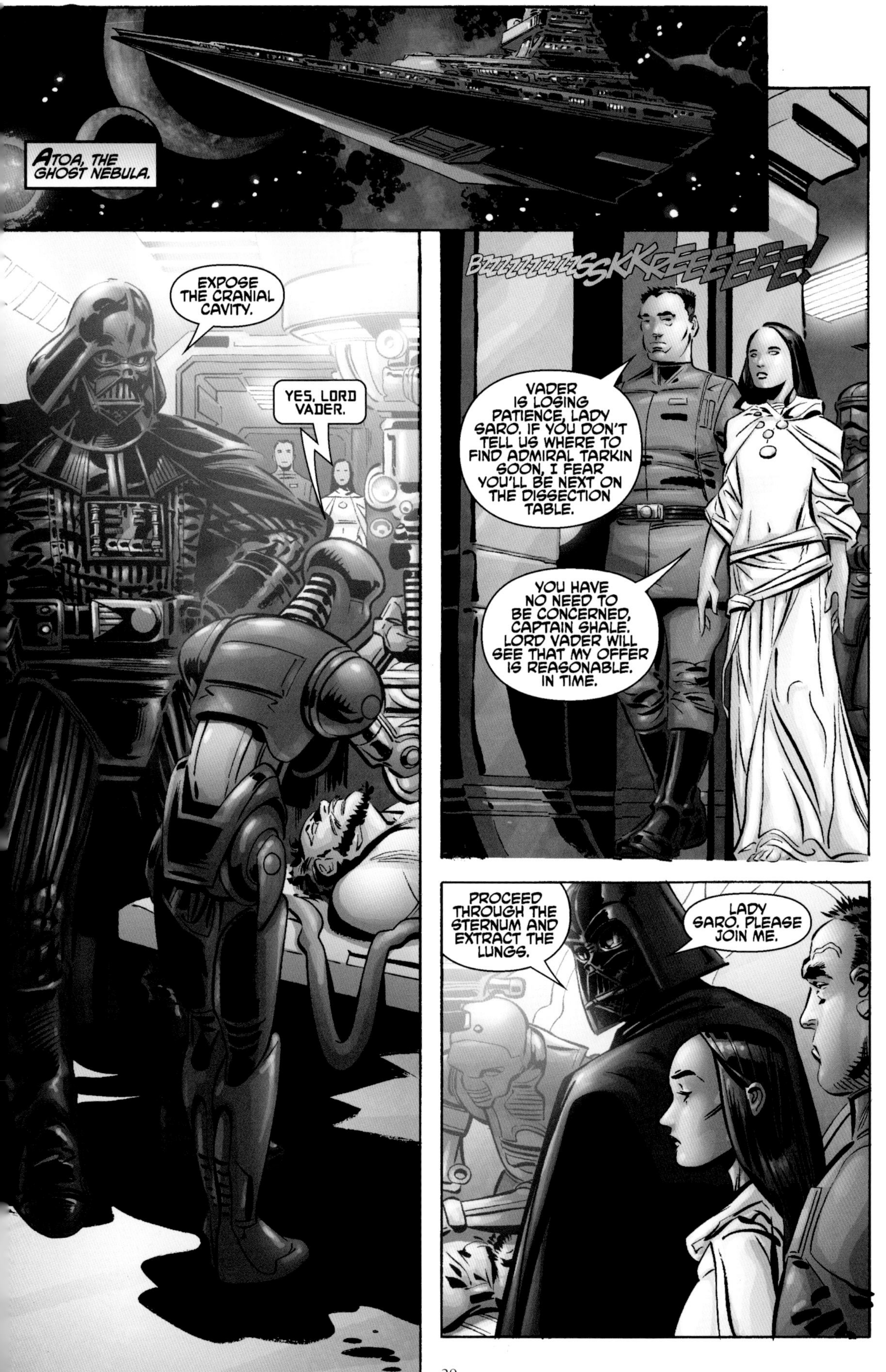
ATOA, THE GHOST NEBULA.
EXPOSE THE CRANIAL CAVITY.
YES, LORD VADER.
BZZZZZZZZSSKKREEEEEEE!
VADER IS LOSING PATIENCE, LADY SARO. IF YOU DON'T TELL US WHERE TO FIND ADMIRAL TARKIN SOON, I FEAR YOU'LL BE NEXT ON THE DISSECTION TABLE.
YOU HAVE NO NEED TO BE CONCERNED, CAPTAIN SHALE. LORD VADER WILL SEE THAT MY OFFER IS REASONABLE. IN TIME.
PROCEED THROUGH THE STERNUM AND EXTRACT THE LUNGS.
LADY SARO. PLEASE JOIN ME.

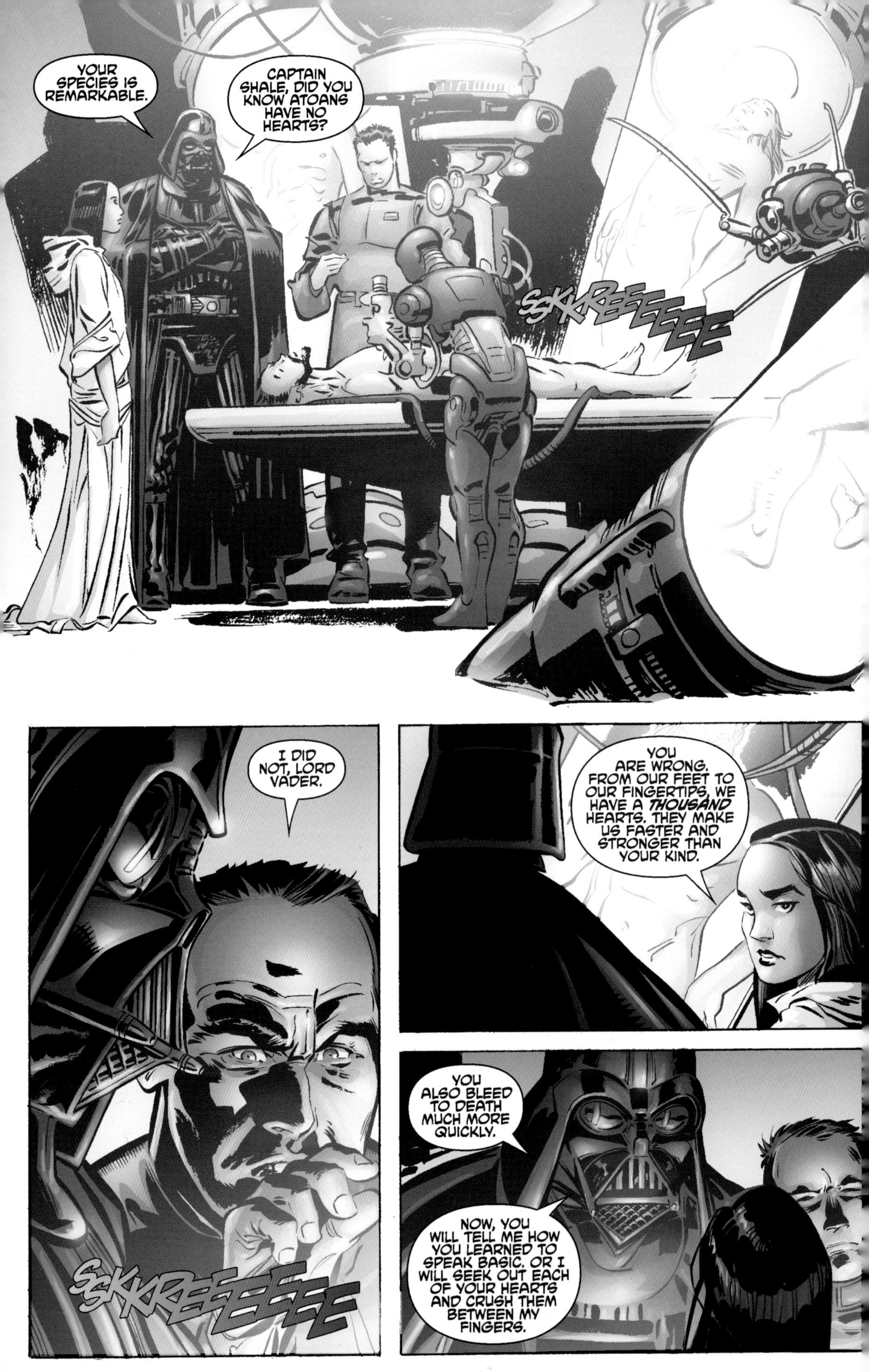
YOUR SPECIES IS REMARKABLE.
CAPTAIN SHALE, DID YOU KNOW ATOANS HAVE NO HEARTS?
SSKKREEEEEEEE
I DID NOT, LORD VADER.
SSKKREEEEEEEE
YOU ARE WRONG. FROM OUR FEET TO OUR FINGERTIPS, WE HAVE A THOUSAND HEARTS. THEY MAKE US FASTER AND STRONGER THAN YOUR KIND.
YOU ALSO BLEED TO DEATH MUCH MORE QUICKLY.
NOW, YOU WILL TELL ME HOW YOU LEARNED TO SPEAK BASIC. OR I WILL SEEK OUT EACH OF YOUR HEARTS AND CRUSH THEM BETWEEN MY FINGERS.

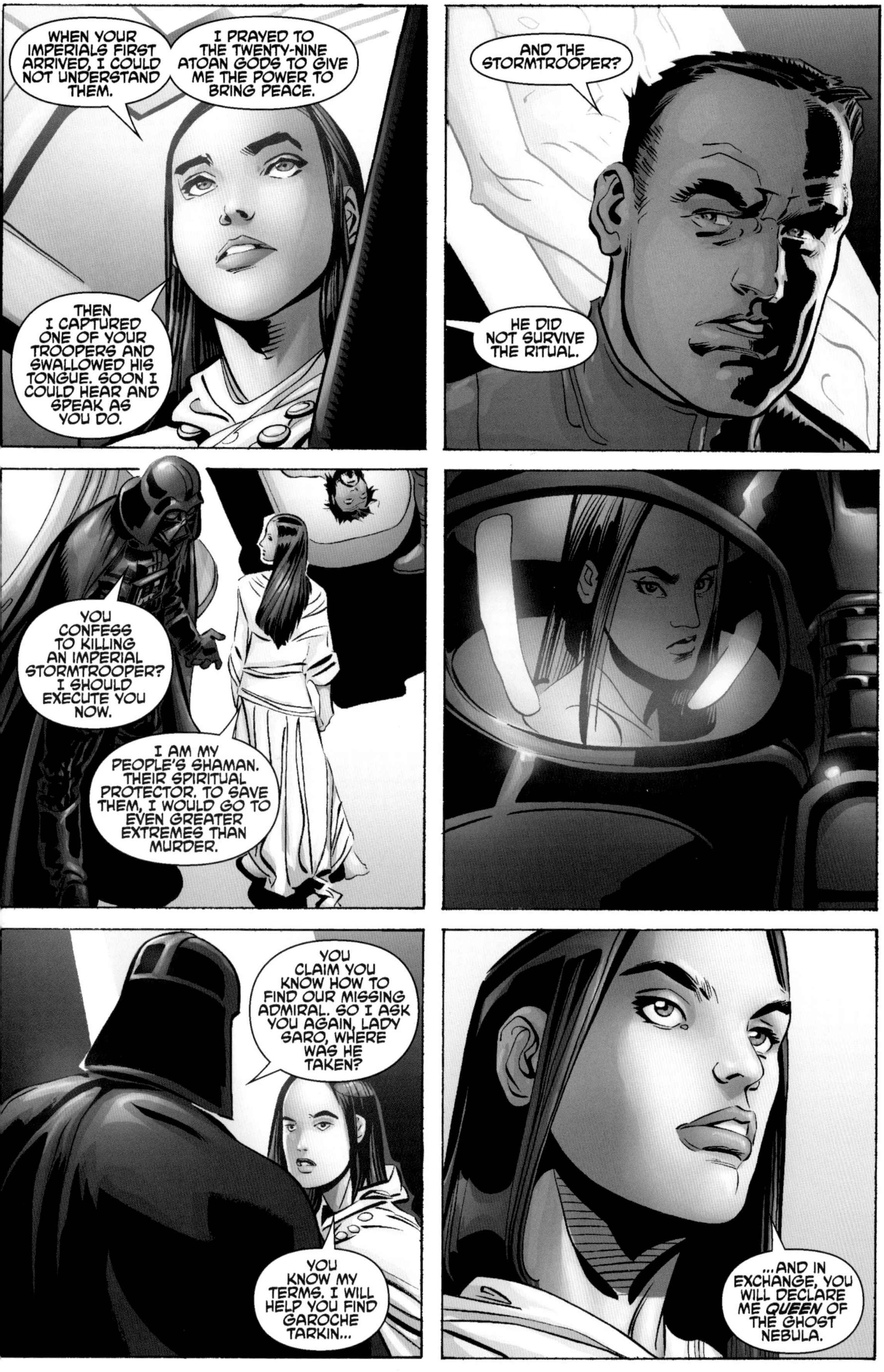
WHEN YOUR IMPERIALS FIRST ARRIVED, I COULD NOT UNDERSTAND THEM.
I PRAYED TO THE TWENTY-NINE ATOAN GODS TO GIVE ME THE POWER TO BRING PEACE.
THEN I CAPTURED ONE OF YOUR TROOPERS AND SWALLOWED HIS TONGUE. SOON I COULD HEAR AND SPEAK AS YOU DO.
AND THE STORMTROOPER?
HE DID NOT SURVIVE THE RITUAL.
YOU CONFESS TO KILLING AN IMPERIAL STORMTROOPER? I SHOULD EXECUTE YOU NOW.
I AM MY PEOPLE'S SHAMAN. THEIR SPIRITUAL PROTECTOR. TO SAVE THEM, I WOULD GO TO EVEN GREATER EXTREMES THAN MURDER.
YOU CLAIM YOU KNOW HOW TO FIND OUR MISSING ADMIRAL. SO I ASK YOU AGAIN, LADY SARO, WHERE WAS HE TAKEN?
YOU KNOW MY TERMS. I WILL HELP YOU FIND GAROCHE TARKIN...
...AND IN EXCHANGE, YOU WILL DECLARE ME *QUEEN* OF THE GHOST NEBULA.

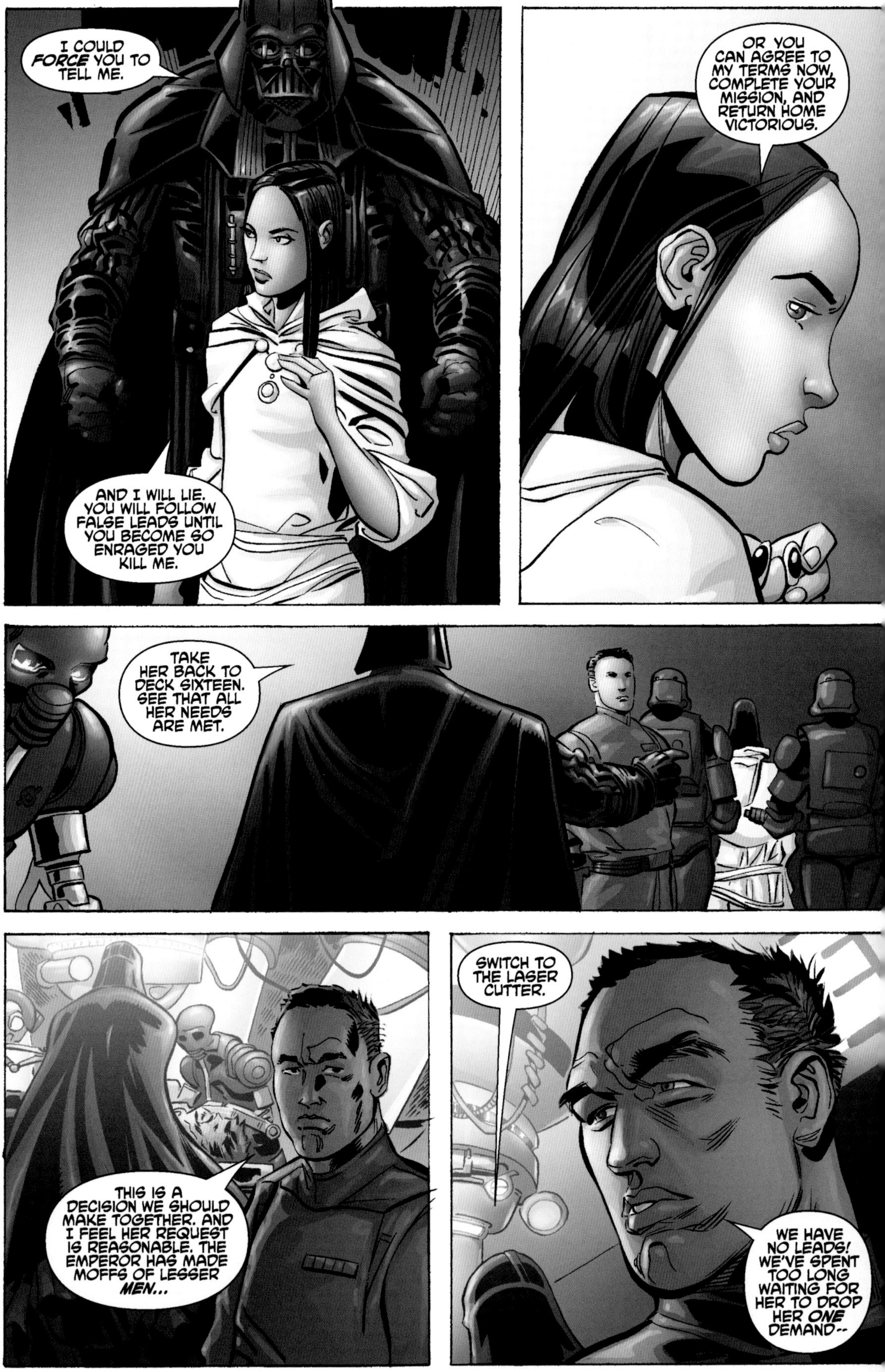
I COULD *FORCE* YOU TO TELL ME.
AND I WILL LIE. YOU WILL FOLLOW FALSE LEADS UNTIL YOU BECOME SO ENRAGED YOU KILL ME.
OR YOU CAN AGREE TO MY TERMS NOW, COMPLETE YOUR MISSION, AND RETURN HOME VICTORIOUS.
TAKE HER BACK TO DECK SIXTEEN. SEE THAT ALL HER NEEDS ARE MET.
THIS IS A DECISION WE SHOULD MAKE TOGETHER. AND I FEEL HER REQUEST IS REASONABLE. THE EMPEROR HAS MADE MOFFS OF LESSER *MEN*...
SWITCH TO THE LASER CUTTER.
WE HAVE NO LEADS! WE'VE SPENT TOO LONG WAITING FOR HER TO DROP HER *ONE* DEMAND--

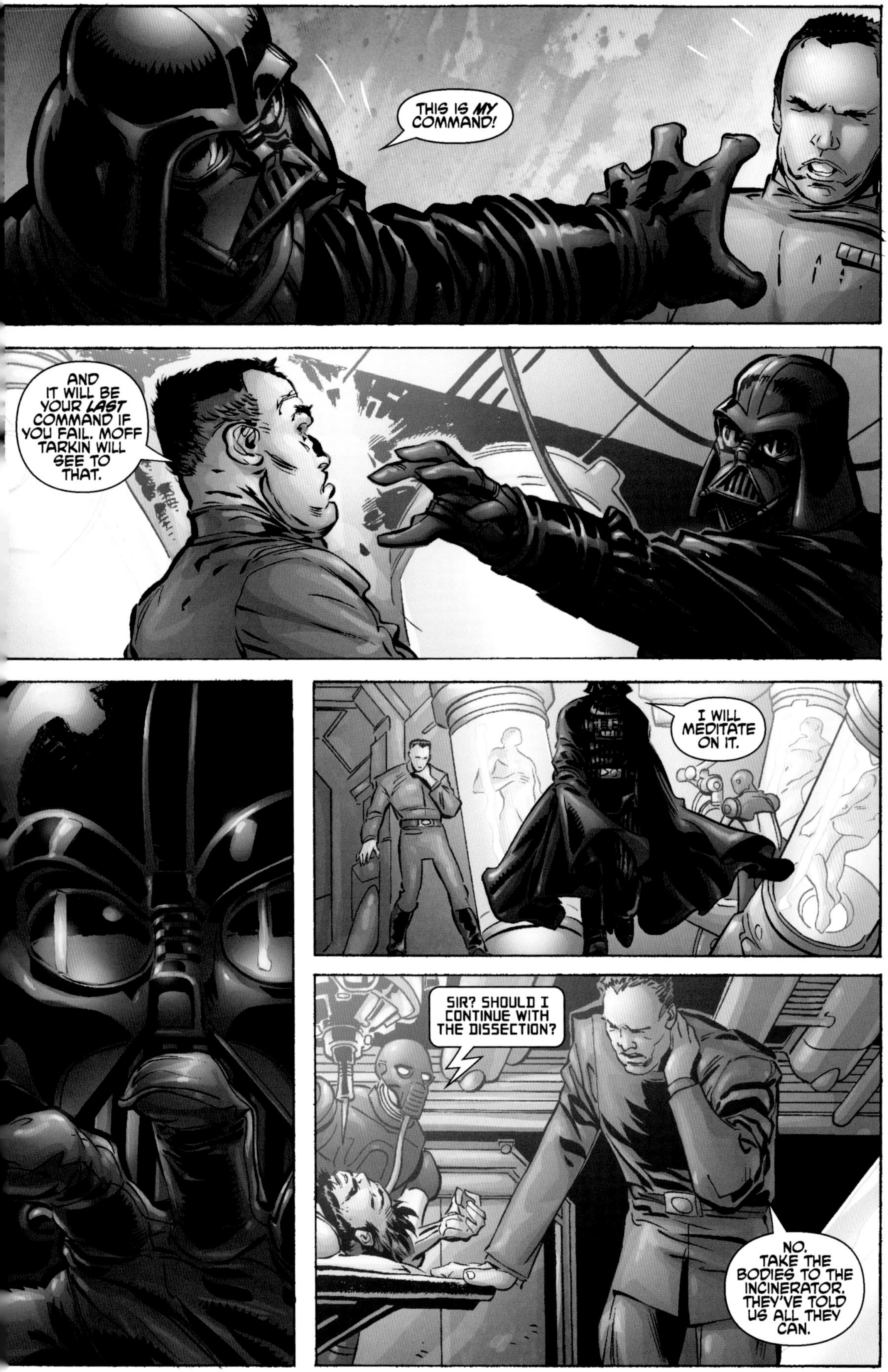
THIS IS *MY* COMMAND!
AND IT WILL BE YOUR *LAST* COMMAND IF YOU FAIL. MOFF TARKIN WILL SEE TO THAT.
I WILL MEDITATE ON IT.
SIR? SHOULD I CONTINUE WITH THE DISSECTION?
NO. TAKE THE BODIES TO THE INCINERATOR. THEY'VE TOLD US ALL THEY CAN.

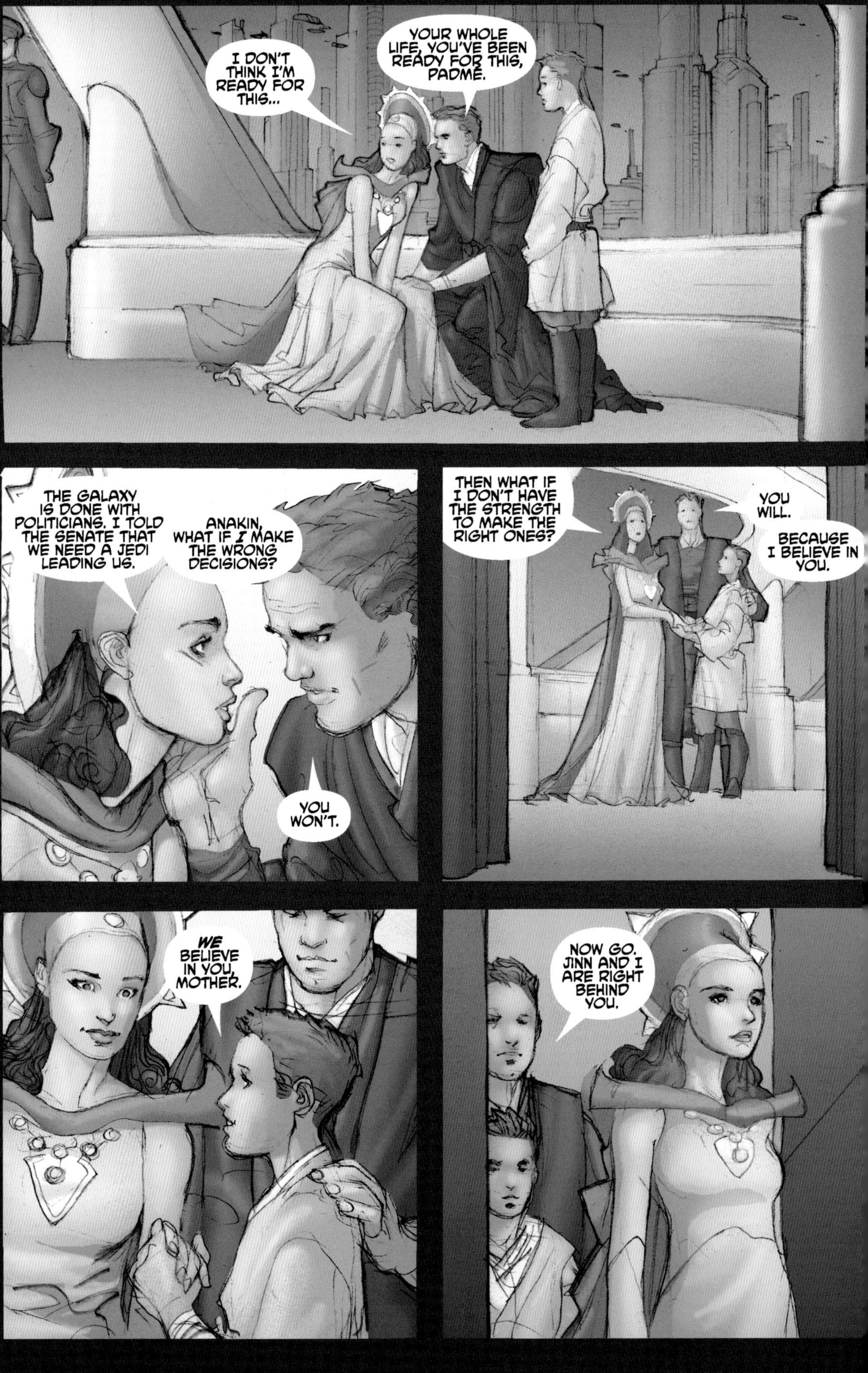
I DON'T THINK I'M READY FOR THIS...
YOUR WHOLE LIFE, YOU'VE BEEN READY FOR THIS, PADMÉ.
THE GALAXY IS DONE WITH POLITICIANS. I TOLD THE SENATE THAT WE NEED A JEDI LEADING US.
ANAKIN, WHAT IF *I* MAKE THE WRONG DECISIONS?
YOU WON'T.
THEN WHAT IF I DON'T HAVE THE STRENGTH TO MAKE THE RIGHT ONES?
YOU WILL.
BECAUSE I BELIEVE IN YOU.
WE BELIEVE IN YOU, MOTHER.
NOW GO. JINN AND I ARE RIGHT BEHIND YOU.

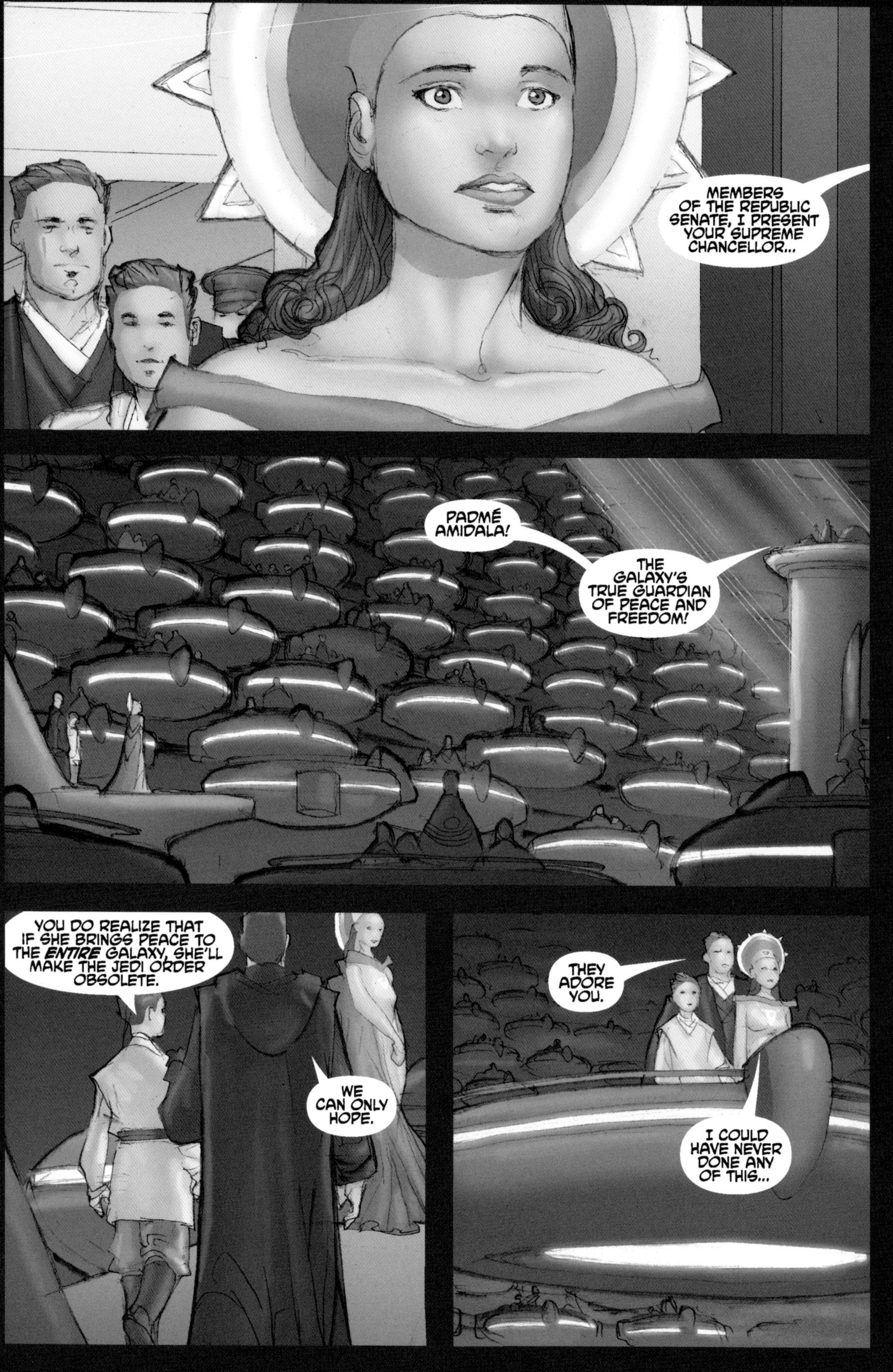
MEMBERS OF THE REPUBLIC SENATE, I PRESENT YOUR SUPREME CHANCELLOR...
PADMÉ AMIDALA!
THE GALAXY'S TRUE GUARDIAN OF PEACE AND FREEDOM!
YOU DO REALIZE THAT IF SHE BRINGS PEACE TO THE *ENTIRE* GALAXY, SHE'LL MAKE THE JEDI ORDER OBSOLETE.
WE CAN ONLY HOPE.
THEY ADORE YOU.
I COULD HAVE NEVER DONE ANY OF THIS...

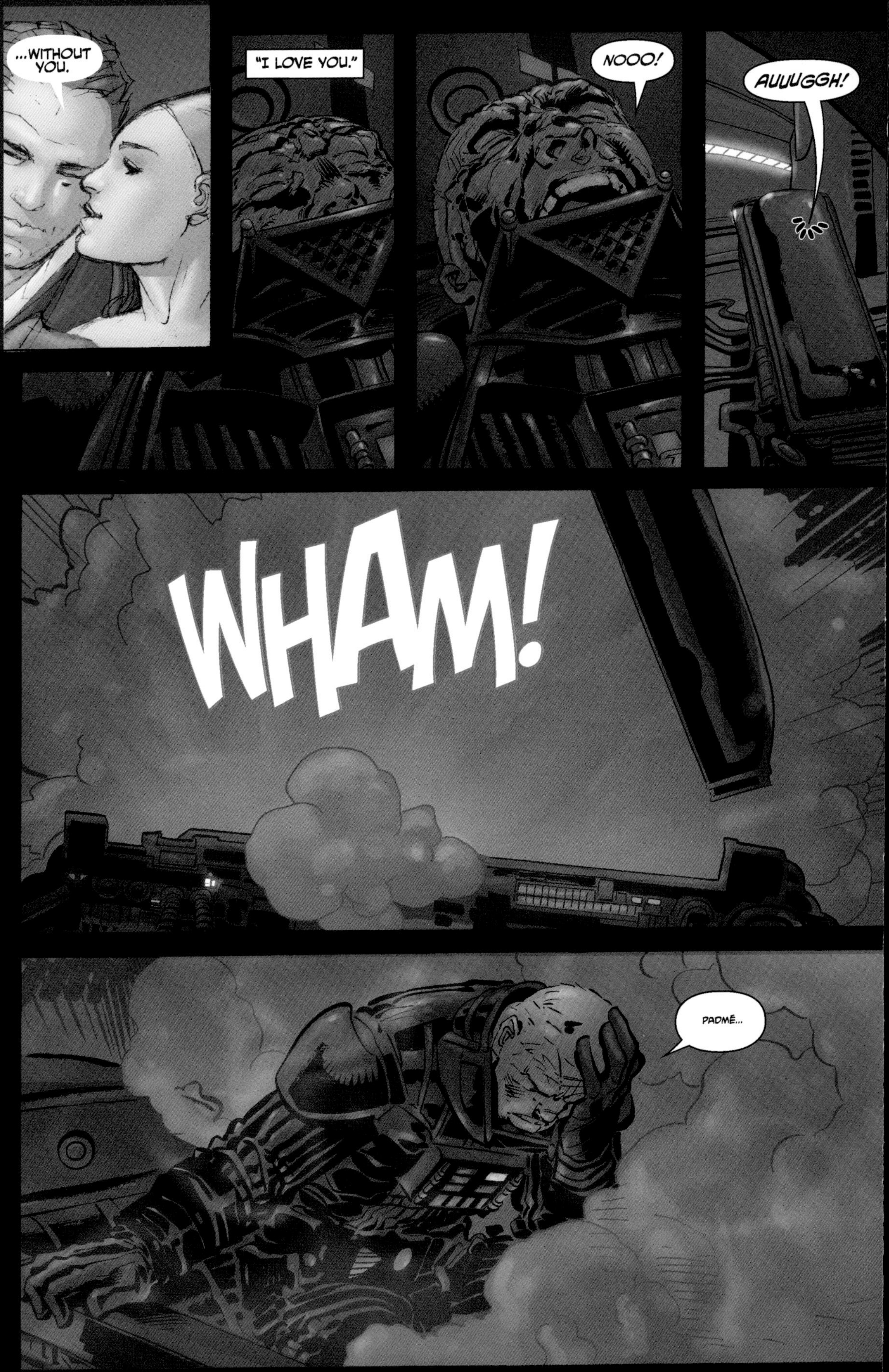

...WITHOUT YOU.
"I LOVE YOU."
NOOO!
AUUUGGH!
WHAM!
PADMÉ...

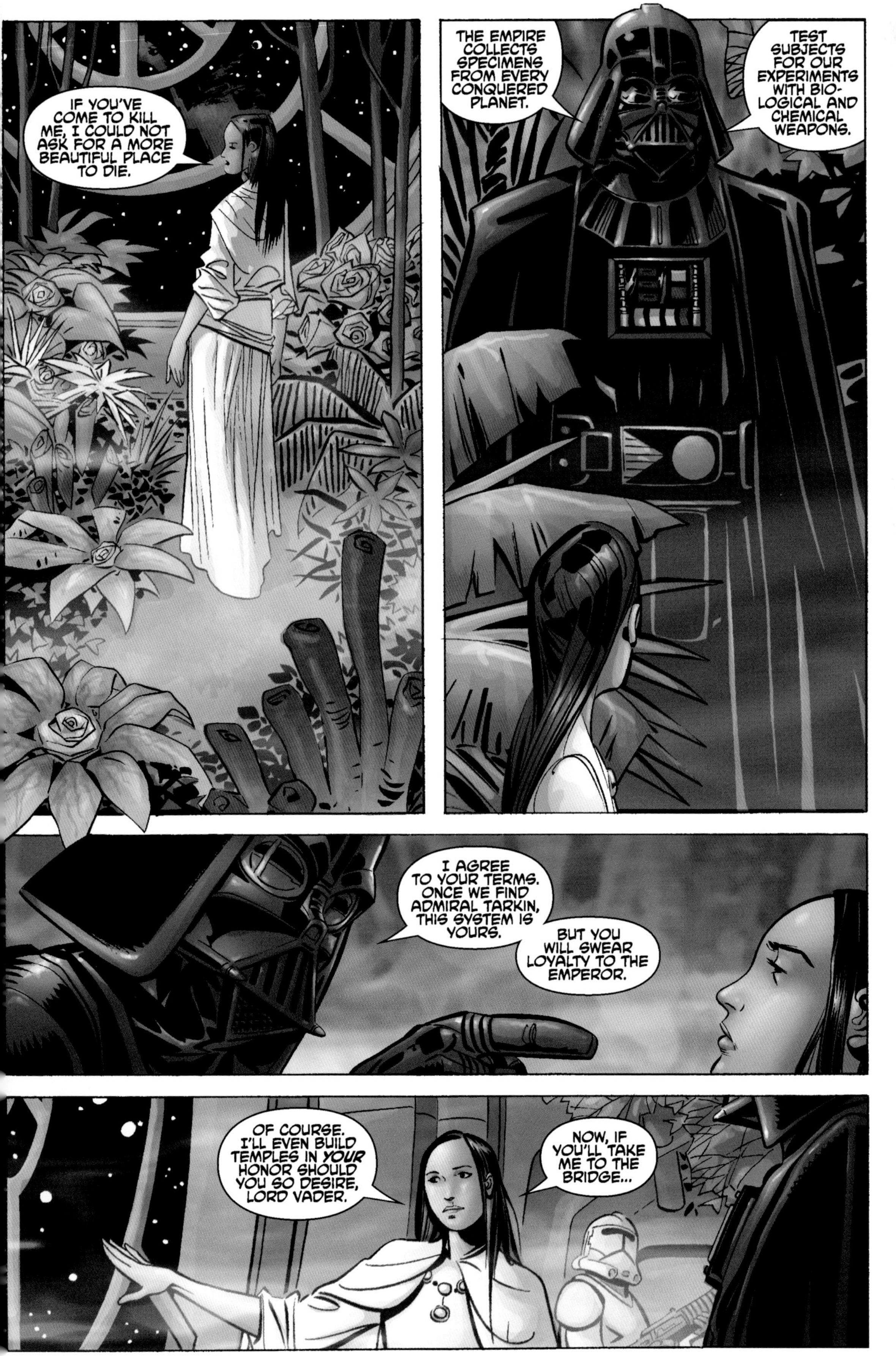
IF YOU'VE COME TO KILL ME, I COULD NOT ASK FOR A MORE BEAUTIFUL PLACE TO DIE.
THE EMPIRE COLLECTS SPECIMENS FROM EVERY CONQUERED PLANET.
TEST SUBJECTS FOR OUR EXPERIMENTS WITH BIO-LOGICAL AND CHEMICAL WEAPONS.
I AGREE TO YOUR TERMS. ONCE WE FIND ADMIRAL TARKIN, THIS SYSTEM IS YOURS.
BUT YOU WILL SWEAR LOYALTY TO THE EMPEROR.
OF COURSE. I'LL EVEN BUILD TEMPLES IN *YOUR* HONOR SHOULD YOU SO DESIRE, LORD VADER.
NOW, IF YOU'LL TAKE ME TO THE BRIDGE...

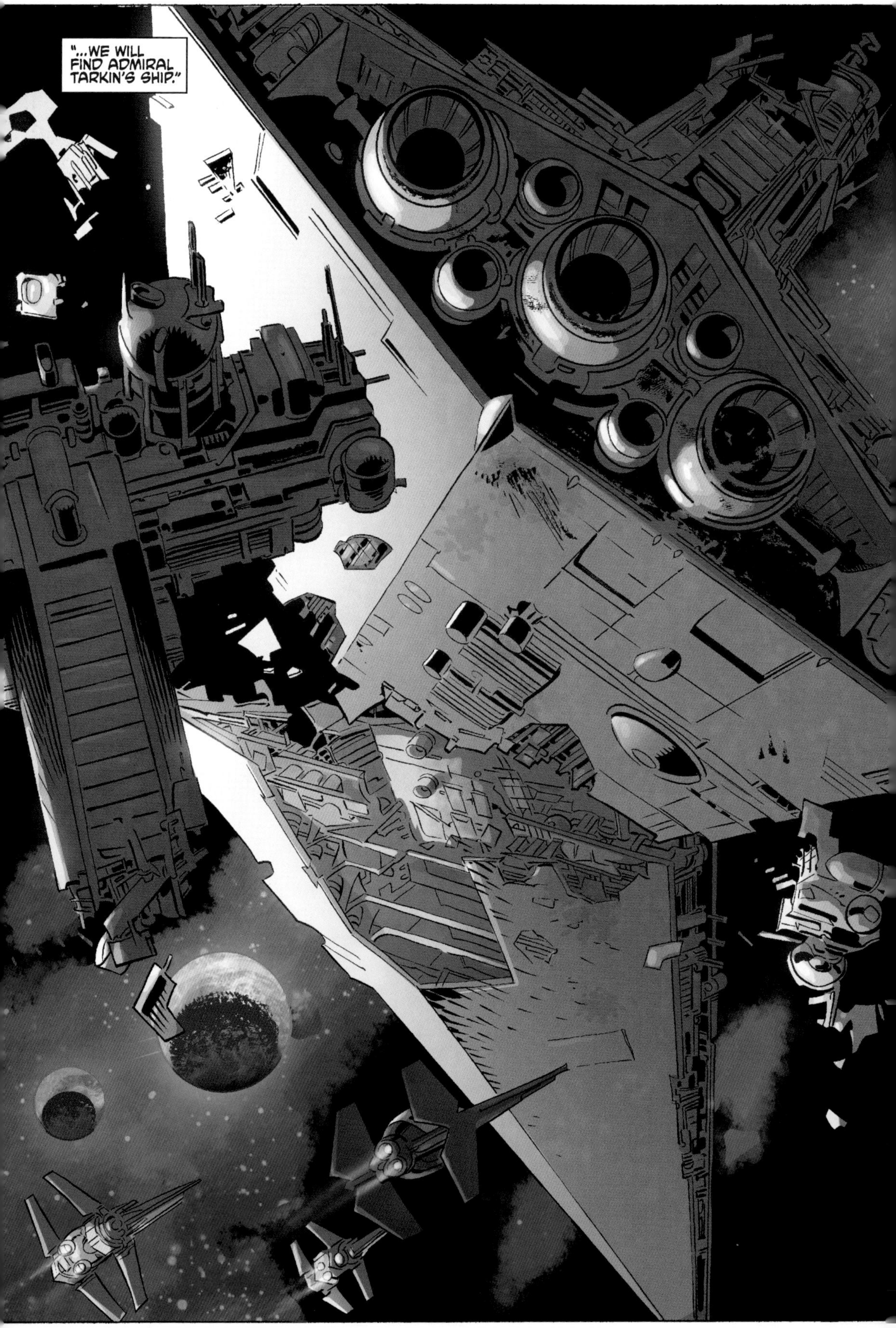
"...WE WILL FIND ADMIRAL TARKIN'S SHIP."

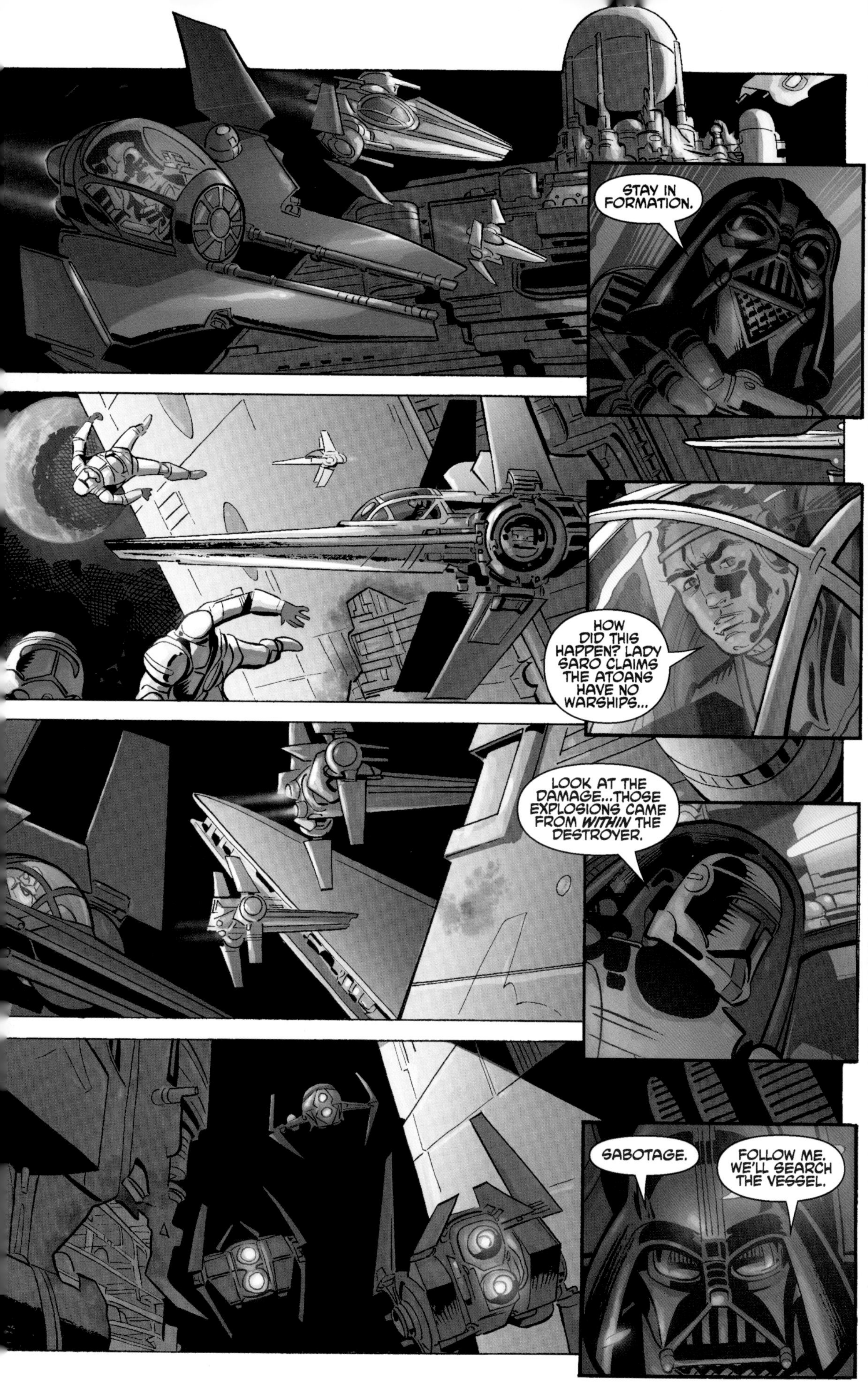
STAY IN FORMATION.
HOW DID THIS HAPPEN? LADY SARO CLAIMS THE ATOANS HAVE NO WARSHIPS...
LOOK AT THE DAMAGE...THOSE EXPLOSIONS CAME FROM *WITHIN* THE DESTROYER.
SABOTAGE.
FOLLOW ME. WE'LL SEARCH THE VESSEL.

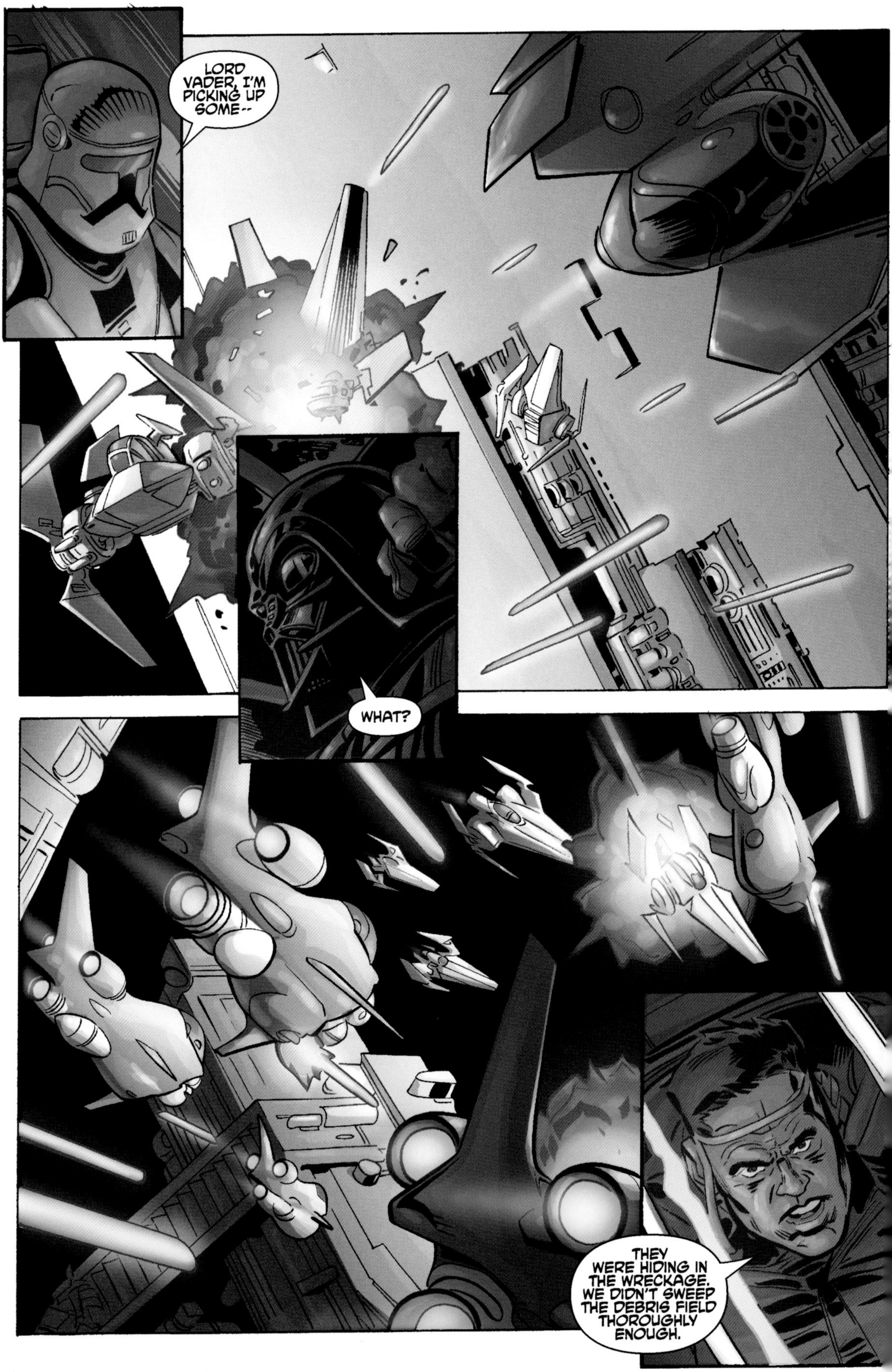
LORD VADER, I'M PICKING UP SOME--
WHAT?
THEY WERE HIDING IN THE WRECKAGE. WE DIDN'T SWEEP THE DEBRIS FIELD THOROUGHLY ENOUGH.

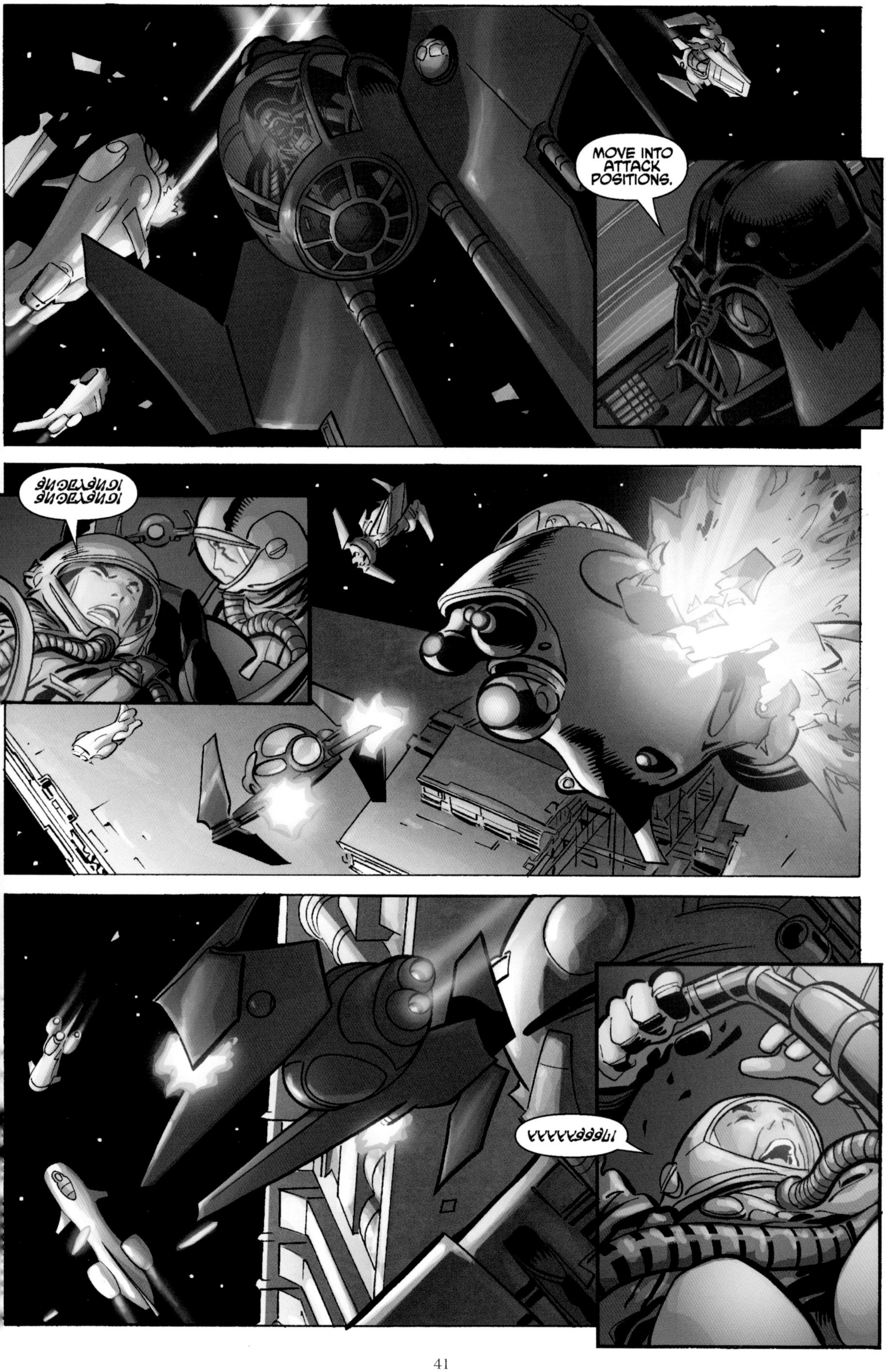
MOVE INTO ATTACK POSITIONS.

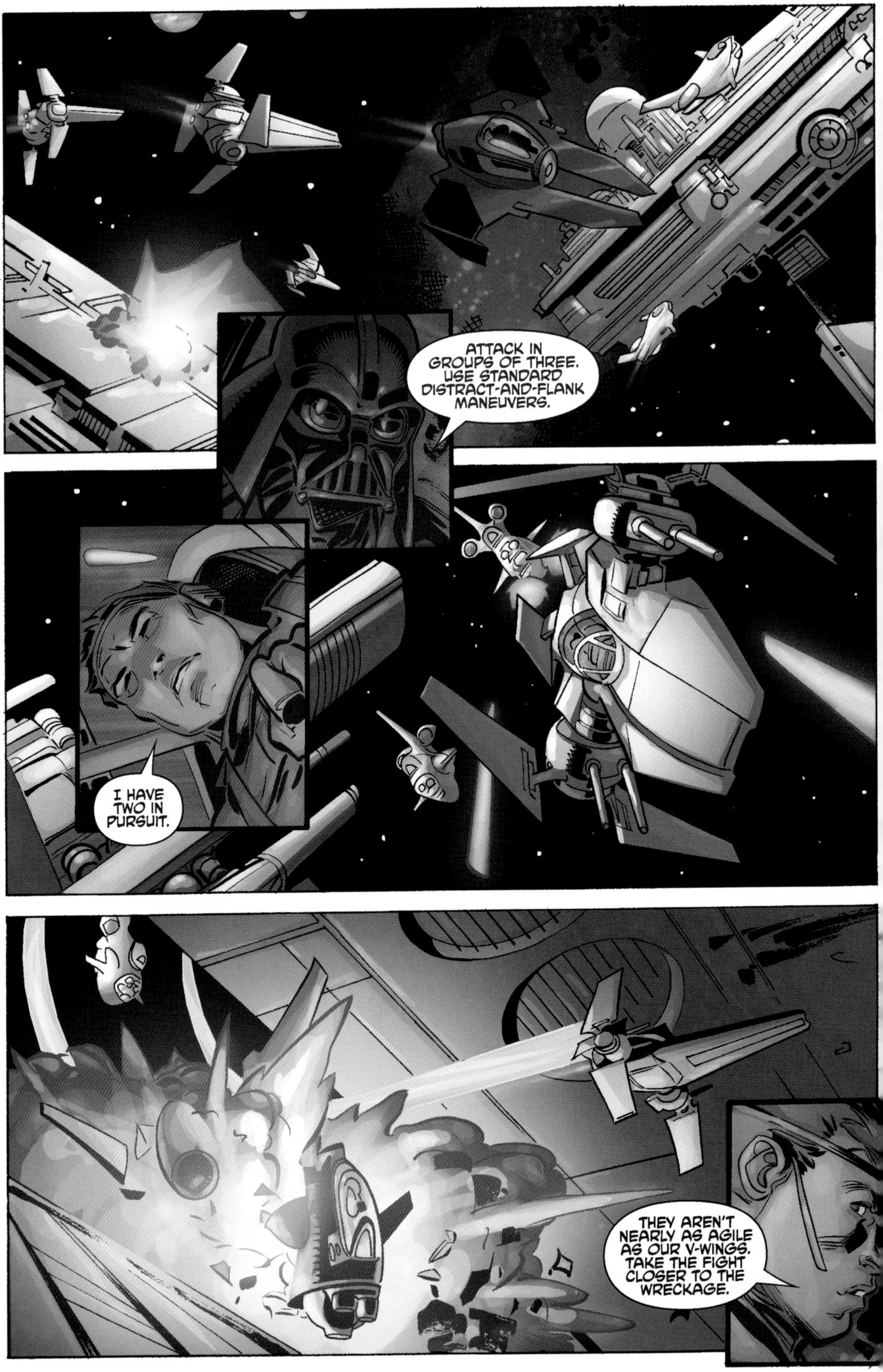
ATTACK IN GROUPS OF THREE. USE STANDARD DISTRACT-AND-FLANK MANEUVERS.
I HAVE TWO IN PURSUIT.
THEY AREN'T NEARLY AS AGILE AS OUR V-WINGS. TAKE THE FIGHT CLOSER TO THE WRECKAGE.

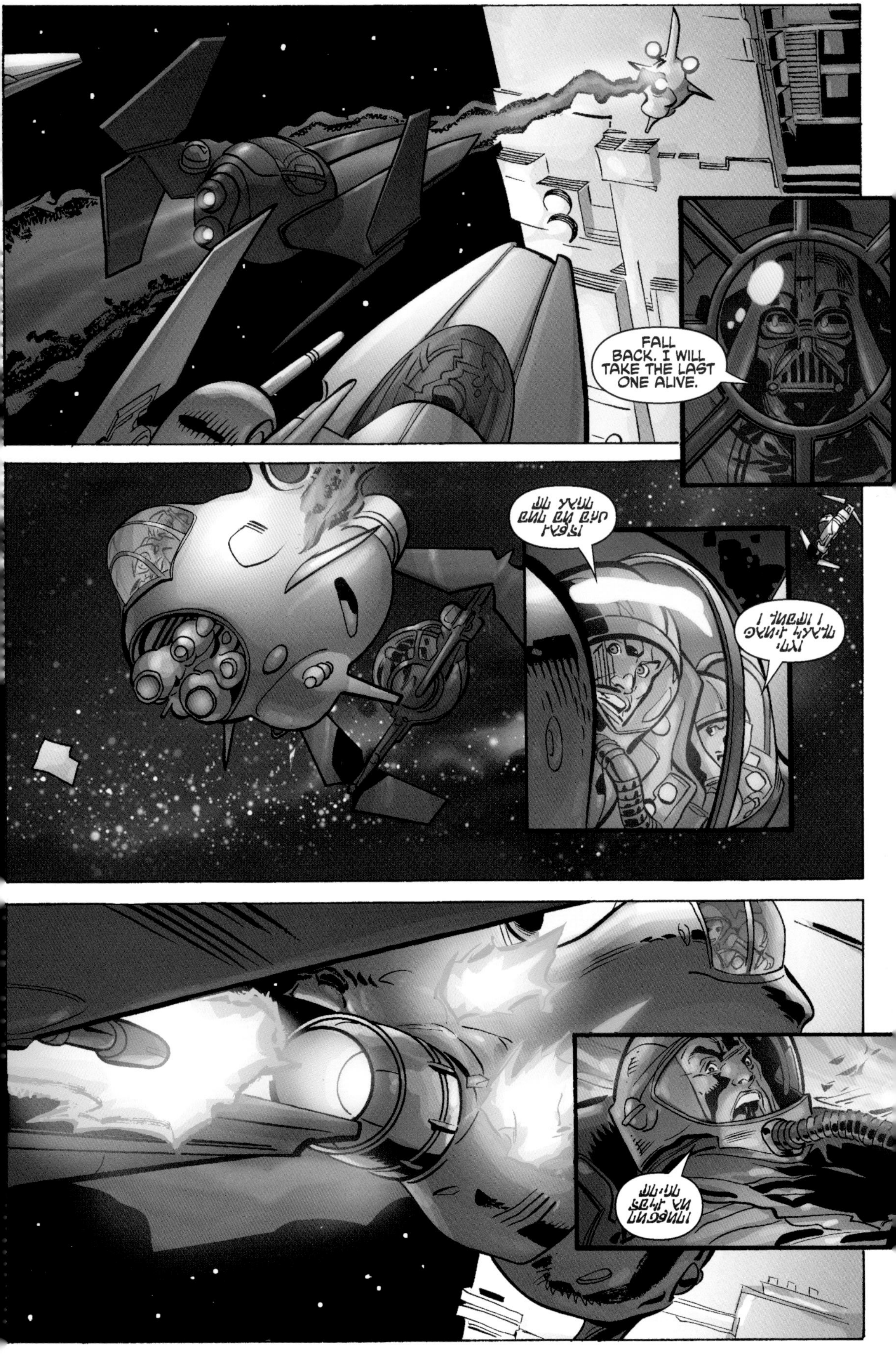
FALL BACK. I WILL TAKE THE LAST ONE ALIVE.

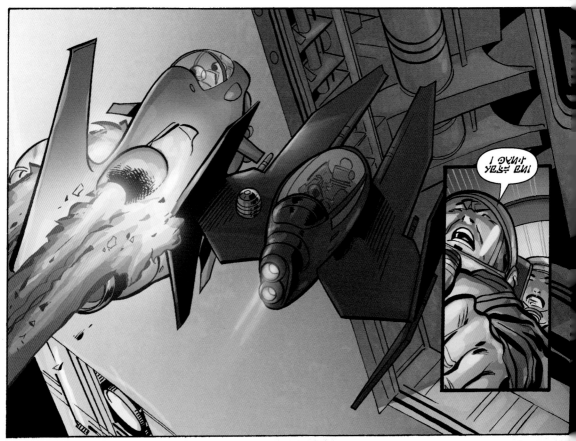

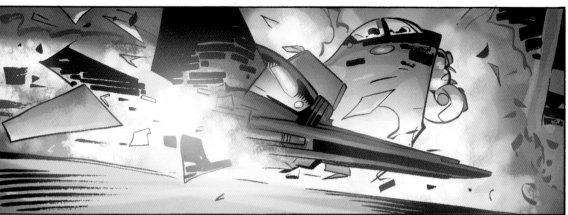

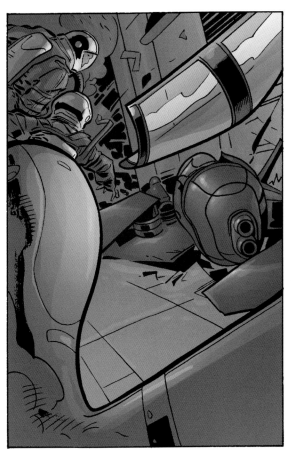

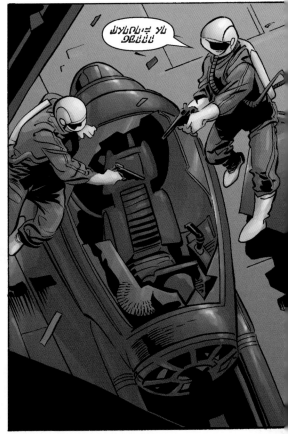

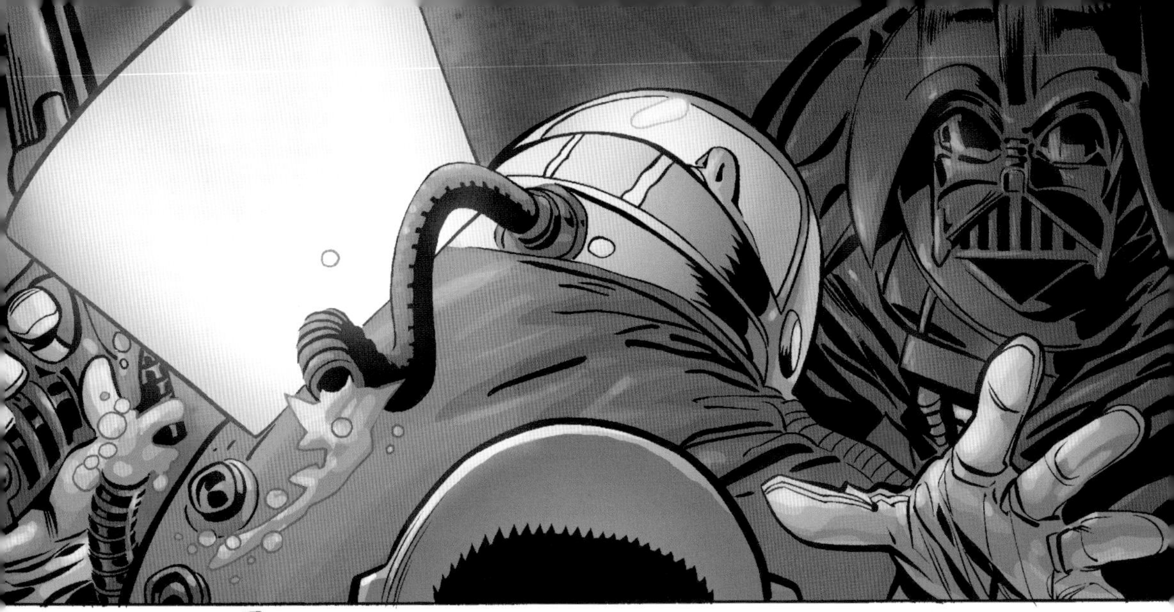

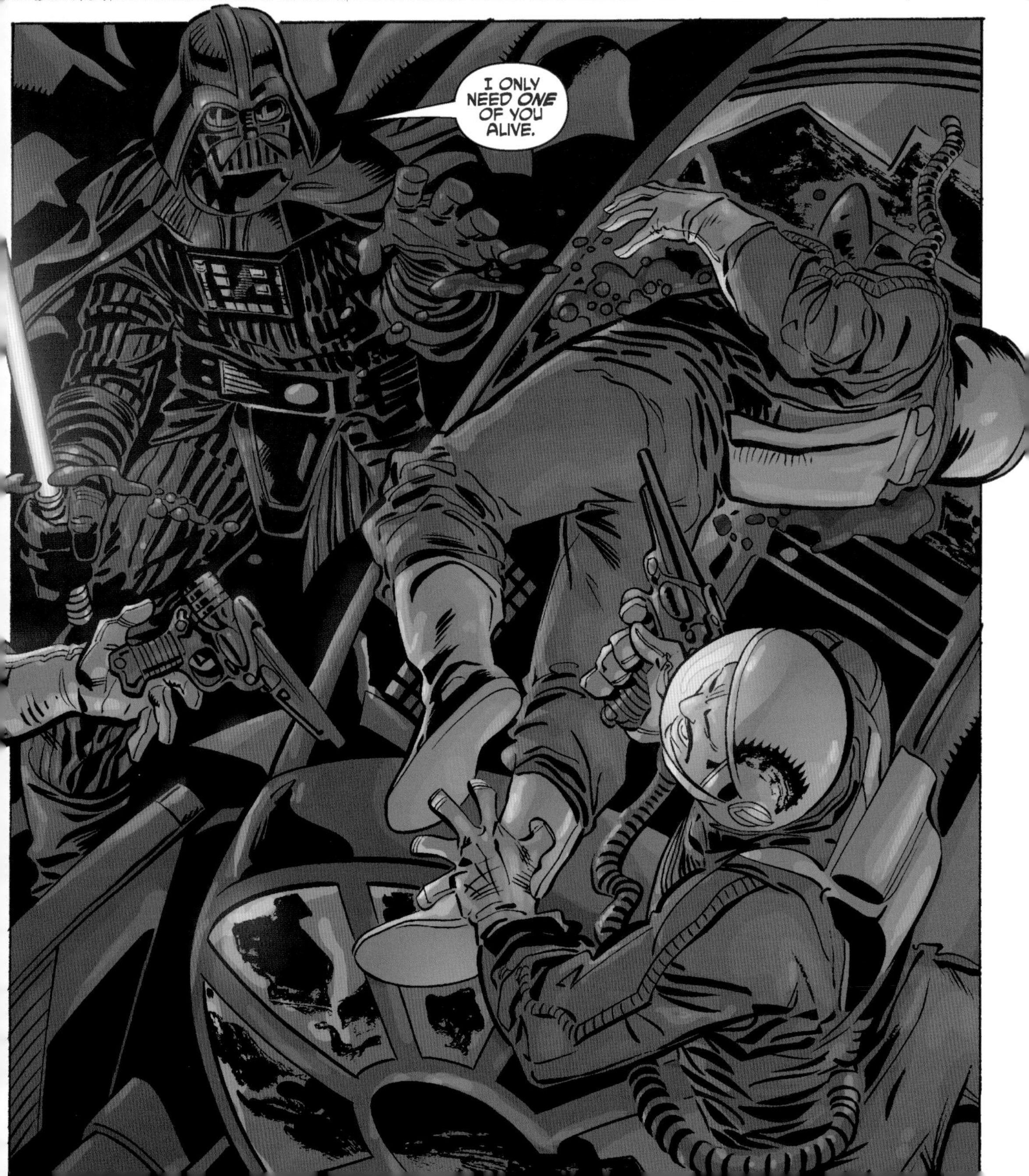
I ONLY NEED ONE OF YOU ALIVE.

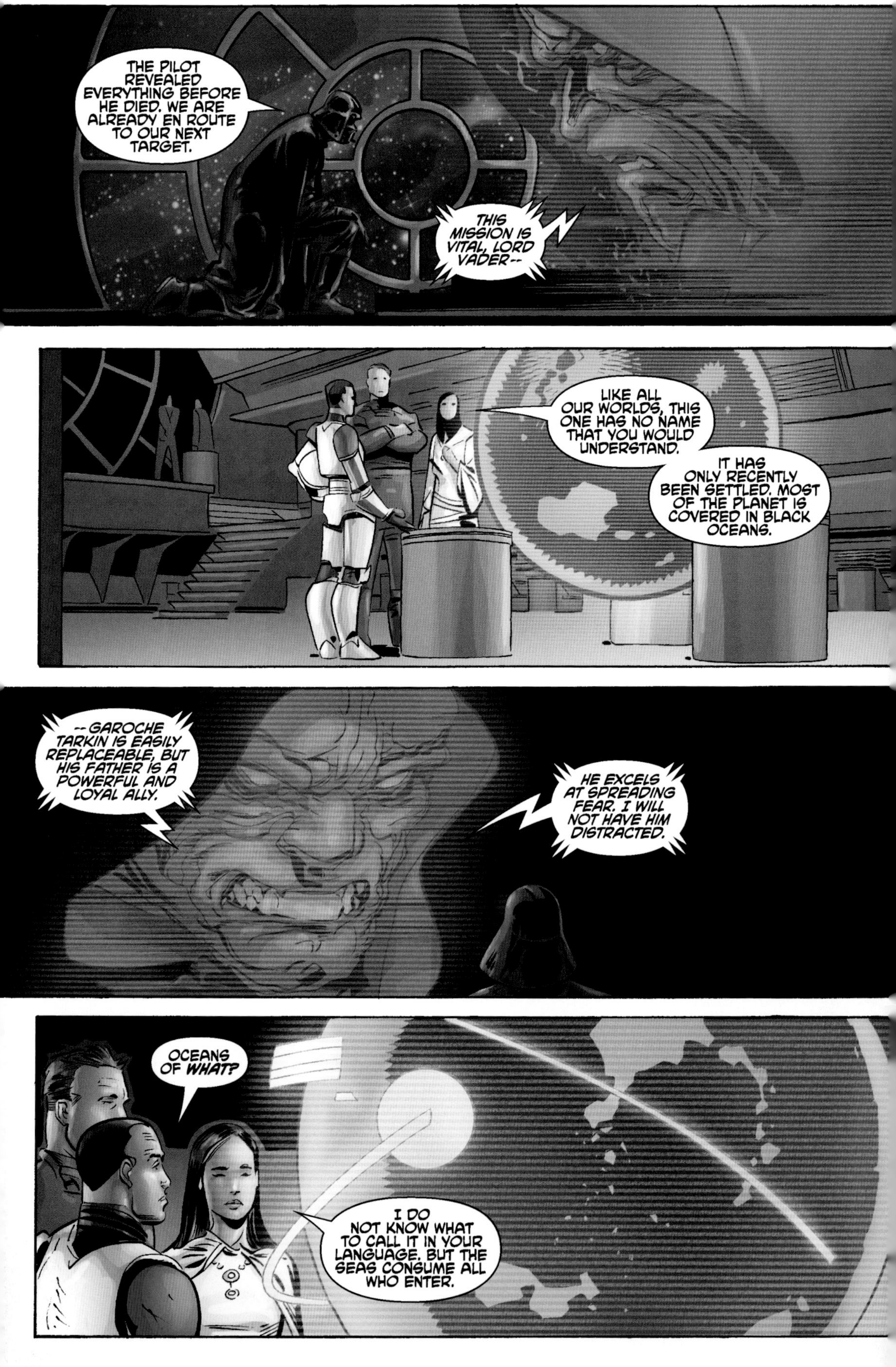
THE PILOT REVEALED EVERYTHING BEFORE HE DIED. WE ARE ALREADY EN ROUTE TO OUR NEXT TARGET.
THIS MISSION IS VITAL, LORD VADER--
LIKE ALL OUR WORLDS, THIS ONE HAS NO NAME THAT YOU WOULD UNDERSTAND.
IT HAS ONLY RECENTLY BEEN SETTLED. MOST OF THE PLANET IS COVERED IN BLACK OCEANS.
--GAROCHE TARKIN IS EASILY REPLACEABLE, BUT HIS FATHER IS A POWERFUL AND LOYAL ALLY.
HE EXCELS AT SPREADING FEAR. I WILL NOT HAVE HIM DISTRACTED.
OCEANS OF WHAT?
I DO NOT KNOW WHAT TO CALL IT IN YOUR LANGUAGE. BUT THE SEAS CONSUME ALL WHO ENTER.

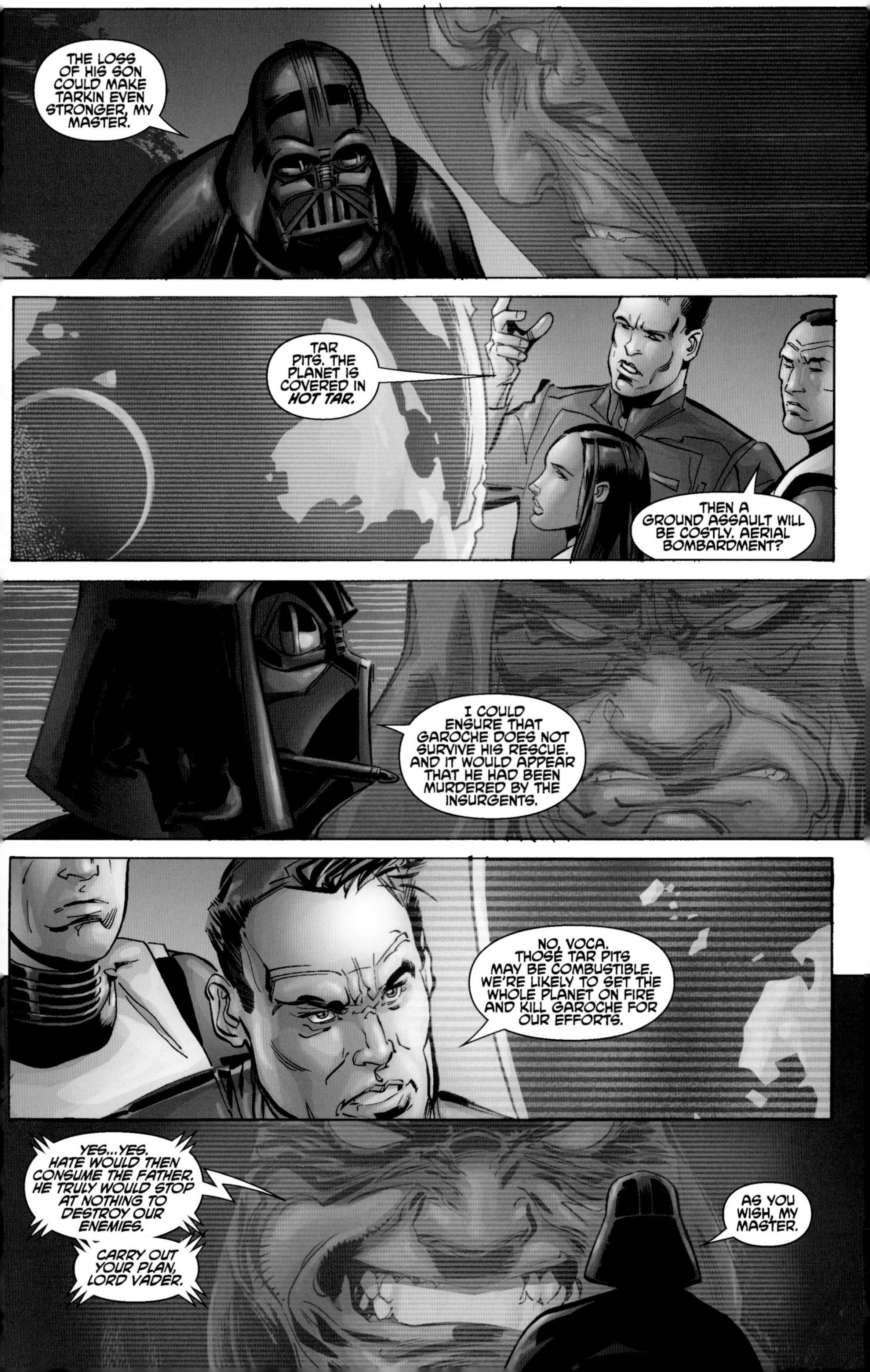
THE LOSS OF HIS SON COULD MAKE TARKIN EVEN STRONGER, MY MASTER.
TAR PITS. THE PLANET IS COVERED IN HOT TAR.
THEN A GROUND ASSAULT WILL BE COSTLY. AERIAL BOMBARDMENT?
I COULD ENSURE THAT GAROCHE DOES NOT SURVIVE HIS RESCUE. AND IT WOULD APPEAR THAT HE HAD BEEN MURDERED BY THE INSURGENTS.
NO, VOCA. THOSE TAR PITS MAY BE COMBUSTIBLE. WE'RE LIKELY TO SET THE WHOLE PLANET ON FIRE AND KILL GAROCHE FOR OUR EFFORTS.
YES...YES. HATE WOULD THEN CONSUME THE FATHER. HE TRULY WOULD STOP AT NOTHING TO DESTROY OUR ENEMIES.
CARRY OUT YOUR PLAN, LORD VADER.
AS YOU WISH, MY MASTER.

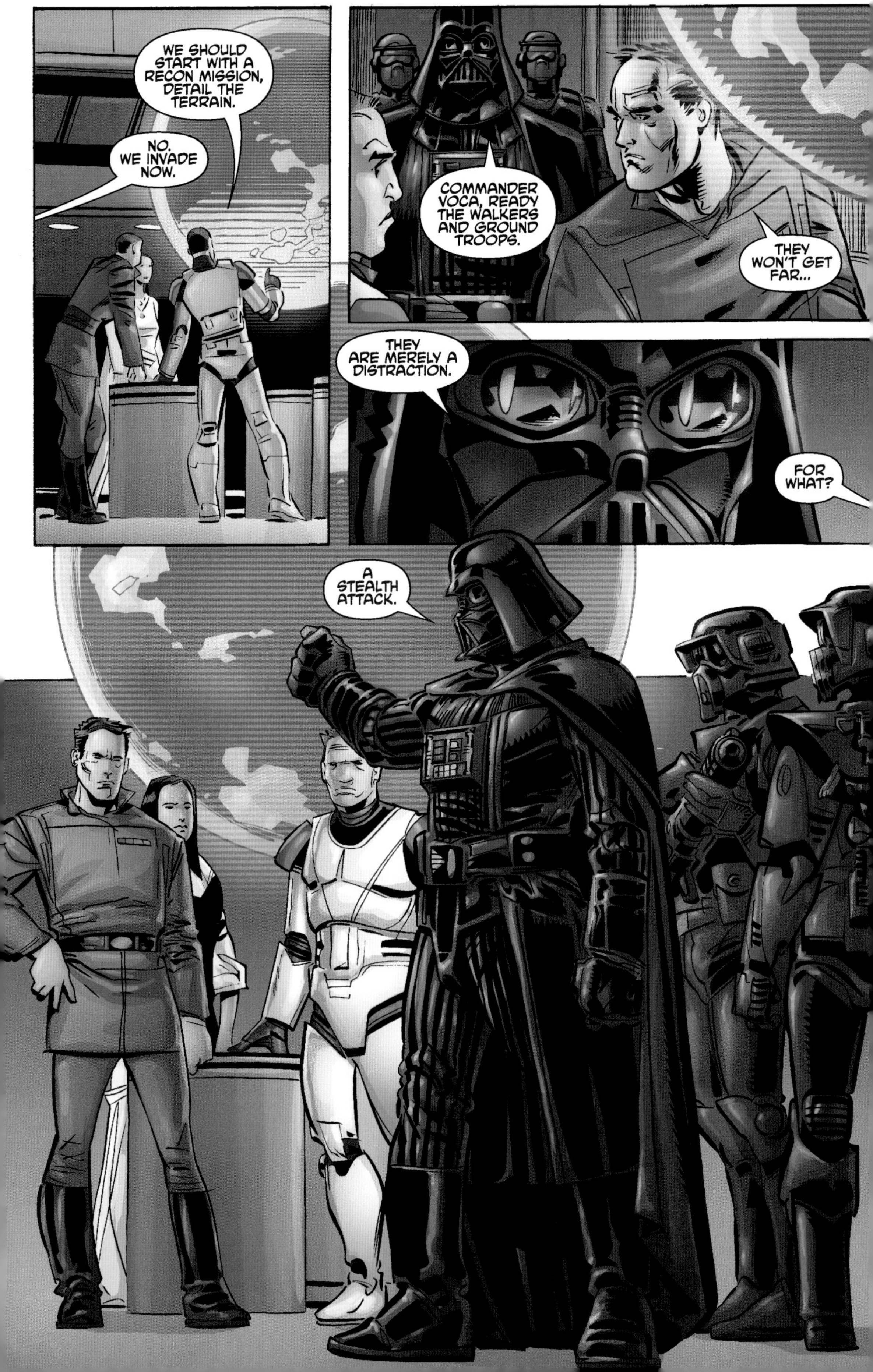
WE SHOULD START WITH A RECON MISSION, DETAIL THE TERRAIN.
NO. WE INVADE NOW.
COMMANDER VOCA, READY THE WALKERS AND GROUND TROOPS.
THEY WON'T GET FAR...
THEY ARE MERELY A DISTRACTION.
FOR WHAT?
A STEALTH ATTACK.

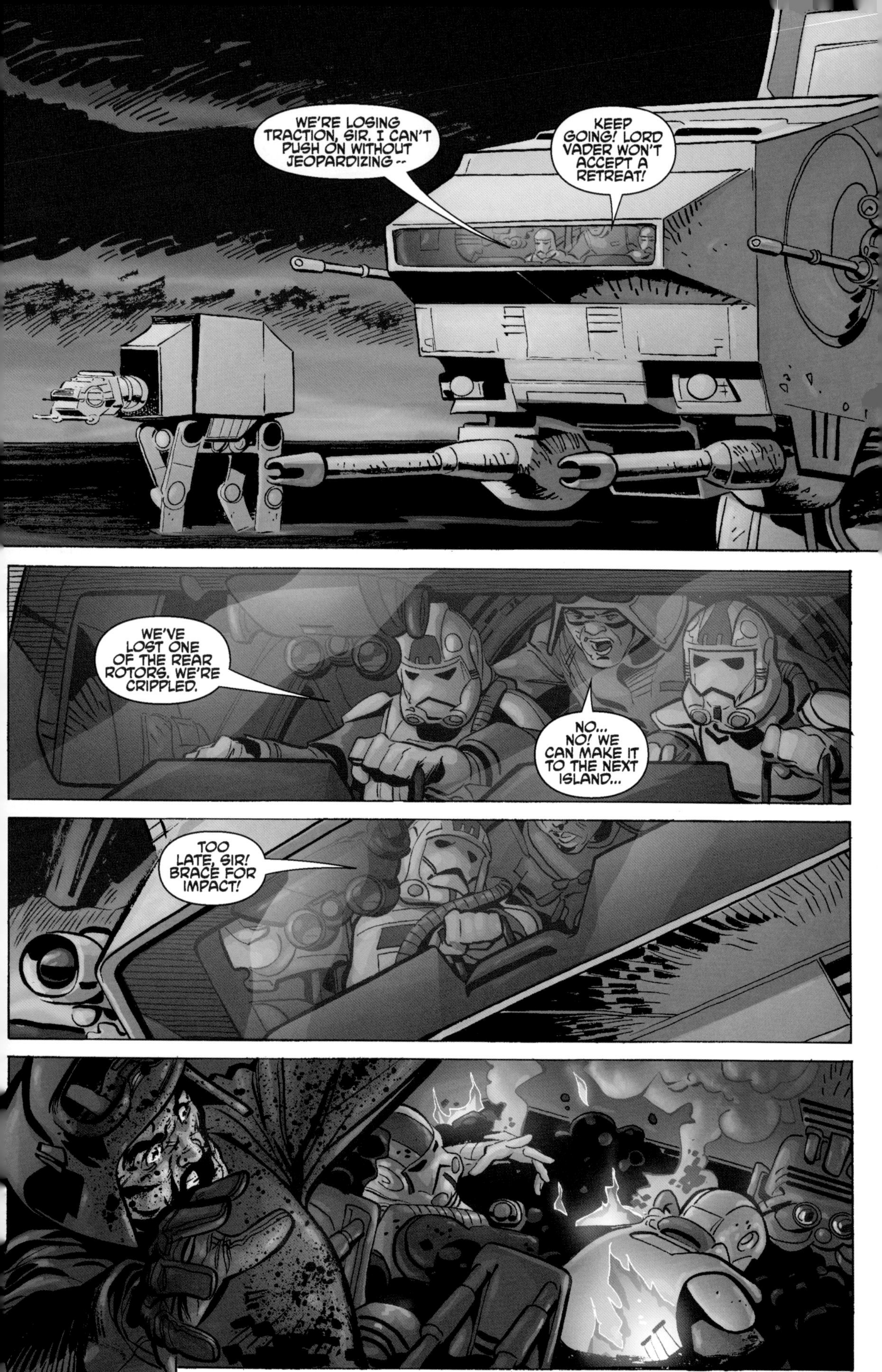
WE'RE LOSING TRACTION, SIR. I CAN'T PUSH ON WITHOUT JEOPARDIZING --
KEEP GOING! LORD VADER WON'T ACCEPT A RETREAT!
WE'VE LOST ONE OF THE REAR ROTORS. WE'RE CRIPPLED.
NO... NO! WE CAN MAKE IT TO THE NEXT ISLAND...
TOO LATE, SIR! BRACE FOR IMPACT!

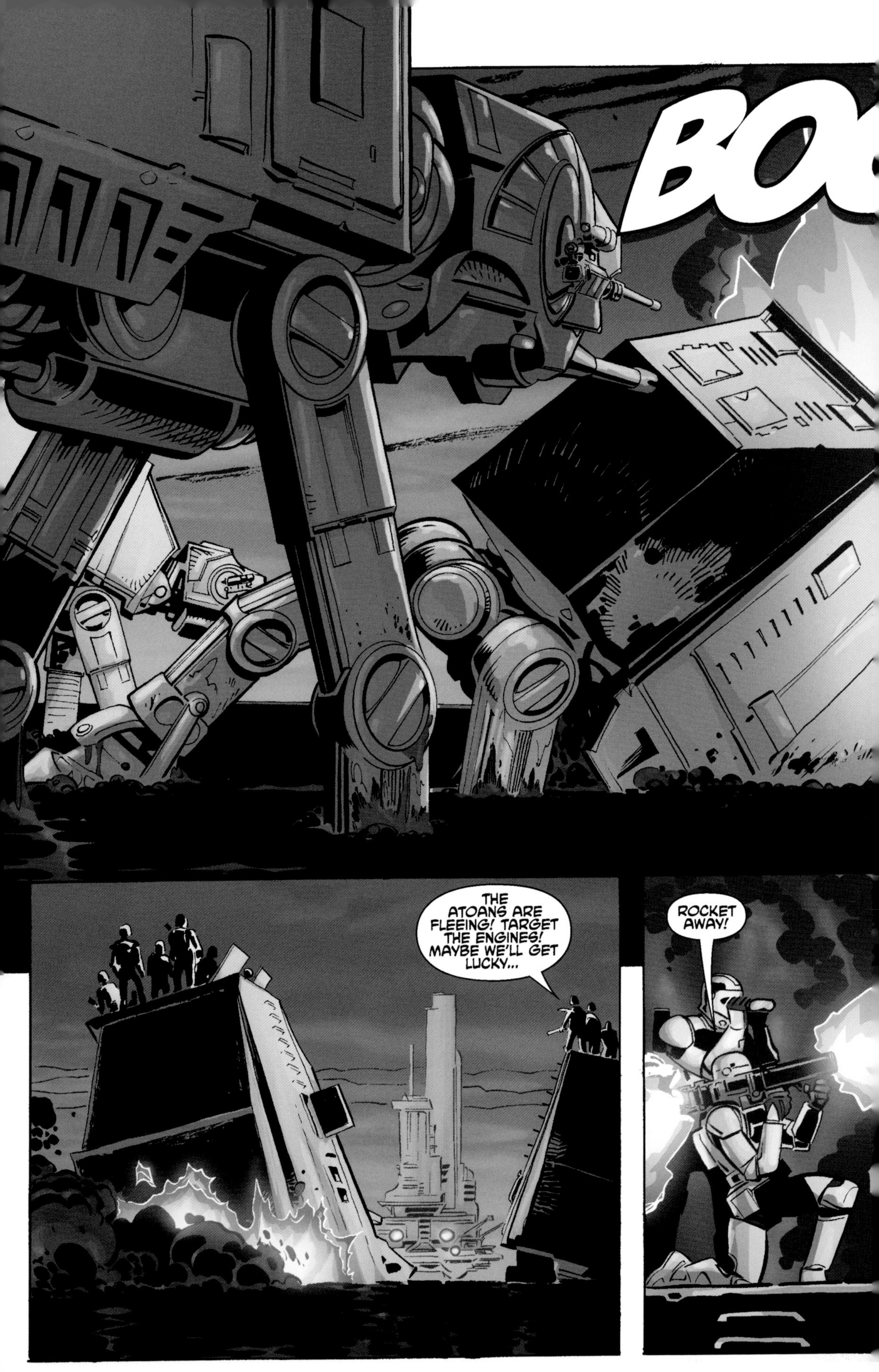
BOO
THE ATOANS ARE FLEEING! TARGET THE ENGINES! MAYBE WE'LL GET LUCKY...
ROCKET AWAY!

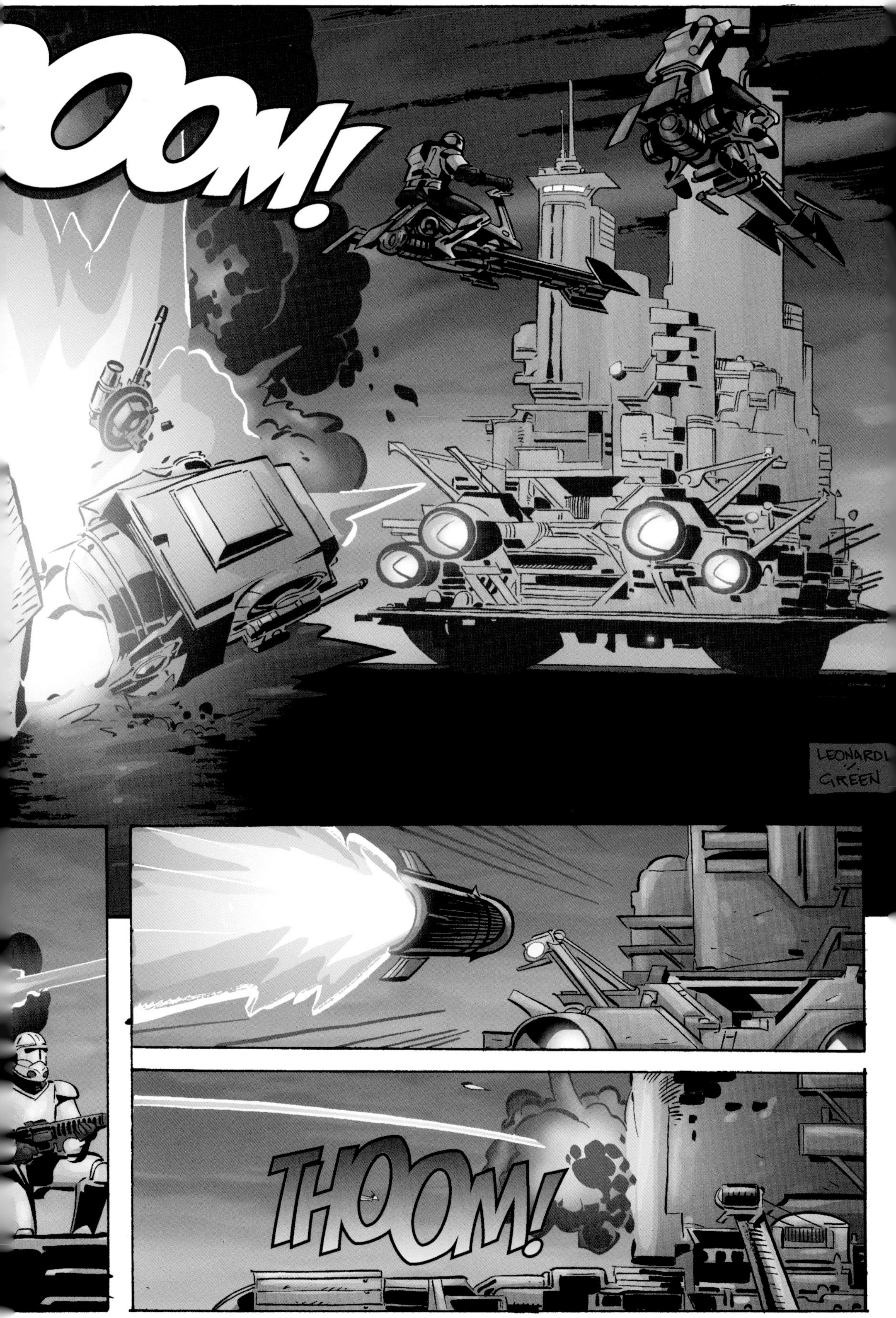
OOM!
LEONARDI
GREEN
THOOM!

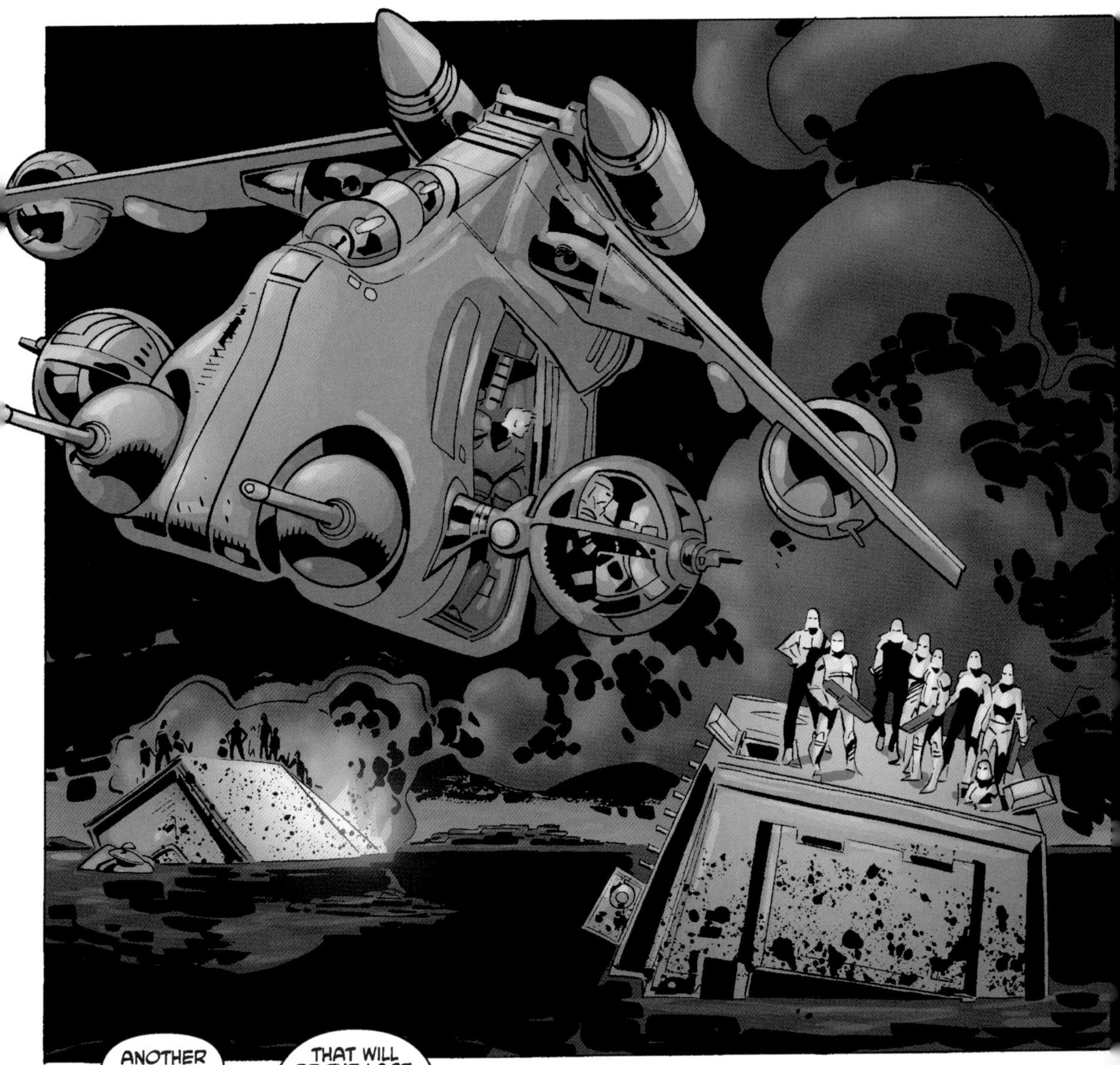

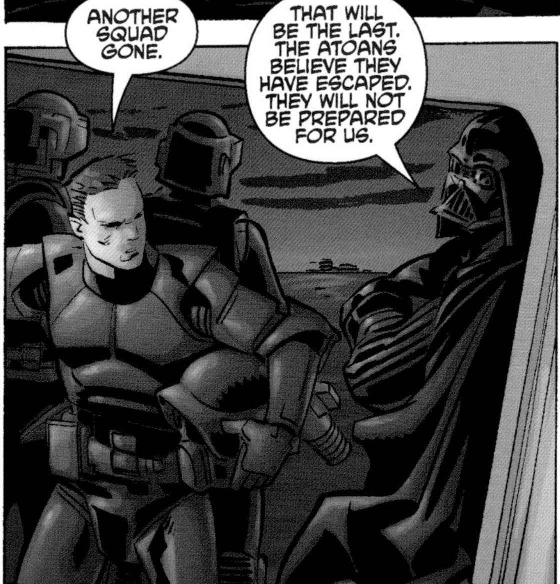
ANOTHER SQUAD GONE.
THAT WILL BE THE LAST. THE ATOANS BELIEVE THEY HAVE ESCAPED. THEY WILL NOT BE PREPARED FOR US.

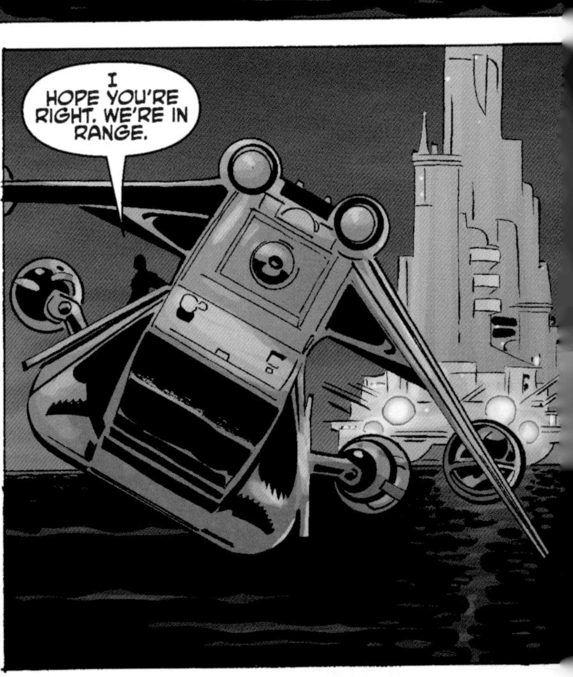
I HOPE YOU'RE RIGHT. WE'RE IN RANGE.

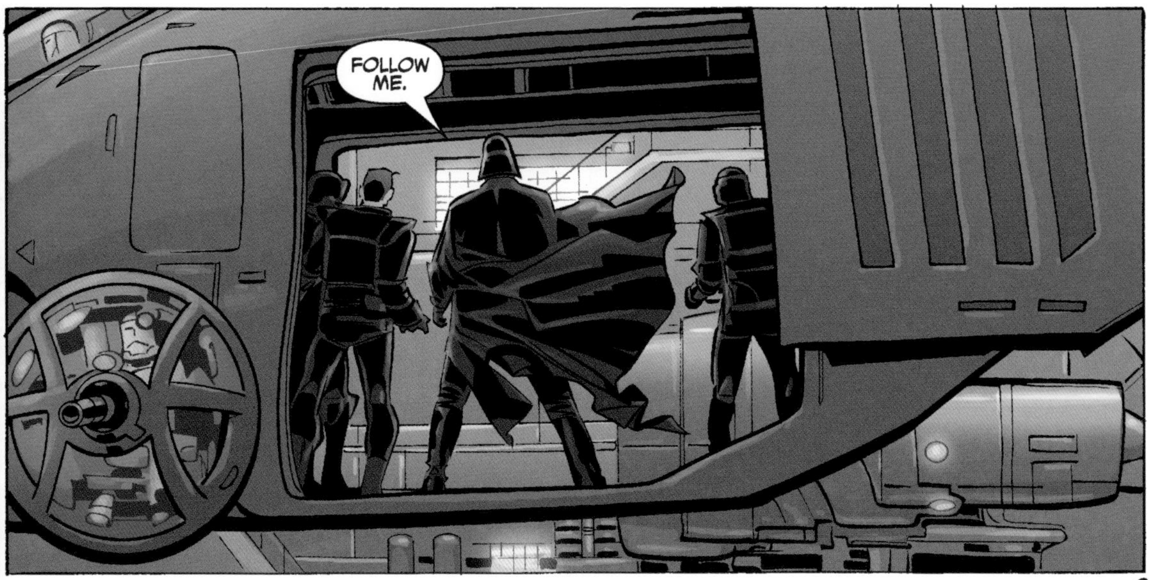
FOLLOW ME.

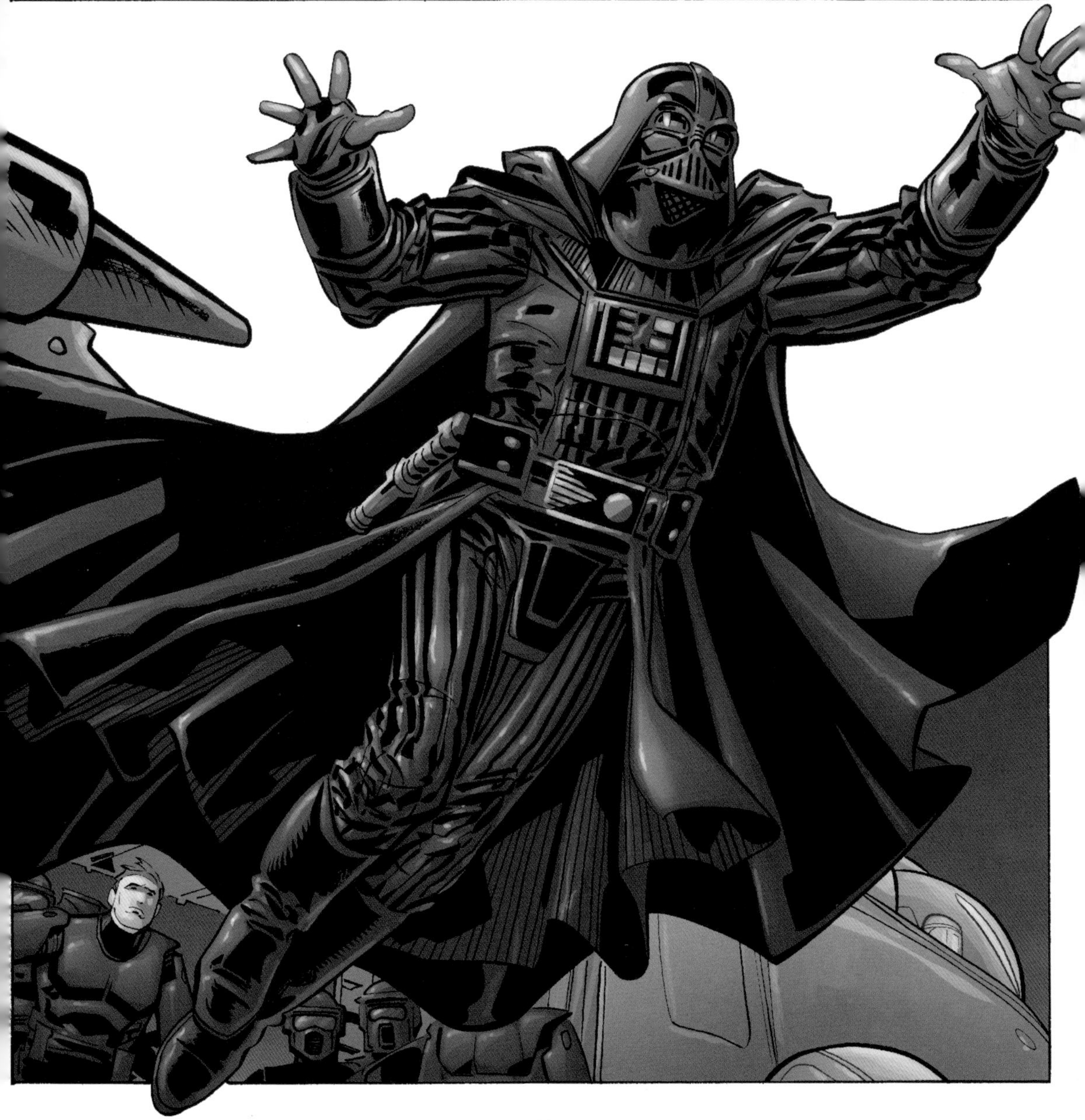

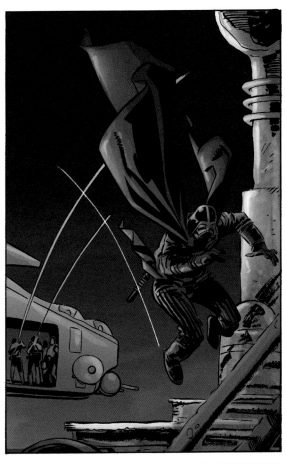

REGROUP ON VADER. GO!

ARE YOU READY?

WHAT DO I NEED TO DO, CAPTAIN SHALE?

JUST HANG ON.

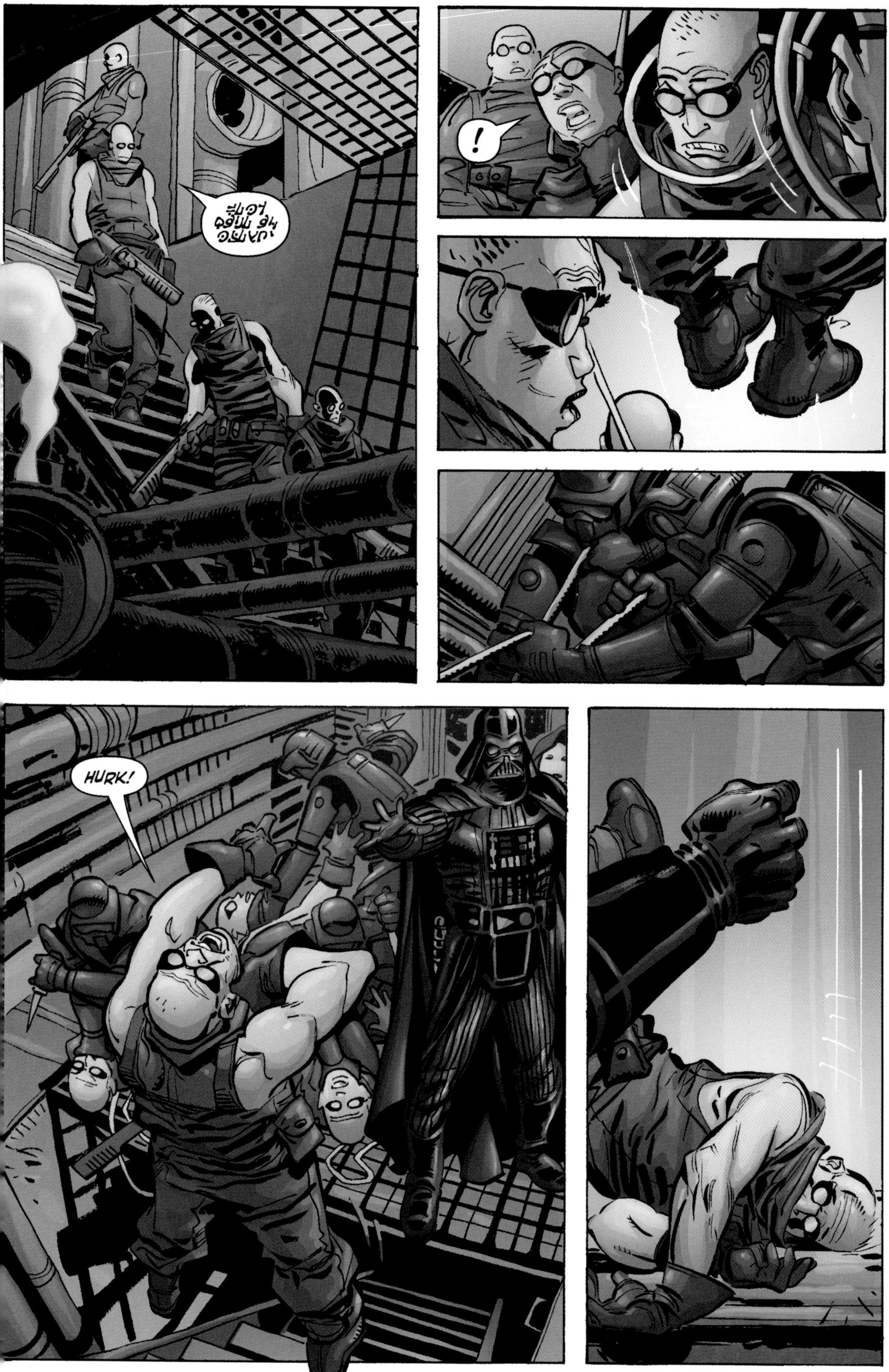
!
HURK!

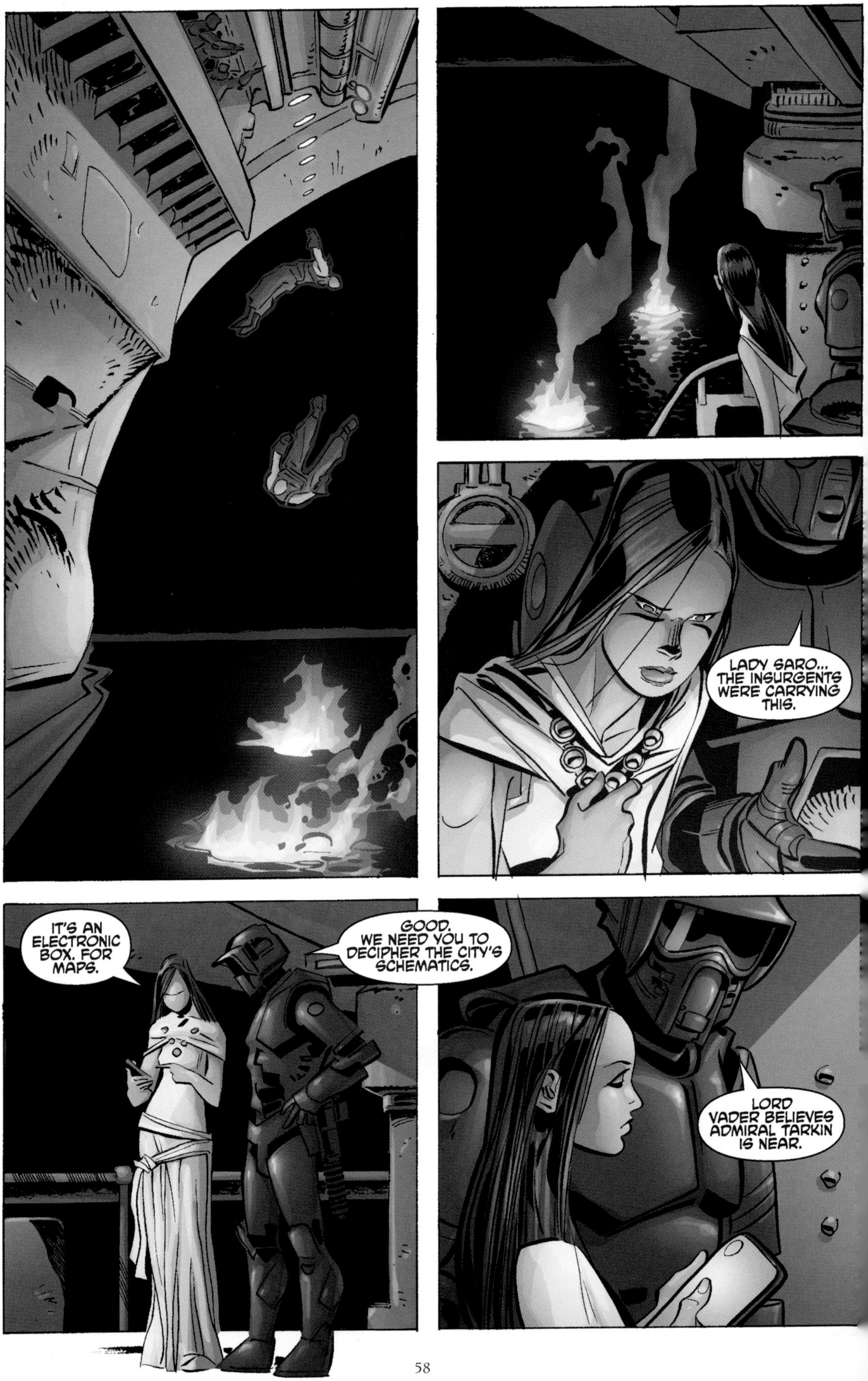
LADY SARO... THE INSURGENTS WERE CARRYING THIS.
IT'S AN ELECTRONIC BOX. FOR MAPS.
GOOD. WE NEED YOU TO DECIPHER THE CITY'S SCHEMATICS.
LORD VADER BELIEVES ADMIRAL TARKIN IS NEAR.

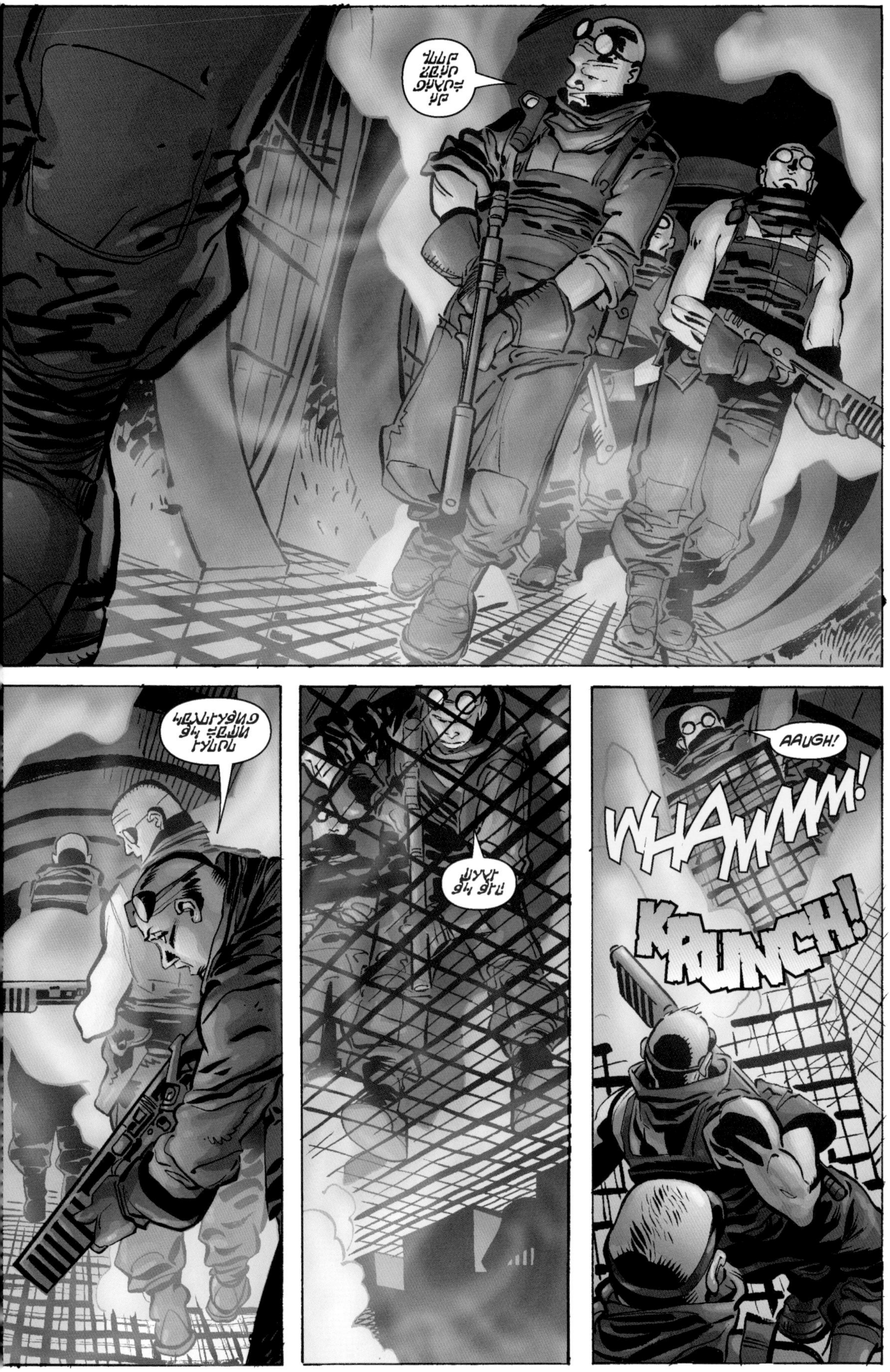
AAUGH!
WHAMMM!
KRUNCH!

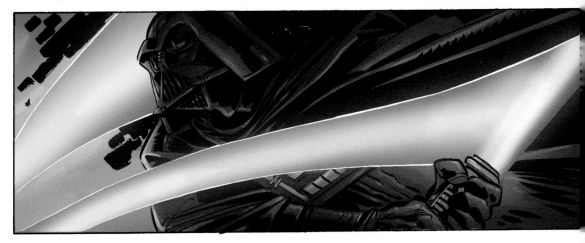

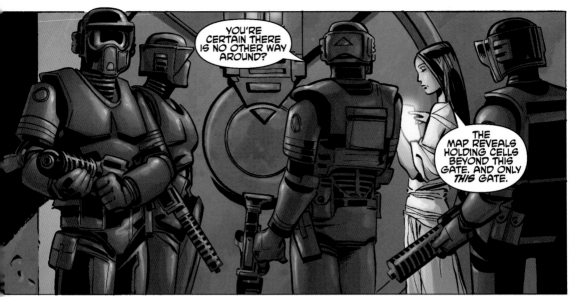

YOU'RE CERTAIN THERE IS NO OTHER WAY AROUND?

THE MAP REVEALS HOLDING CELLS BEYOND THIS GATE. AND ONLY *THIS* GATE.

HMM. BREACHING MINES WILL BRING AN ARMED RESPONSE. OR A TOTAL LOCK-DOWN OF OUR POSITION.

WE'LL GIVE LORD VADER A FEW MOMENTS MORE TO SECURE THIS SECTION OF --

THIS WAY.

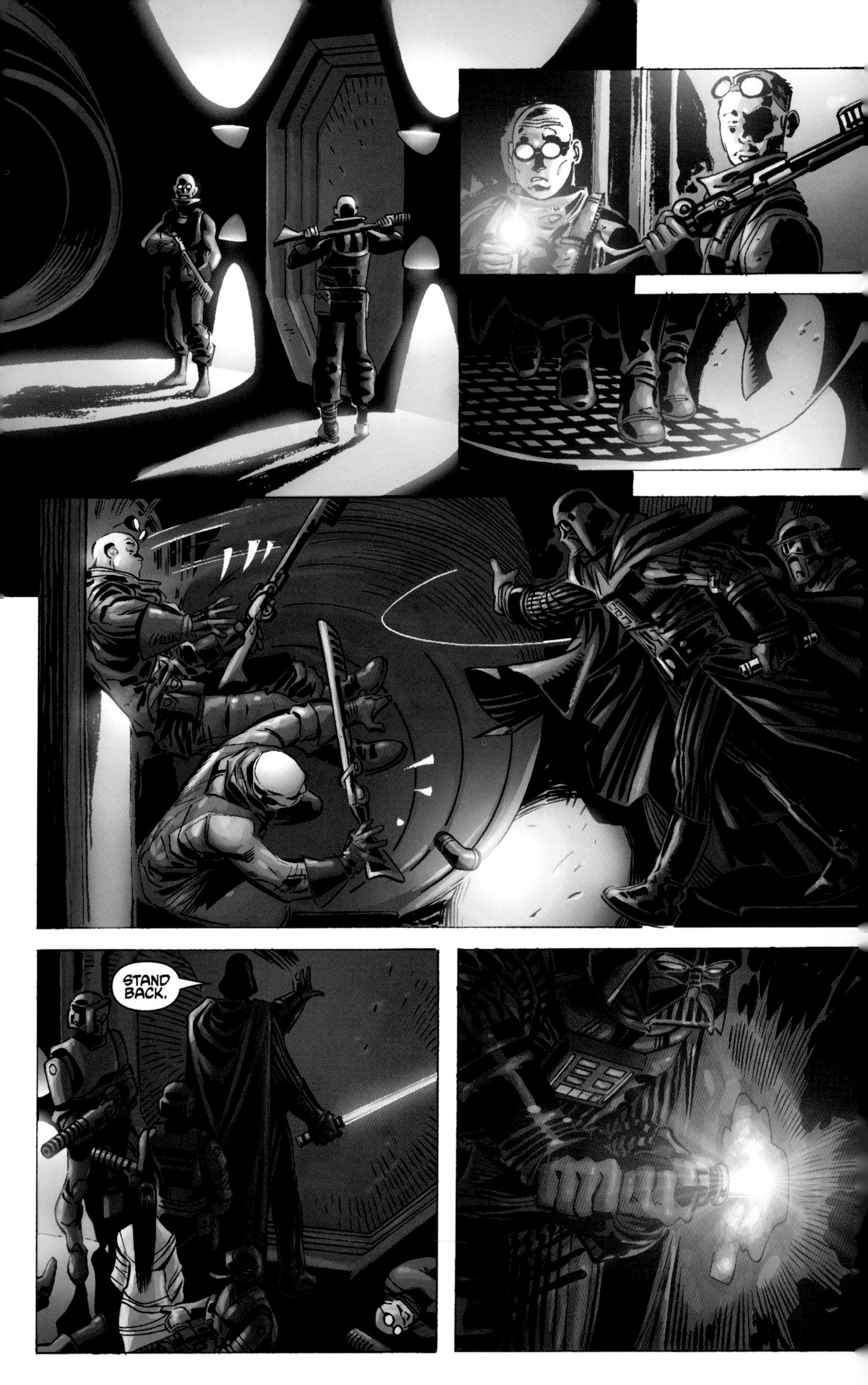
STAND BACK.

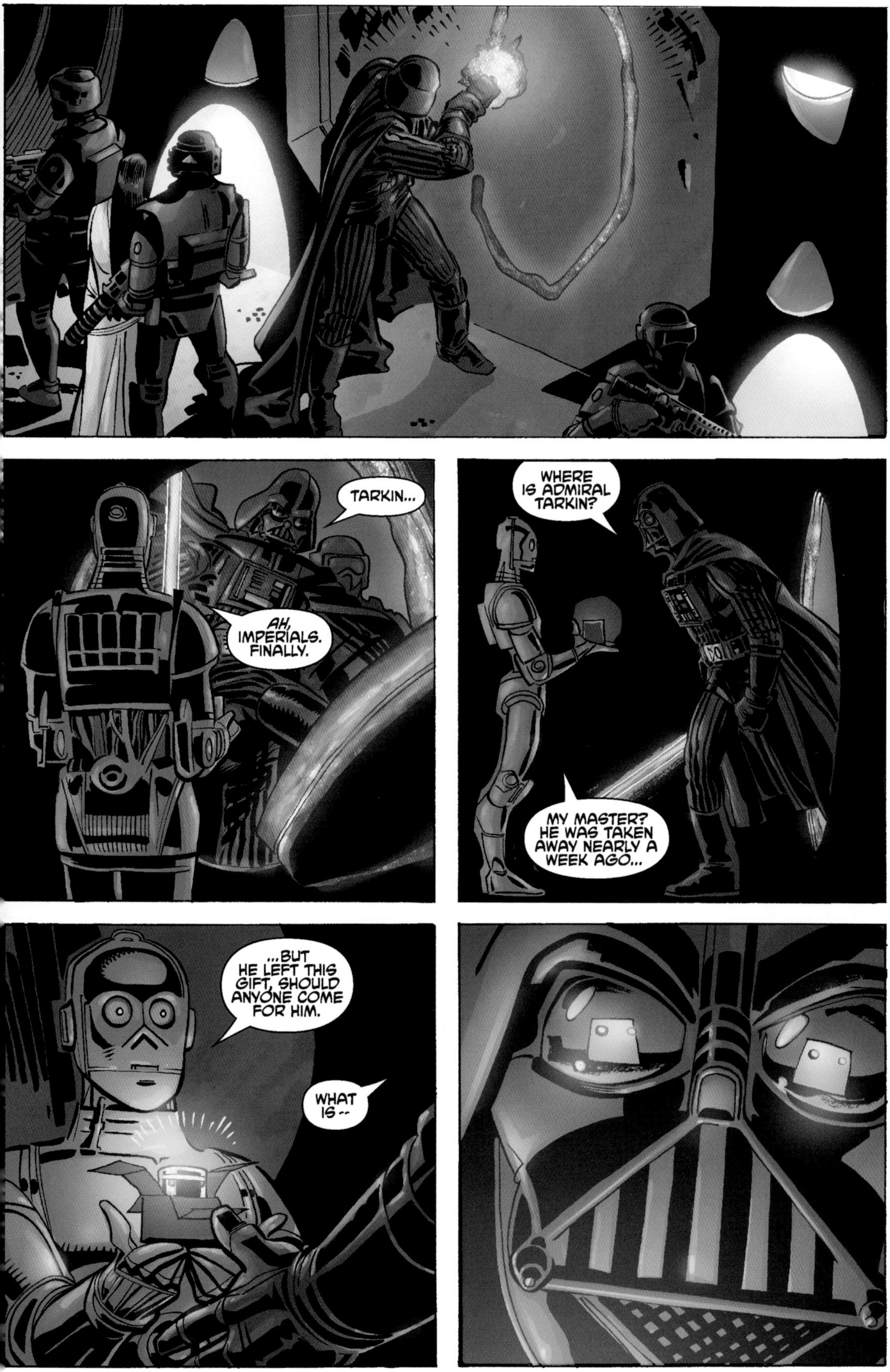
TARKIN...
AH, IMPERIALS. FINALLY.
WHERE IS ADMIRAL TARKIN?
MY MASTER? HE WAS TAKEN AWAY NEARLY A WEEK AGO...
...BUT HE LEFT THIS GIFT, SHOULD ANYONE COME FOR HIM.
WHAT IS --

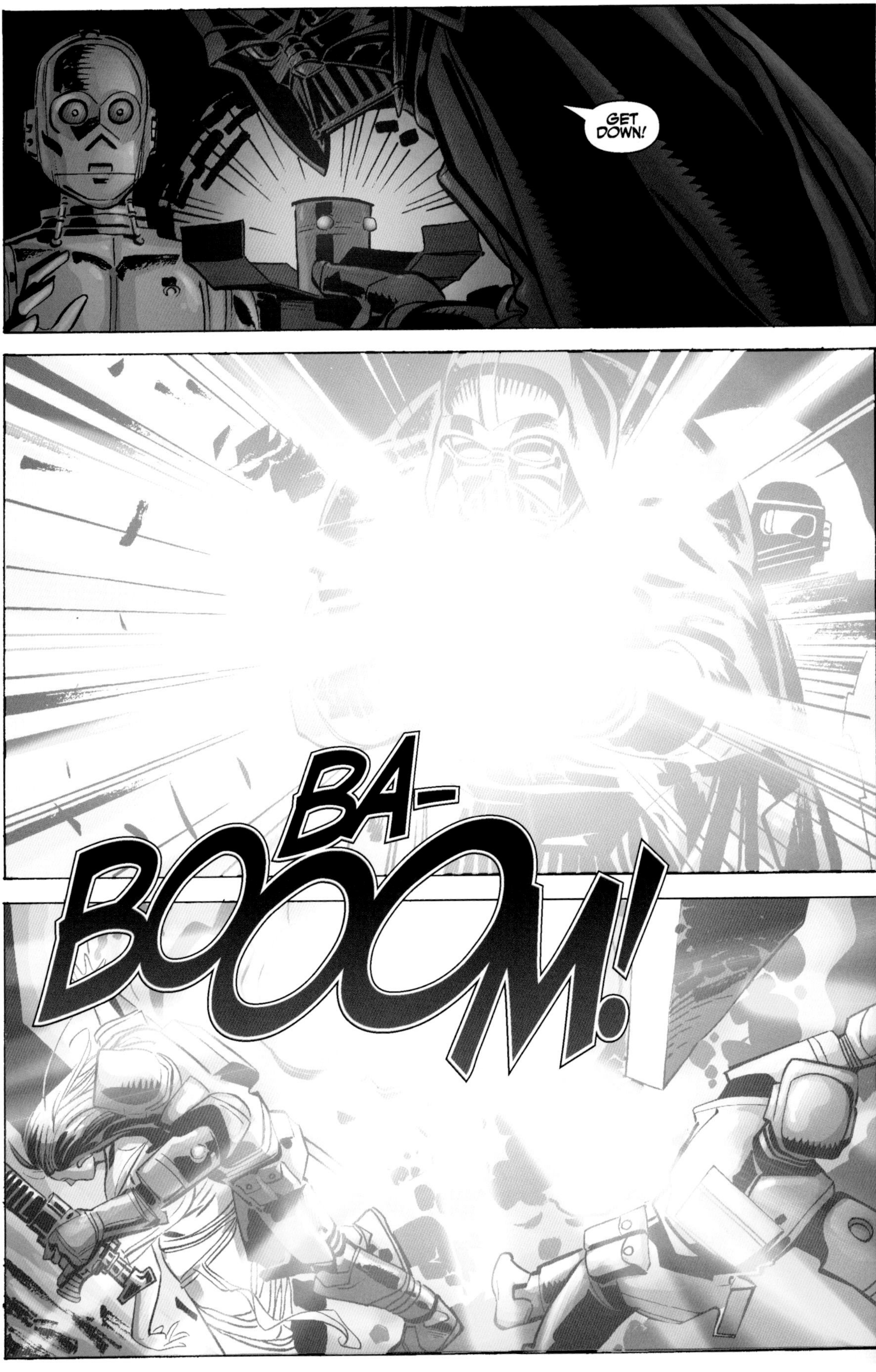
GET DOWN!
BA-BOOOM!

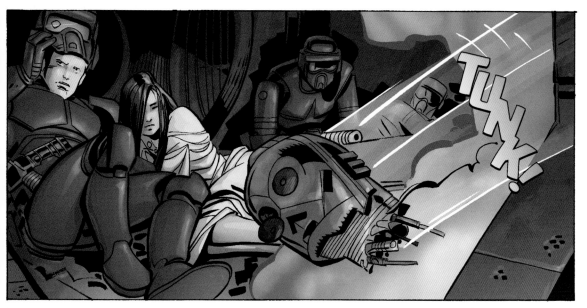

NO MORE ATTACKING FROM THE SHADOWS...

NOW WE TAKE THE BRIDGE.

KRA-KOOM!

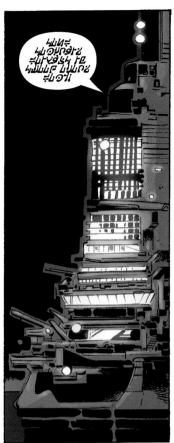

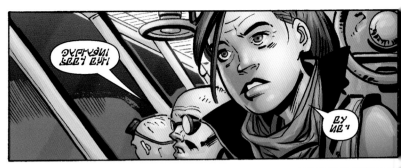

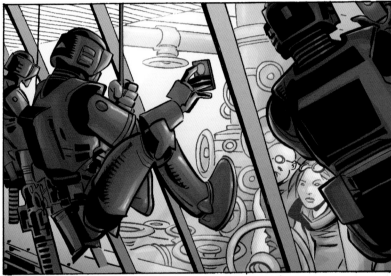

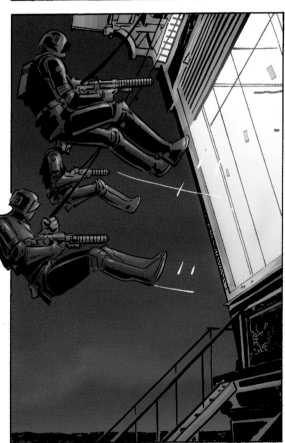

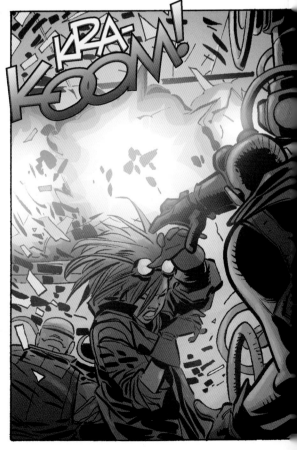

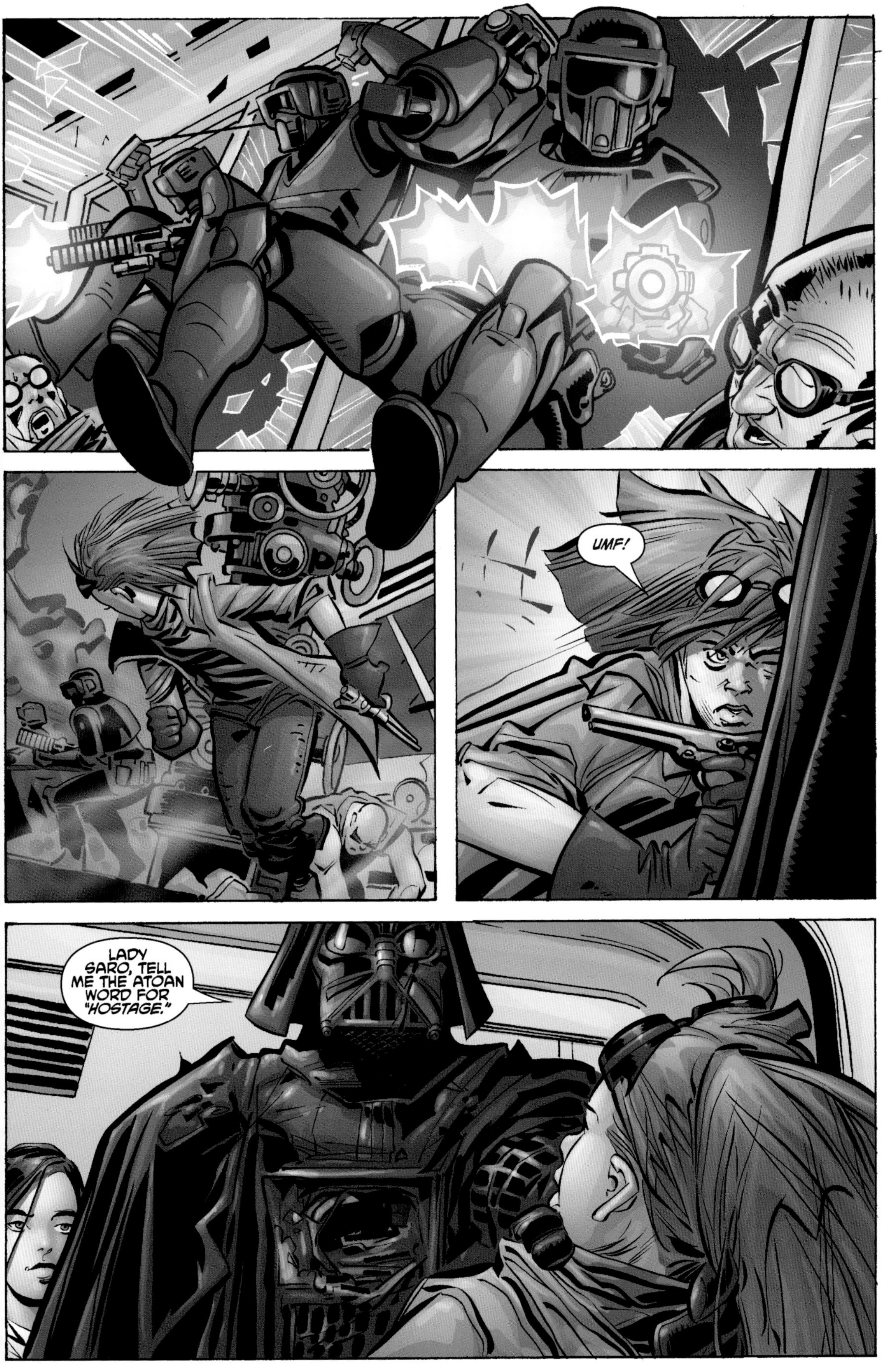
UMF!
LADY SARO, TELL ME THE ATOAN WORD FOR "HOSTAGE."

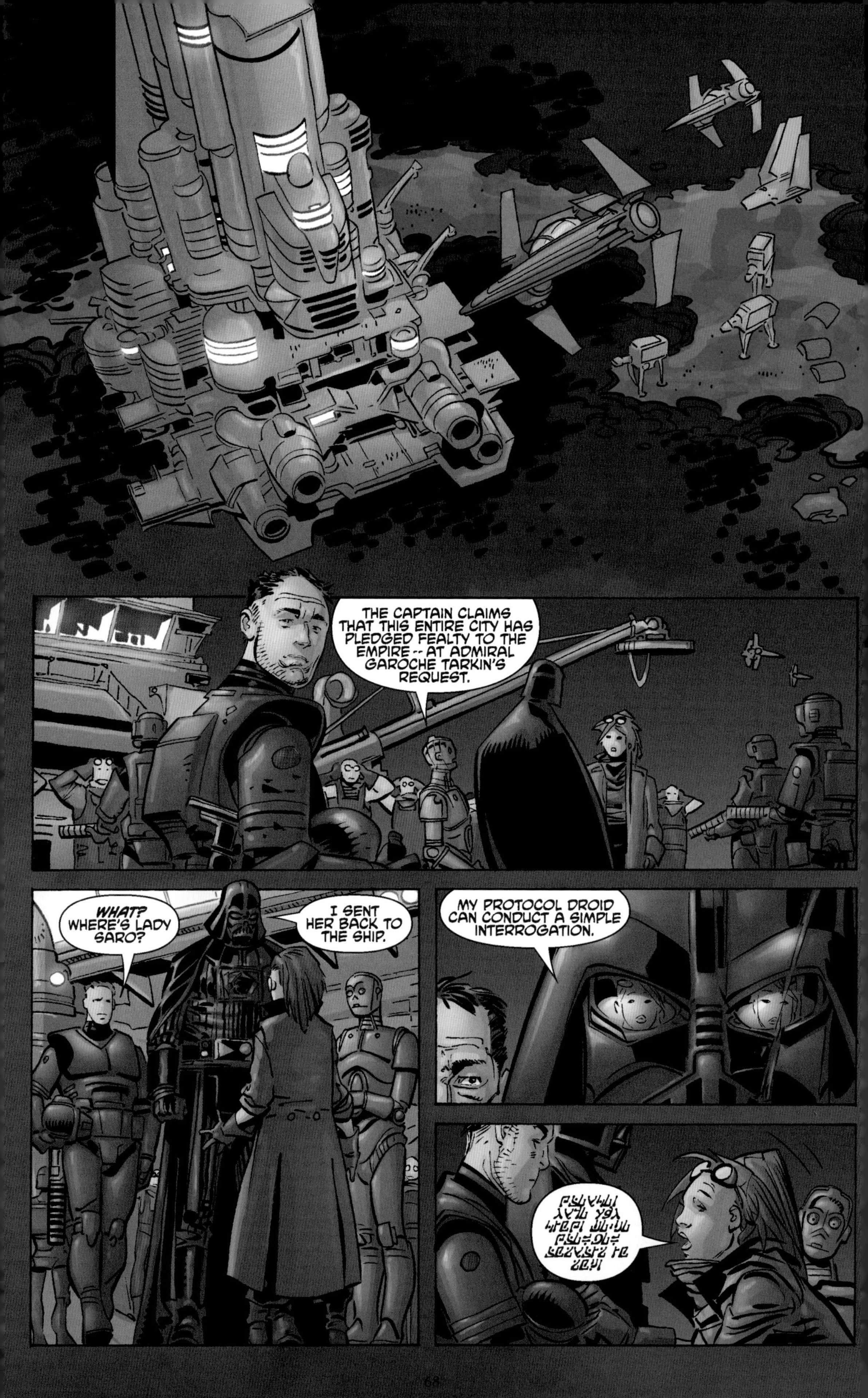
THE CAPTAIN CLAIMS THAT THIS ENTIRE CITY HAS PLEDGED FEALTY TO THE EMPIRE -- AT ADMIRAL GAROCHE TARKIN'S REQUEST.
WHAT? WHERE'S LADY SARO?
I SENT HER BACK TO THE SHIP.
MY PROTOCOL DROID CAN CONDUCT A SIMPLE INTERROGATION.

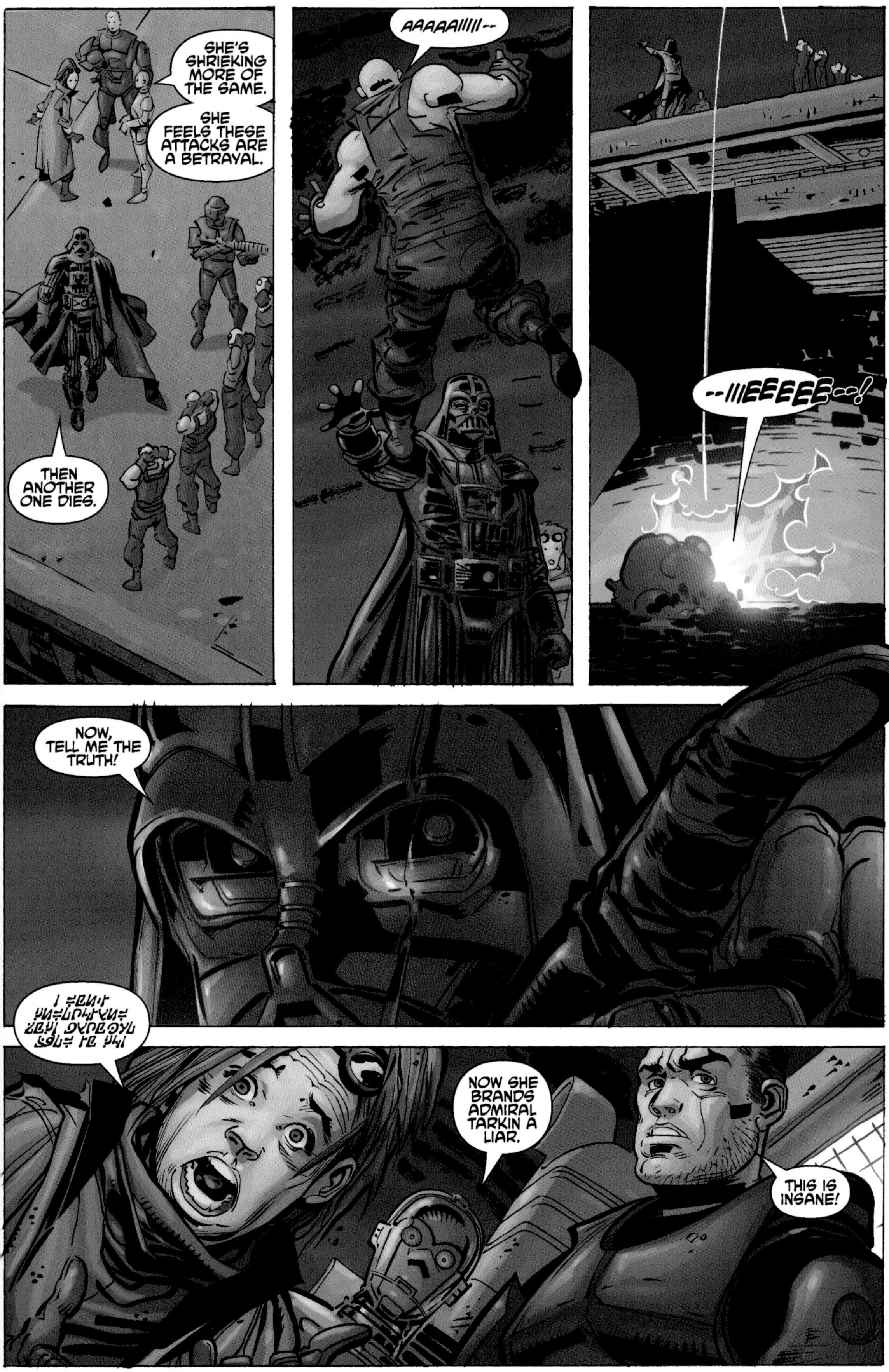
SHE'S SHRIEKING MORE OF THE SAME.
SHE FEELS THESE ATTACKS ARE A BETRAYAL.
THEN ANOTHER ONE DIES.
AAAAAIIIII--
--IIIEEEEEE--!
NOW, TELL ME THE TRUTH!
NOW SHE BRANDS ADMIRAL TARKIN A LIAR.
THIS IS INSANE!

AAAAAGH!

...ꟼꟼꟼꟼꟼꟼ ꟼꟼꟼ ꟼꟼꟼꟼ ꟼꟼꟼꟼꟼ ꟼꟼ ꟼꟼꟼꟼ

PSSHAK!

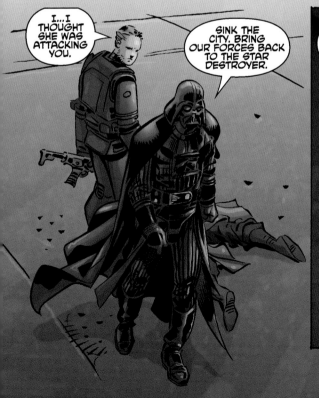

I...I THOUGHT SHE WAS ATTACKING YOU.

SINK THE CITY. BRING OUR FORCES BACK TO THE STAR DESTROYER.

AND THEN WE WILL DISCUSS THESE CHARGES AGAINST ADMIRAL TARKIN.

YOUR FRIEND.

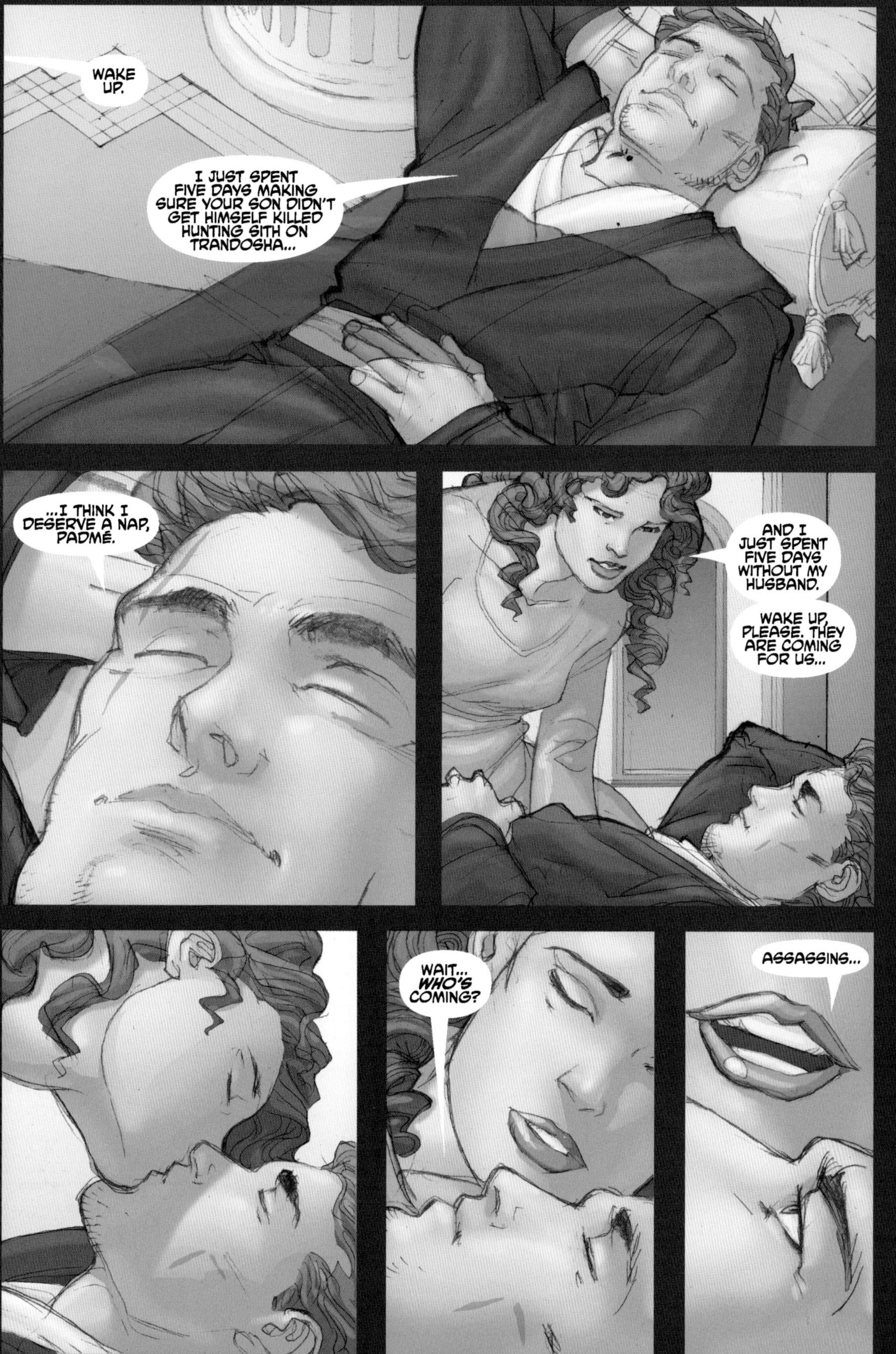
WAKE UP.
I JUST SPENT FIVE DAYS MAKING SURE YOUR SON DIDN'T GET HIMSELF KILLED HUNTING SITH ON TRANDOSHA...
...I THINK I DESERVE A NAP, PADMÉ.
AND I JUST SPENT FIVE DAYS WITHOUT MY HUSBAND.
WAKE UP, PLEASE. THEY ARE COMING FOR US...
WAIT... *WHO'S* COMING?
ASSASSINS...

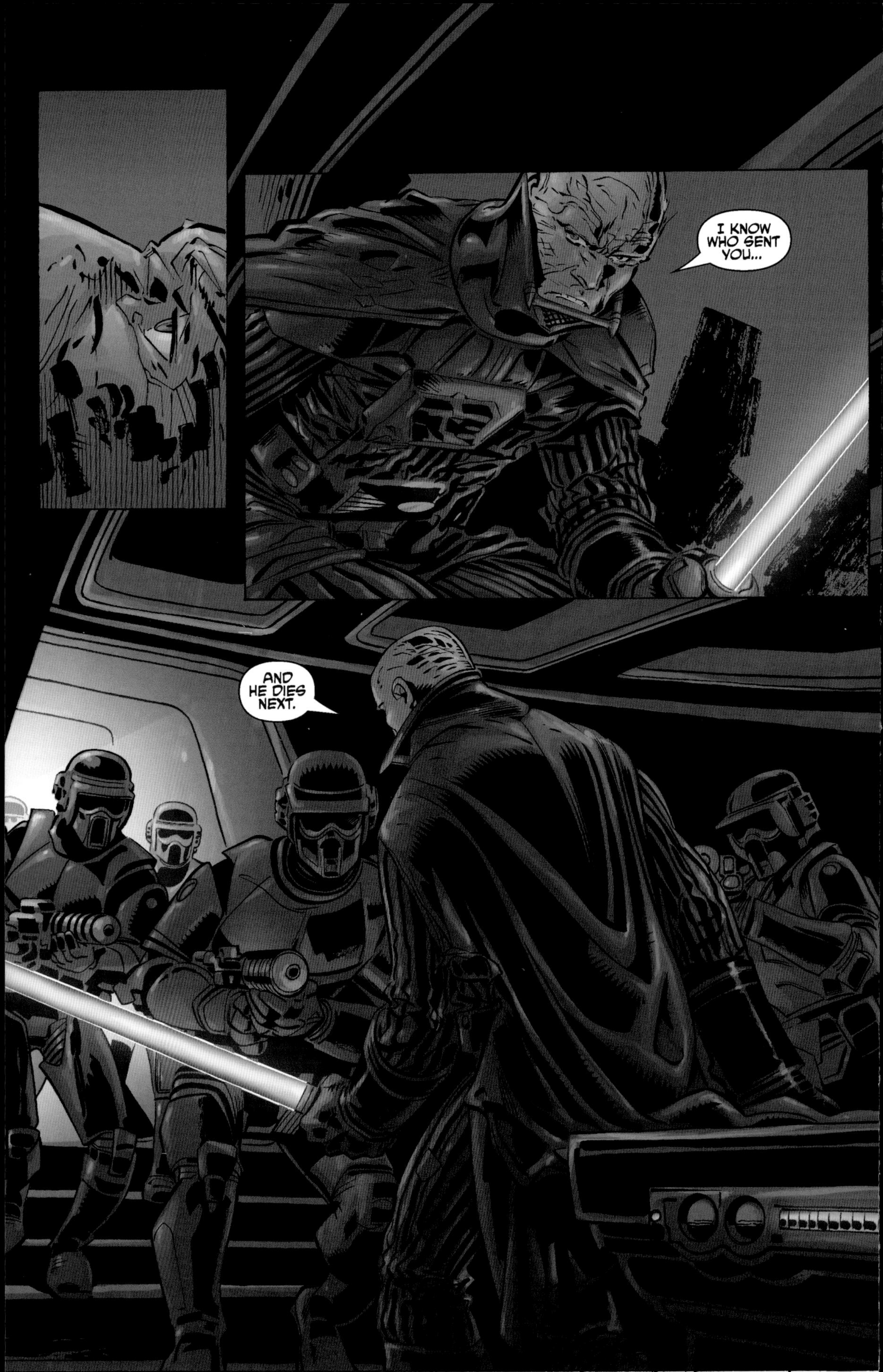
I KNOW WHO SENT YOU...
AND HE DIES NEXT.

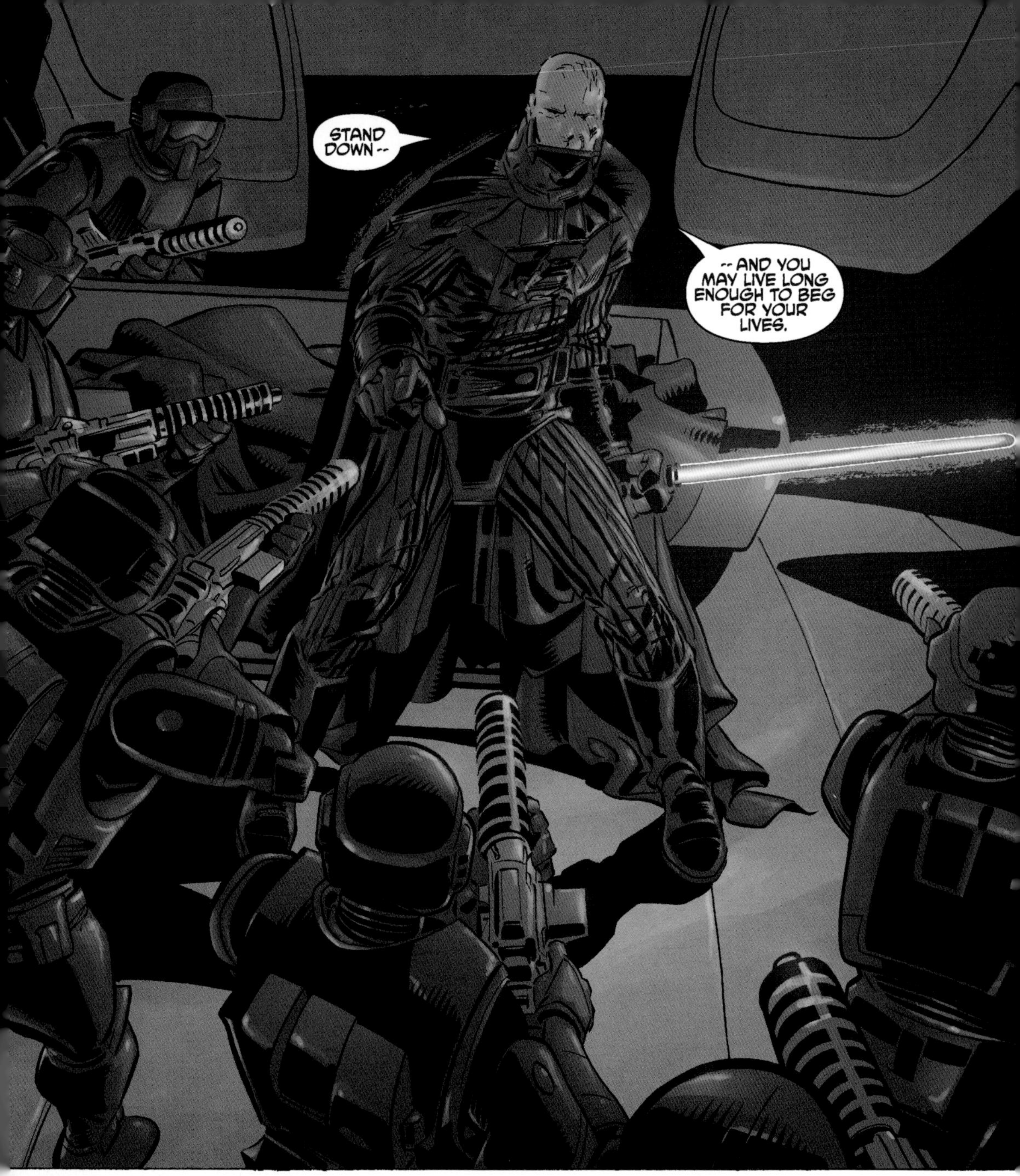
STAND DOWN --
-- AND YOU MAY LIVE LONG ENOUGH TO BEG FOR YOUR LIVES.

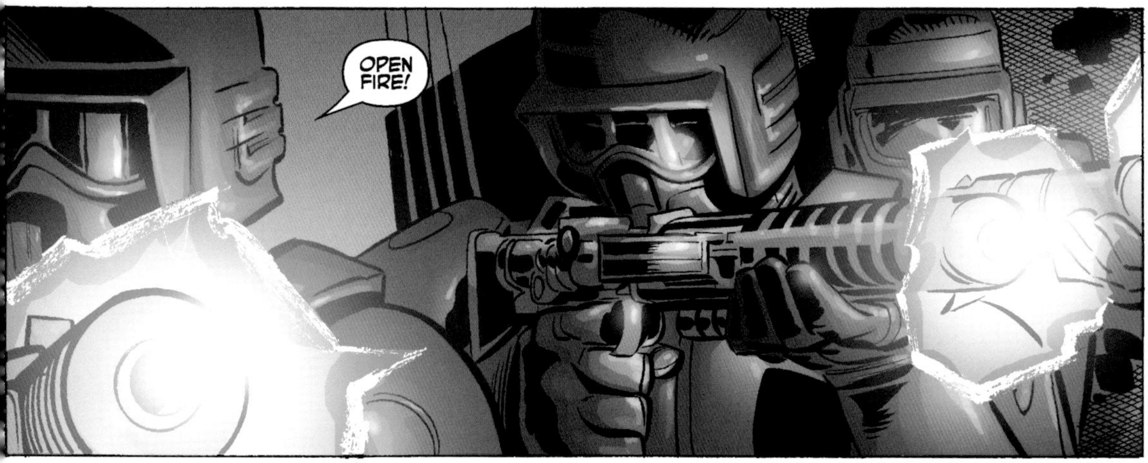
OPEN FIRE!

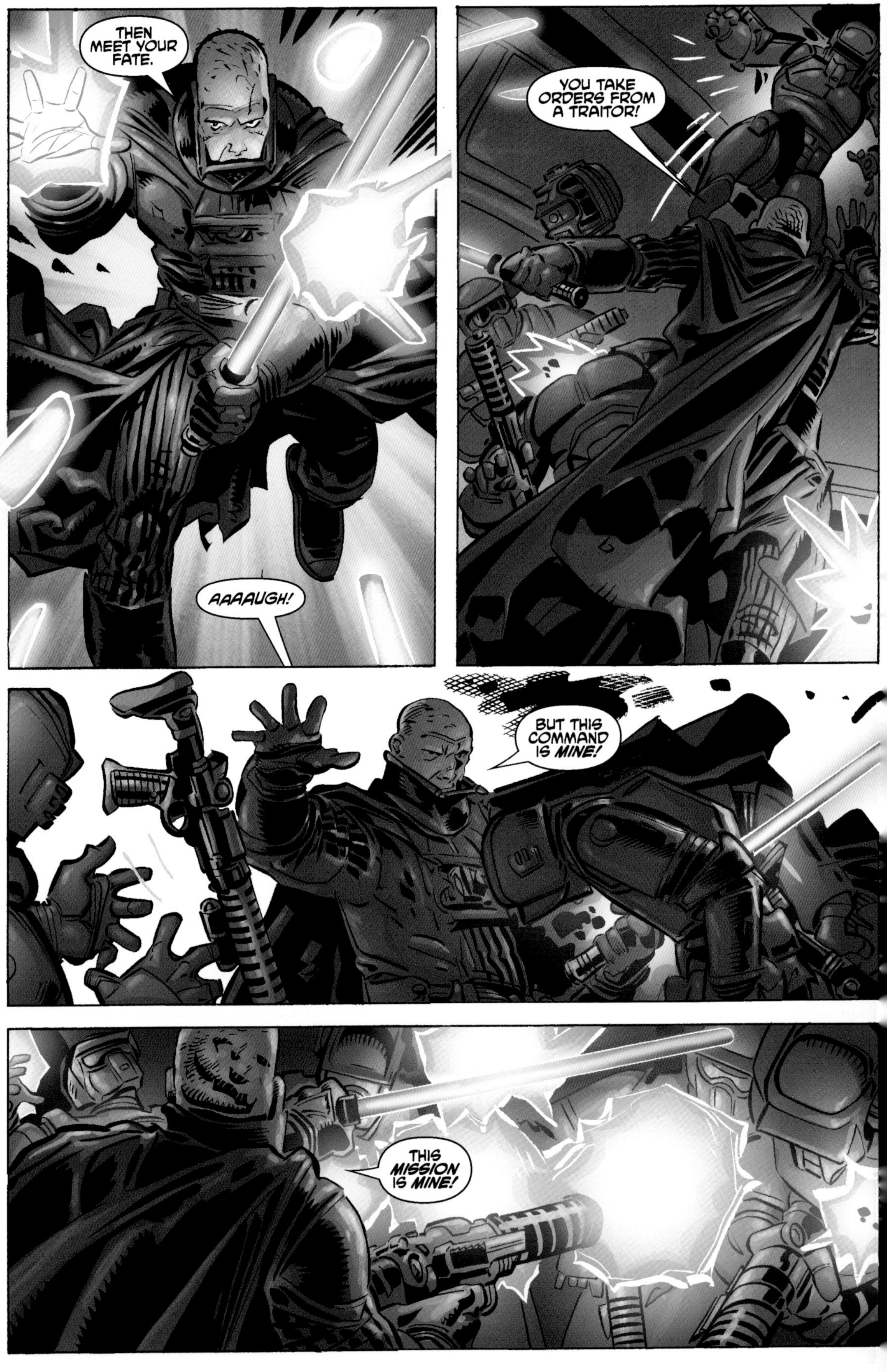
THEN MEET YOUR FATE.
AAAAUGH!
YOU TAKE ORDERS FROM A TRAITOR!
BUT THIS COMMAND IS *MINE!*
THIS *MISSION* IS *MINE!*

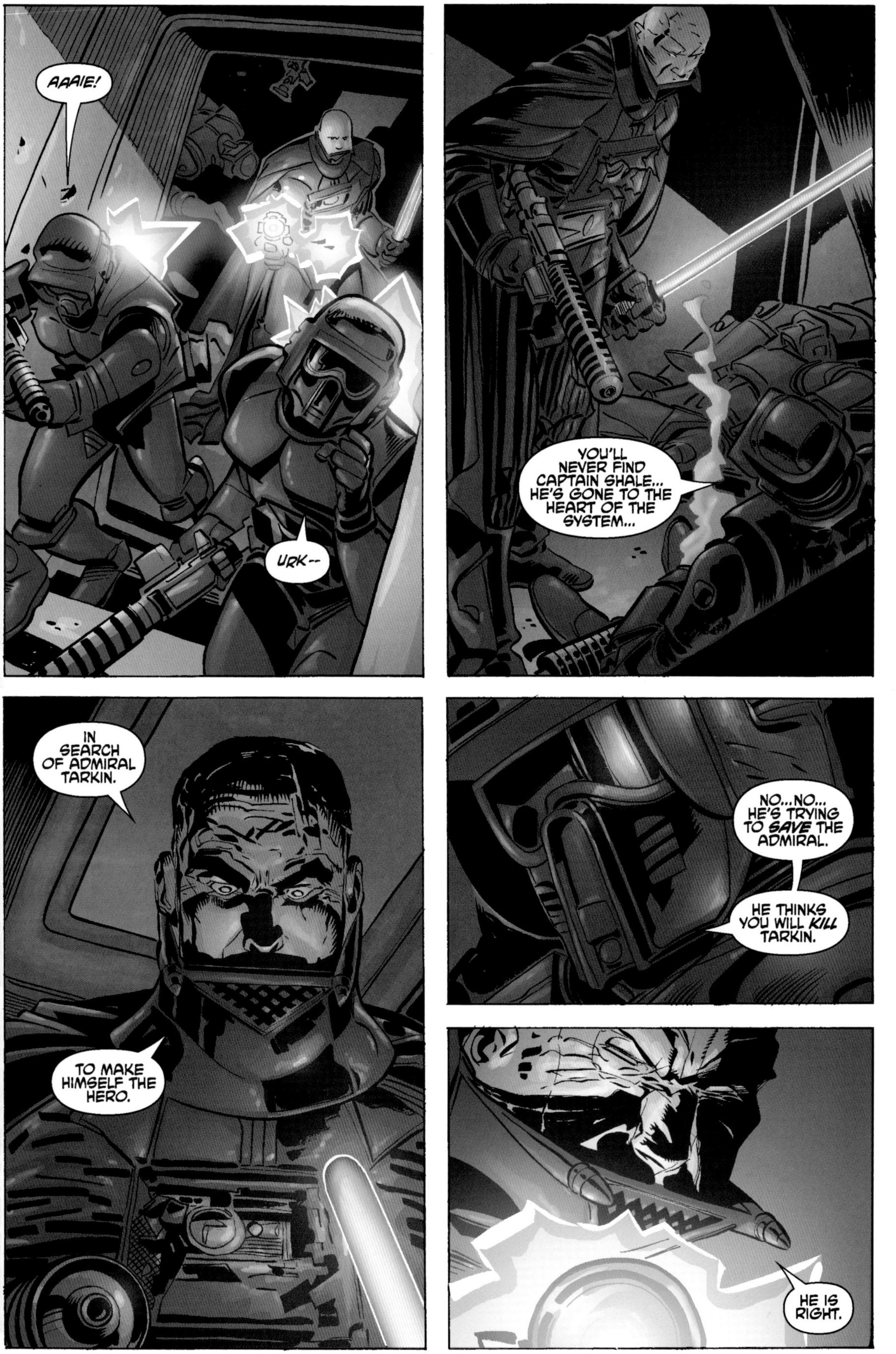
AAAIE!
URK--
YOU'LL NEVER FIND CAPTAIN SHALE... HE'S GONE TO THE HEART OF THE SYSTEM...
IN SEARCH OF ADMIRAL TARKIN.
TO MAKE HIMSELF THE HERO.
NO...NO... HE'S TRYING TO *SAVE* THE ADMIRAL.
HE THINKS YOU WILL *KILL* TARKIN.
HE IS RIGHT.

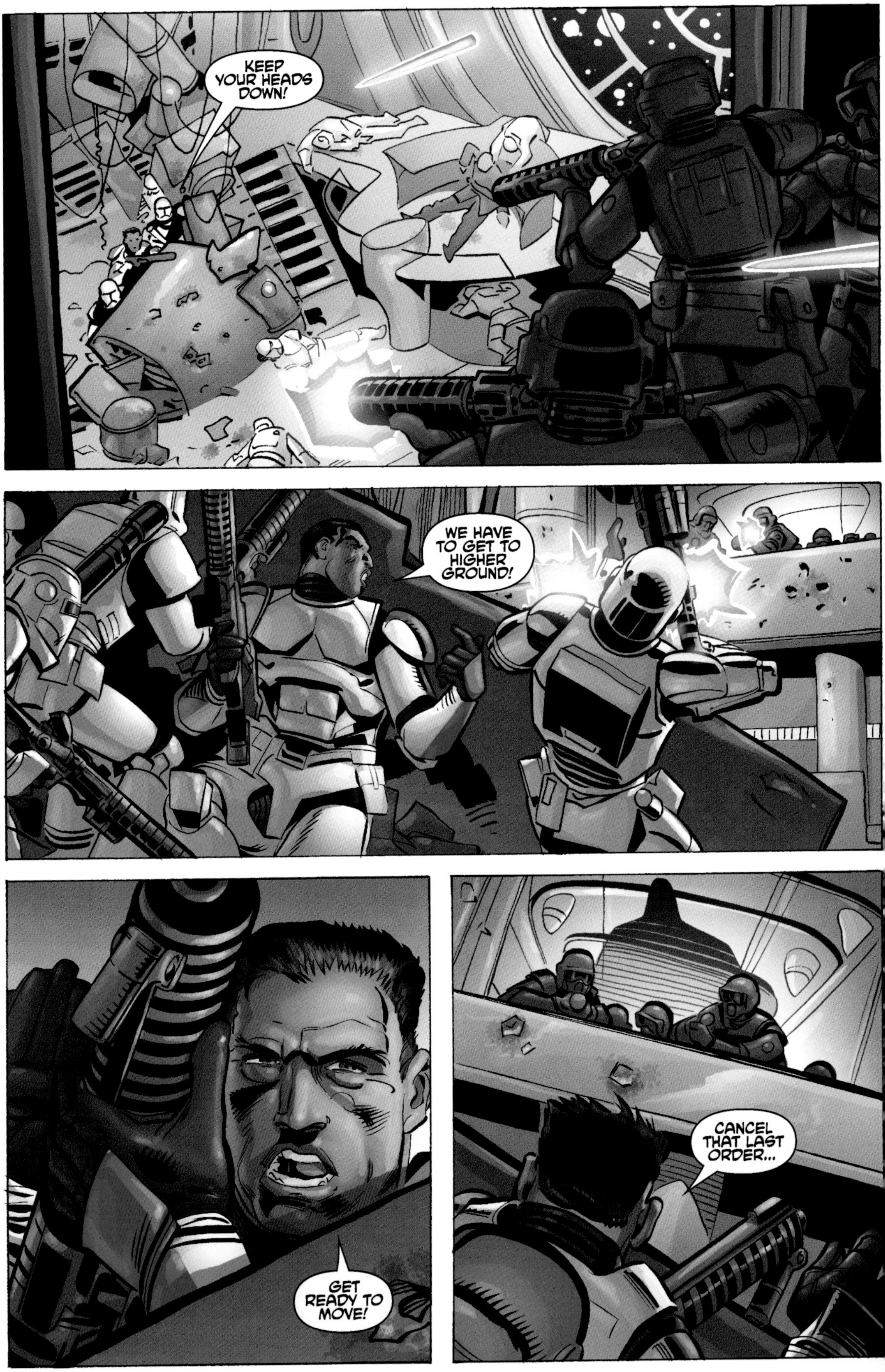
KEEP YOUR HEADS DOWN!
WE HAVE TO GET TO HIGHER GROUND!
GET READY TO MOVE!
CANCEL THAT LAST ORDER...

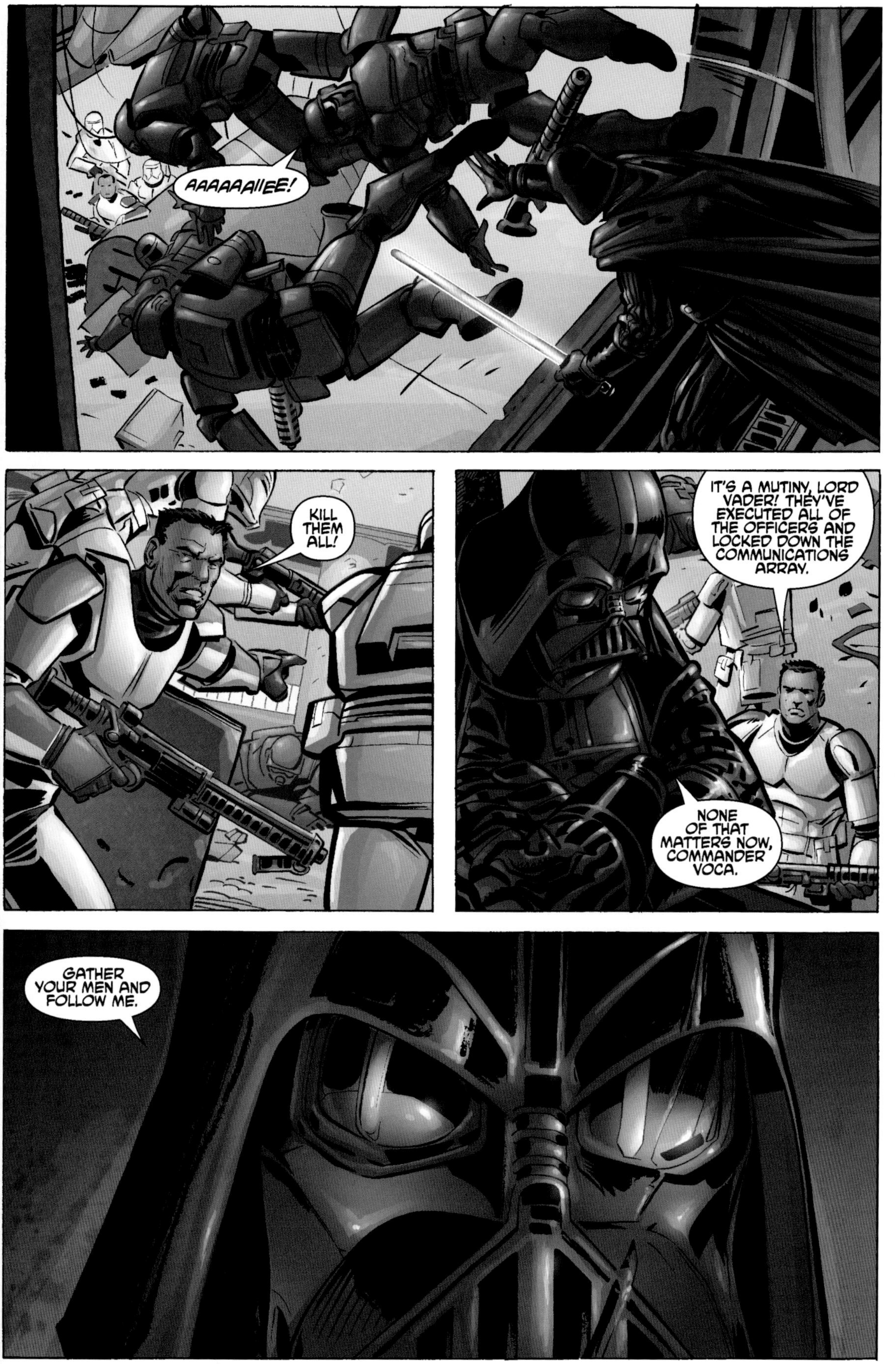

AAAAAAIIEE!
KILL THEM ALL!
IT'S A MUTINY, LORD VADER! THEY'VE EXECUTED ALL OF THE OFFICERS AND LOCKED DOWN THE COMMUNICATIONS ARRAY.
NONE OF THAT MATTERS NOW, COMMANDER VOCA.
GATHER YOUR MEN AND FOLLOW ME.

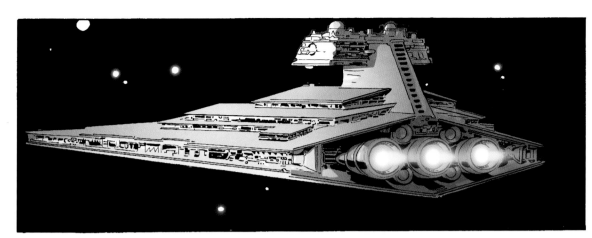

SEND YOUR ENGINEERS TO SHALE'S HANGAR AND ACTIVATE THE TRACKING DE--

BOOOOOOM

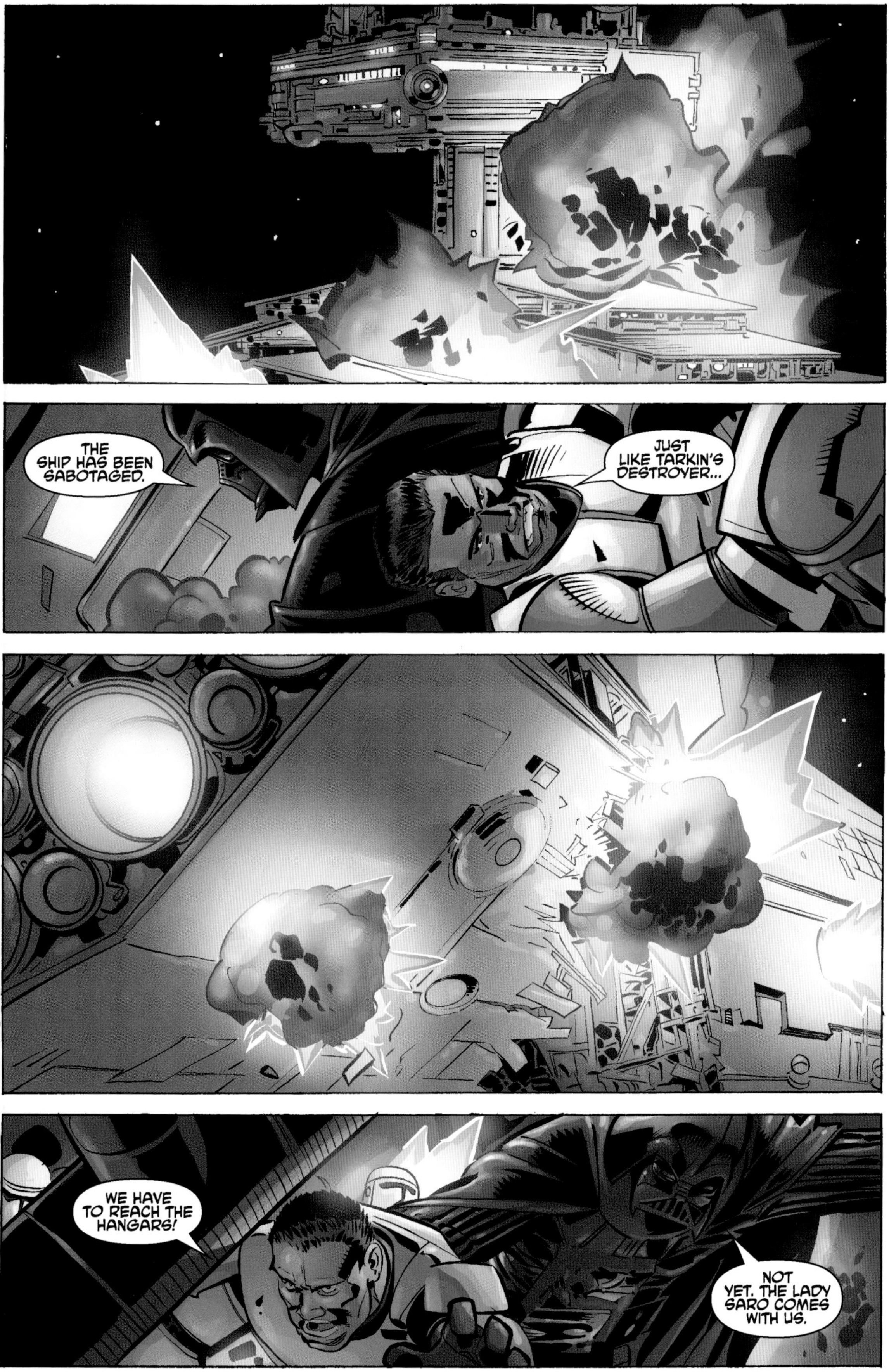
THE SHIP HAS BEEN SABOTAGED.
JUST LIKE TARKIN'S DESTROYER...
WE HAVE TO REACH THE HANGARS!
NOT YET. THE LADY SARO COMES WITH US.

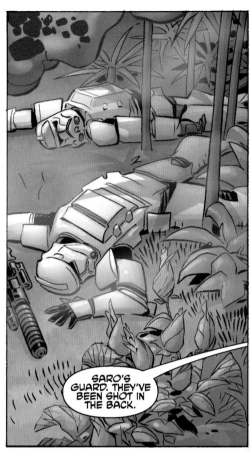

SARO'S GUARD. THEY'VE BEEN SHOT IN THE BACK.

SHALE MUST HAVE TAKEN THE LADY SARO BEFORE HE FLED.

THERE'S NOTHING MORE FOR US HERE.

NOW WE HUNT THESE COWARDS.

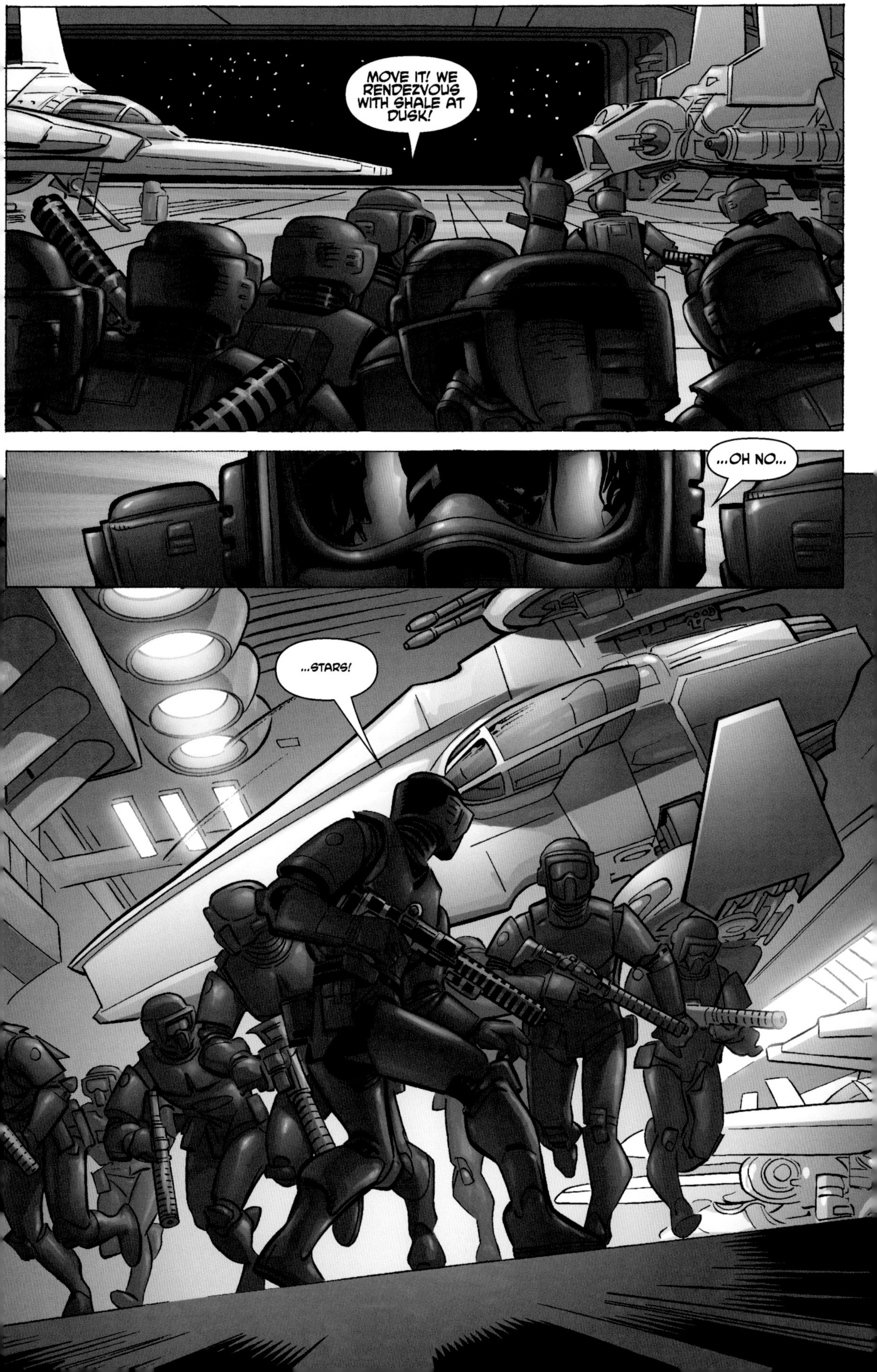
MOVE IT! WE RENDEZVOUS WITH SHALE AT DUSK!
...OH NO...
...STARS!

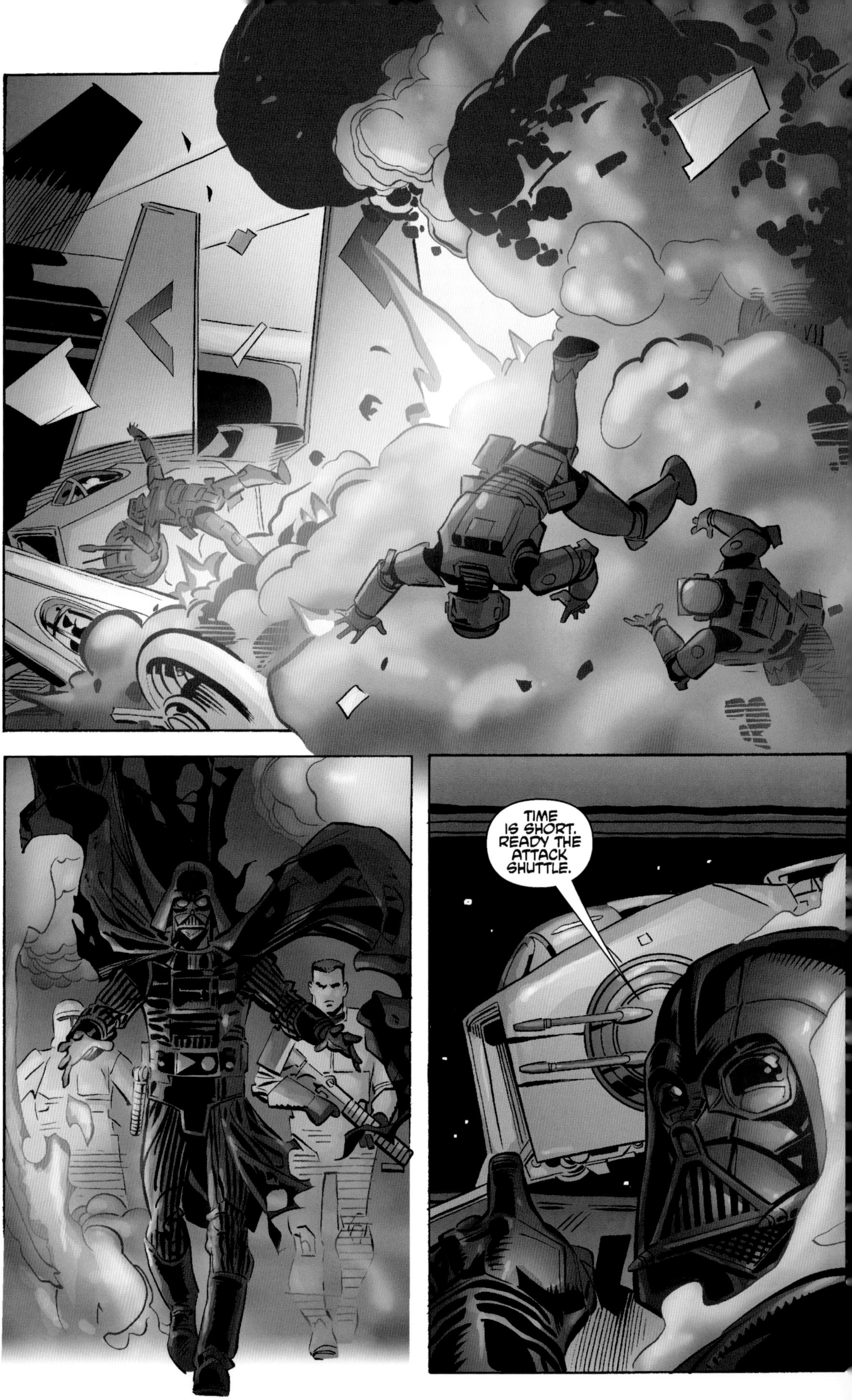
TIME IS SHORT. READY THE ATTACK SHUTTLE.

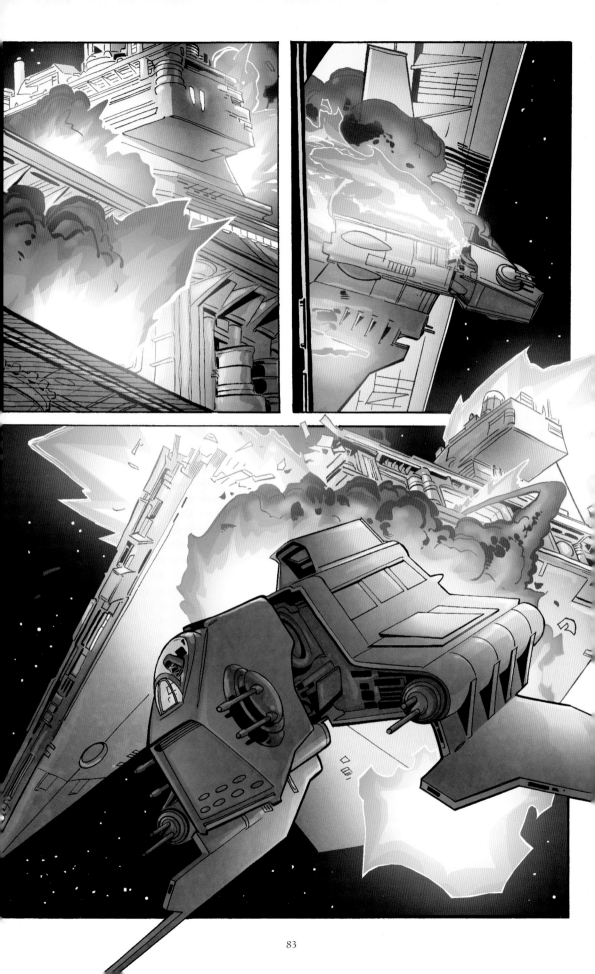

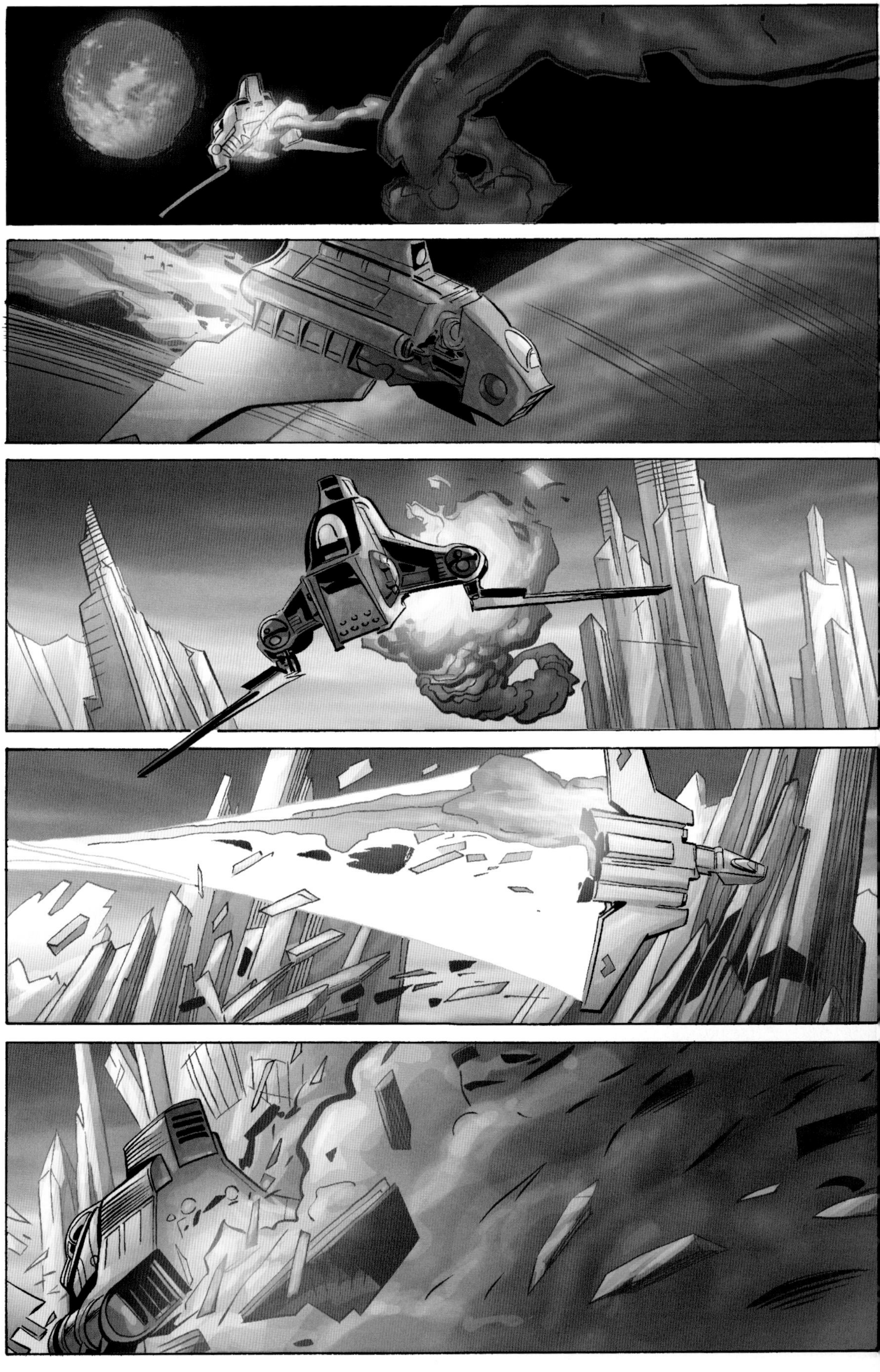

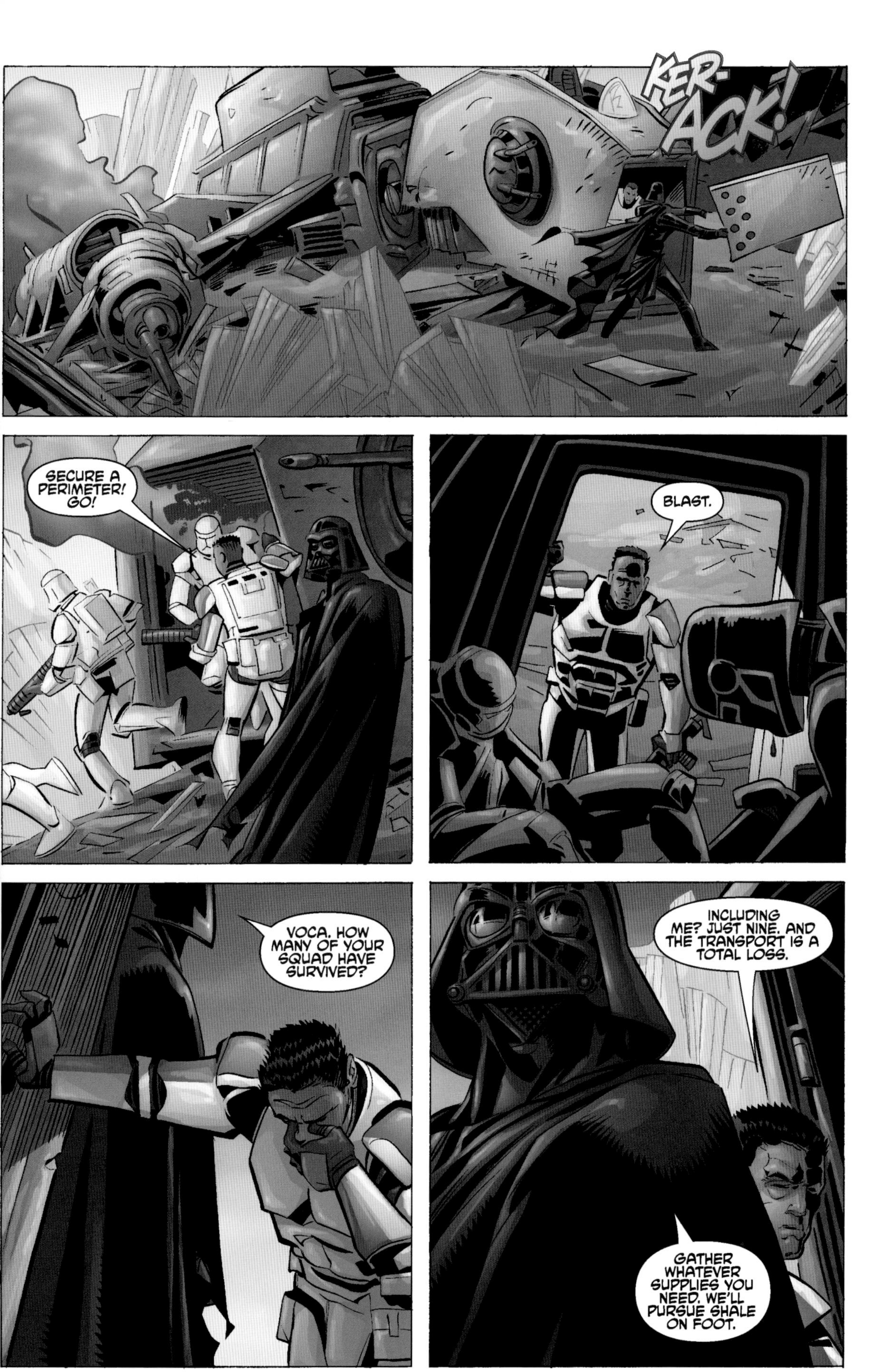
KER-ACK!
SECURE A PERIMETER! GO!
BLAST.
VOCA. HOW MANY OF YOUR SQUAD HAVE SURVIVED?
INCLUDING ME? JUST NINE. AND THE TRANSPORT IS A TOTAL LOSS.
GATHER WHATEVER SUPPLIES YOU NEED. WE'LL PURSUE SHALE ON FOOT.

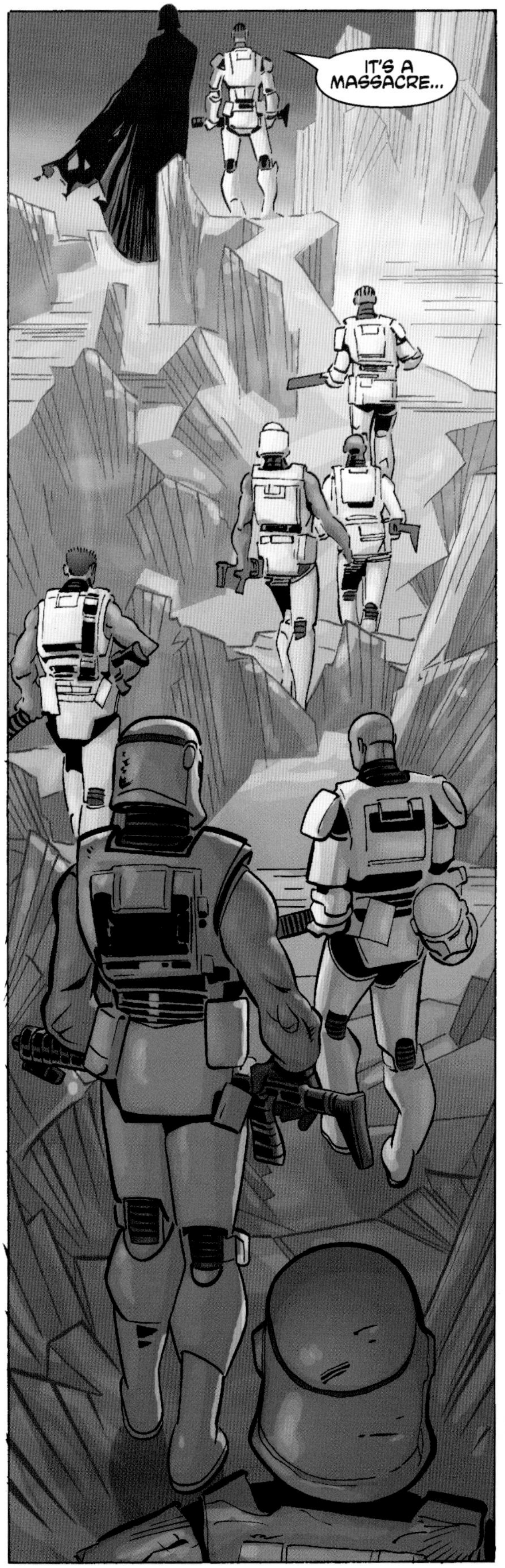
IT'S A MASSACRE...
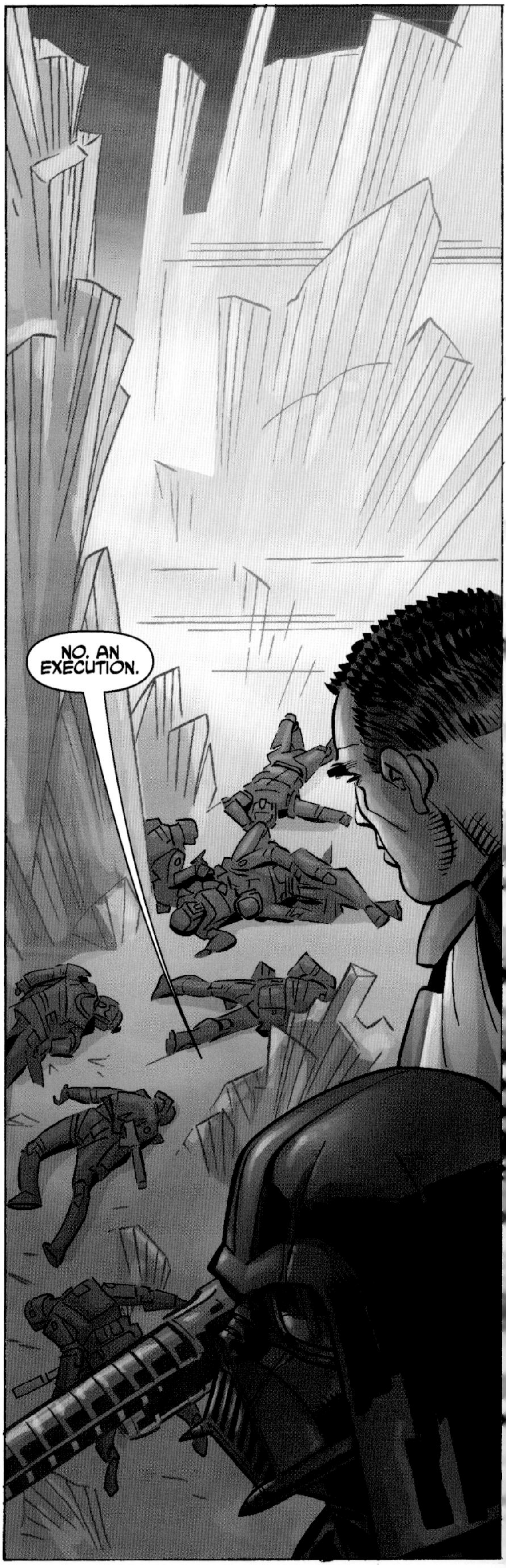
NO. AN EXECUTION.

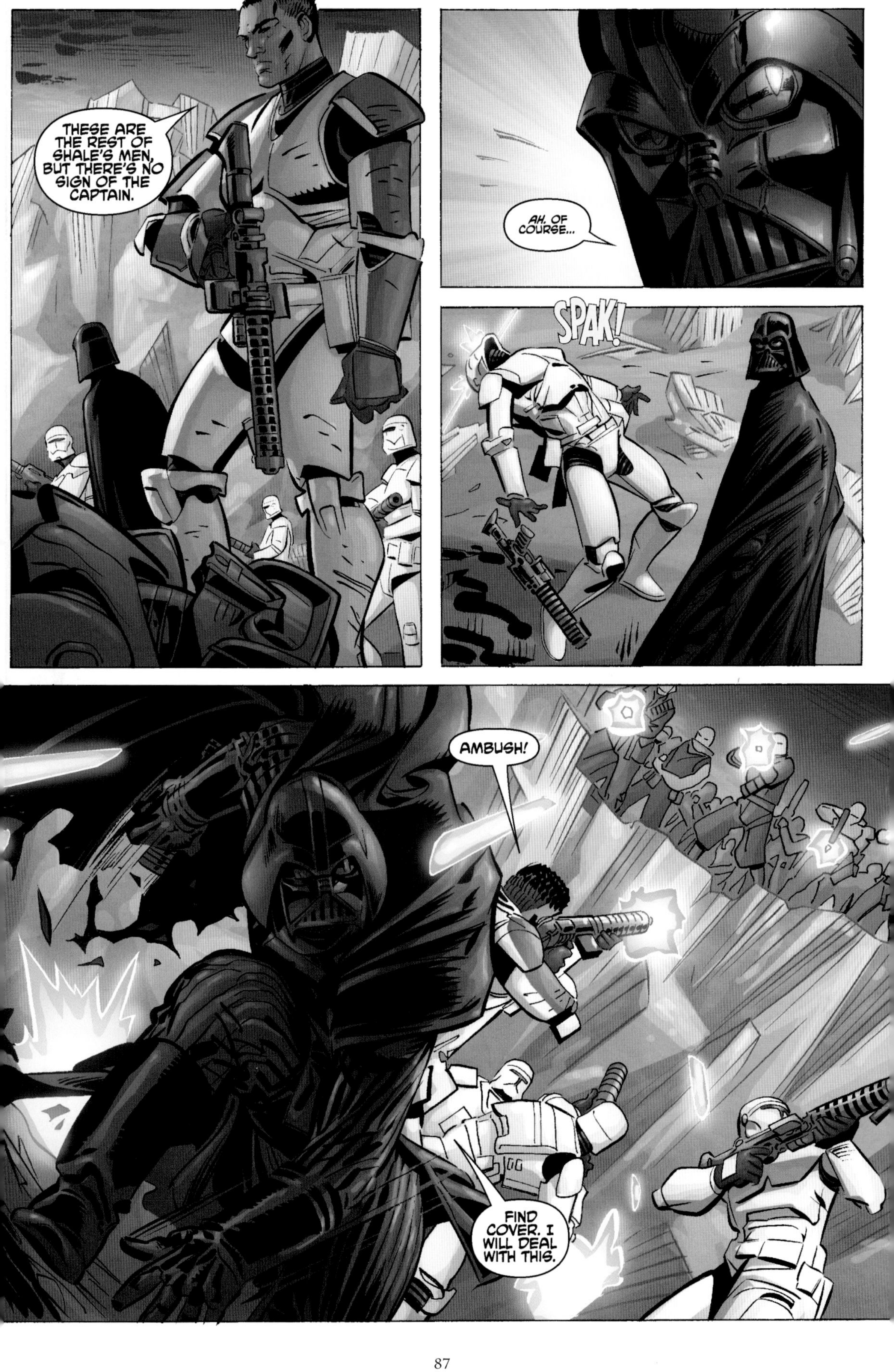
THESE ARE THE REST OF SHALE'S MEN, BUT THERE'S NO SIGN OF THE CAPTAIN.
AH. OF COURSE...
SPAK!
AMBUSH!
FIND COVER. I WILL DEAL WITH THIS.

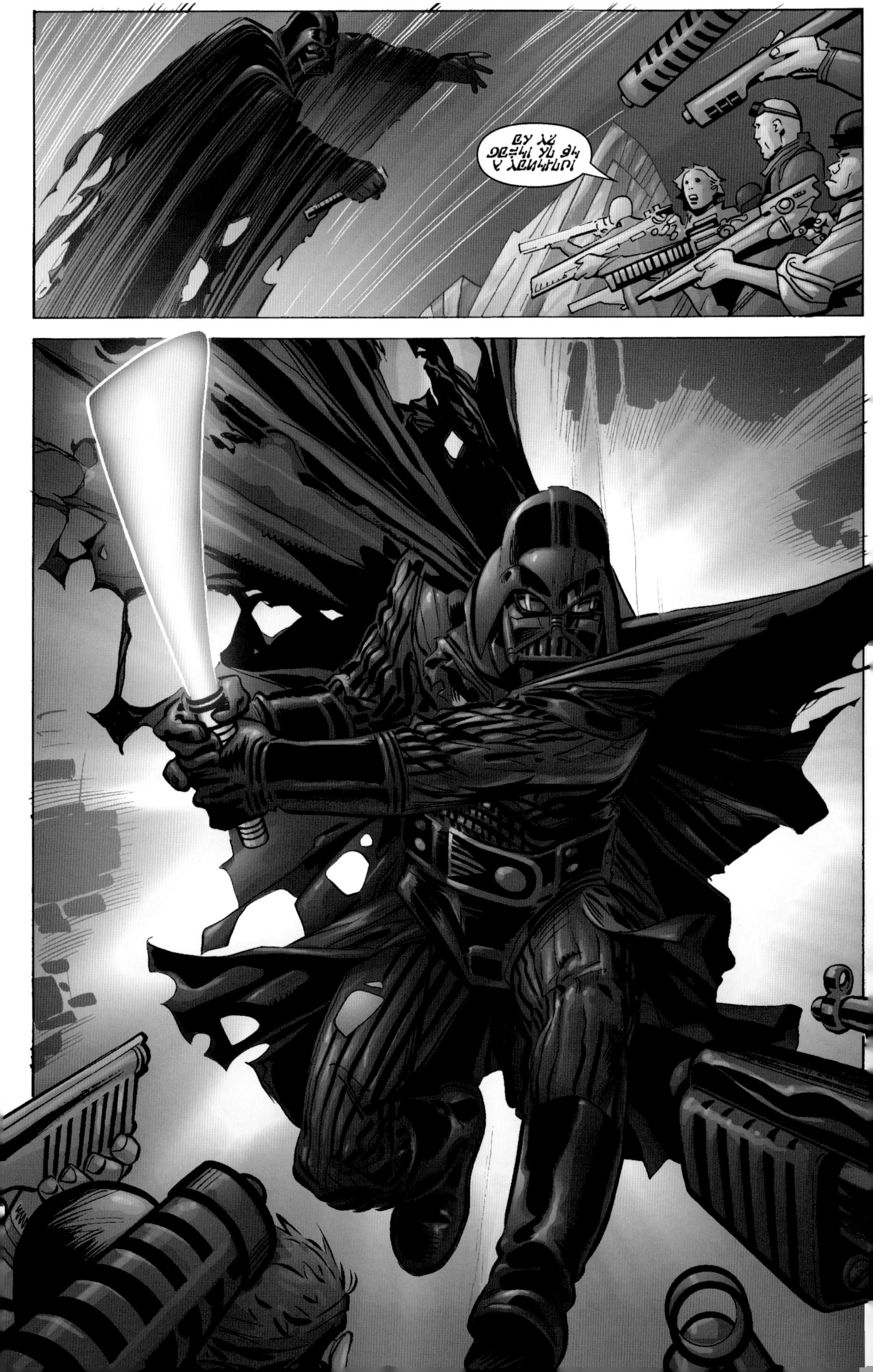

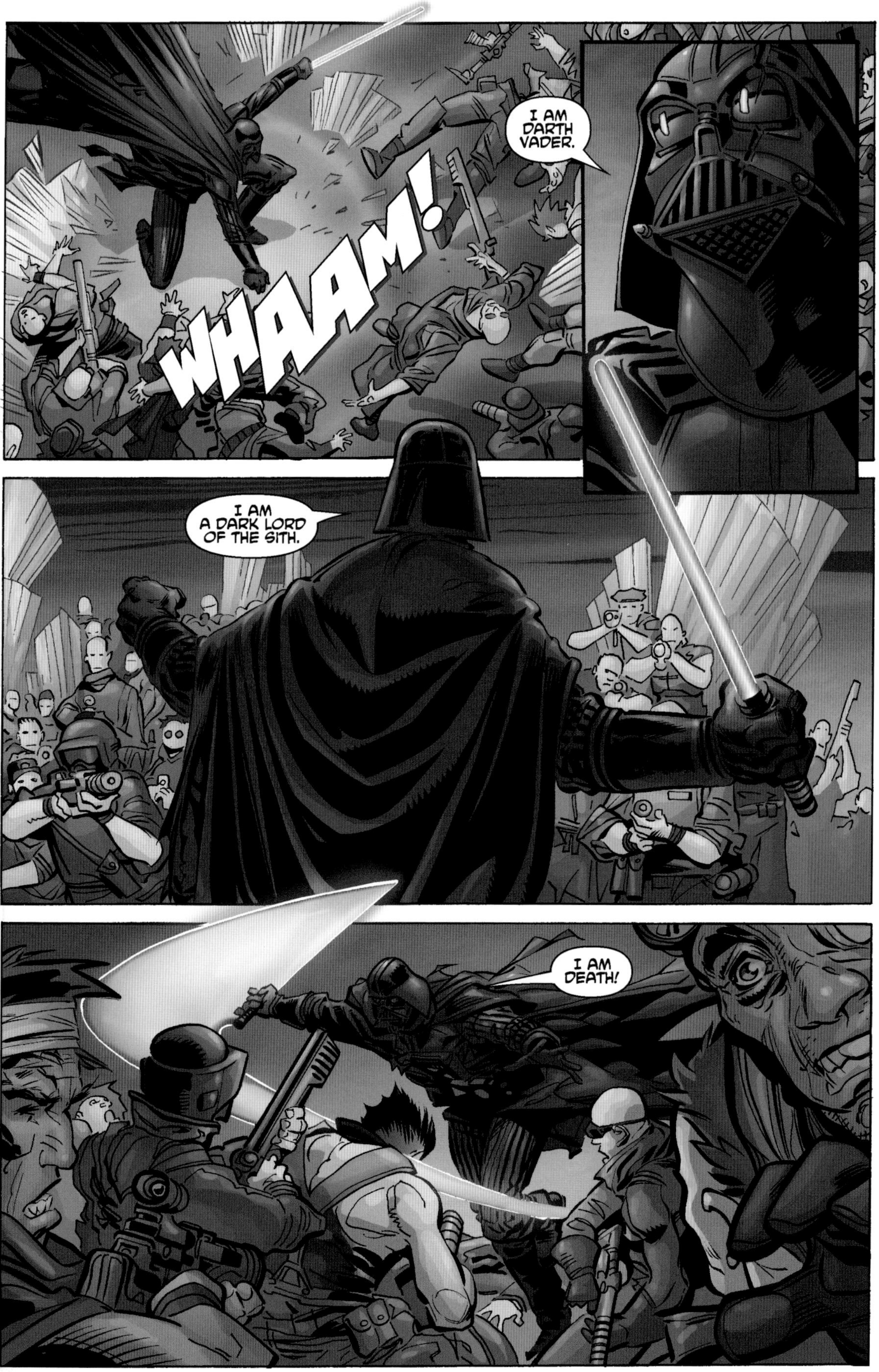
WHAAM!
I AM DARTH VADER.
I AM A DARK LORD OF THE SITH.
I AM DEATH!

FOLLOW THE RAVINE! HURRY!

LADY SARO...

SHALE...

I'M SORRY, COMMANDER.

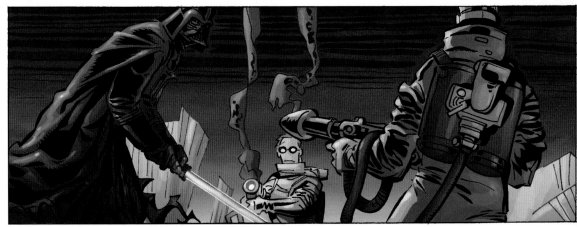

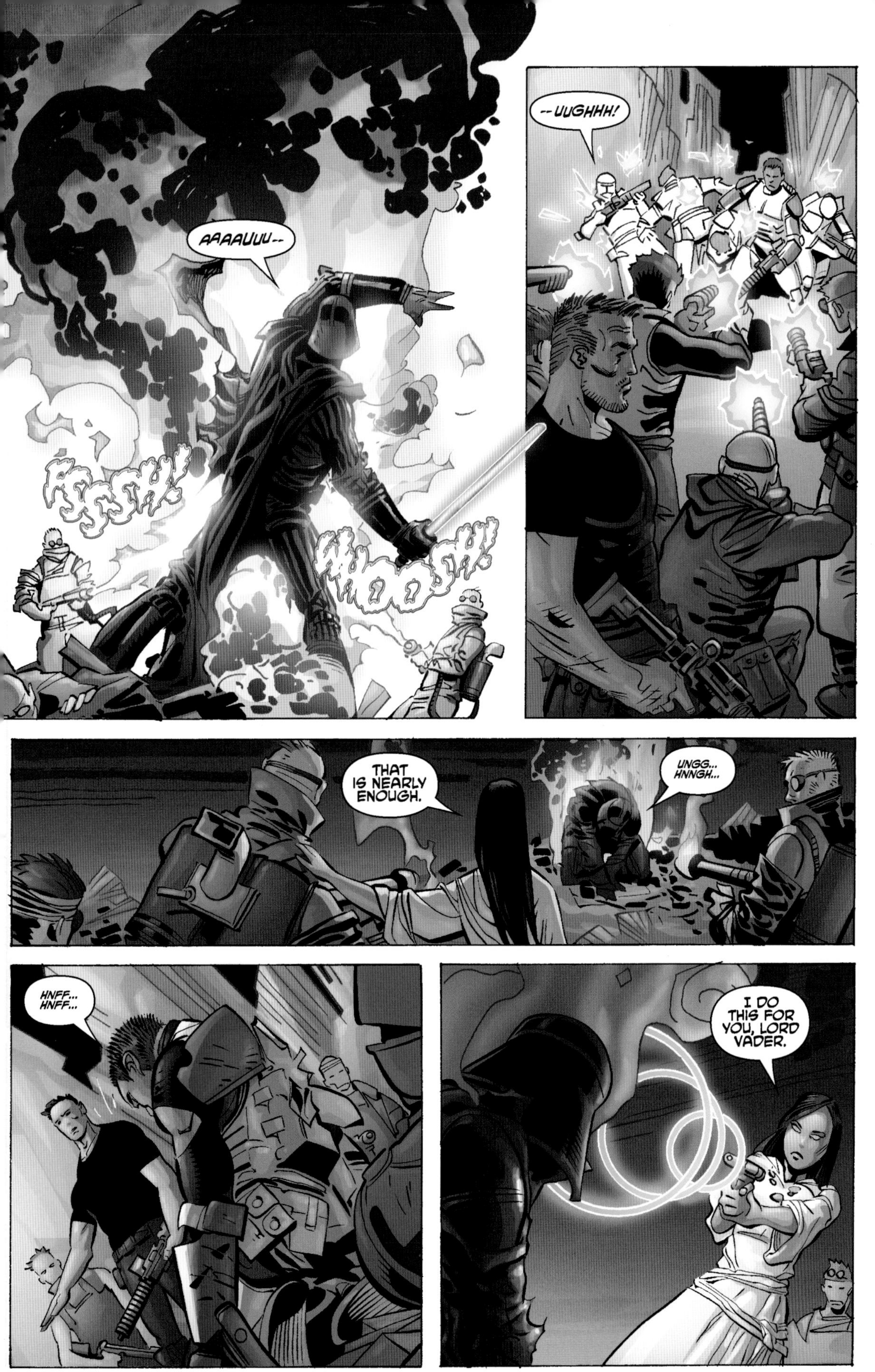
AAAAUUU--
FSSSH!
WHOOSH!
--UUGHHH!
THAT IS NEARLY ENOUGH.
UNGG... HNNGH...
HNFF... HNFF...
I DO THIS FOR YOU, LORD VADER.

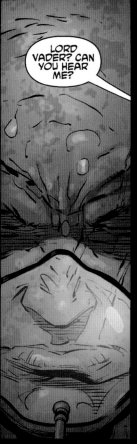

LORD VADER? CAN YOU HEAR ME?

UNNNHH...

ADMIRAL TARKIN. *GAROCHE TARKIN.*

WELCOME TO THE HEART OF THE GHOST NEBULA.

WHY AM I... *UNNNHH...AM I STILL ALIVE?*

BECAUSE YOU'VE SOMEHOW WILLED YOURSELF BACK FROM THE DEAD. JUST AS SARO TOLD ME YOU WOULD.

AND SHE WON'T LET ME KILL YOU, AS LONG AS SHE THINKS YOU CAN STILL BE TURNED TO OUR CAUSE.

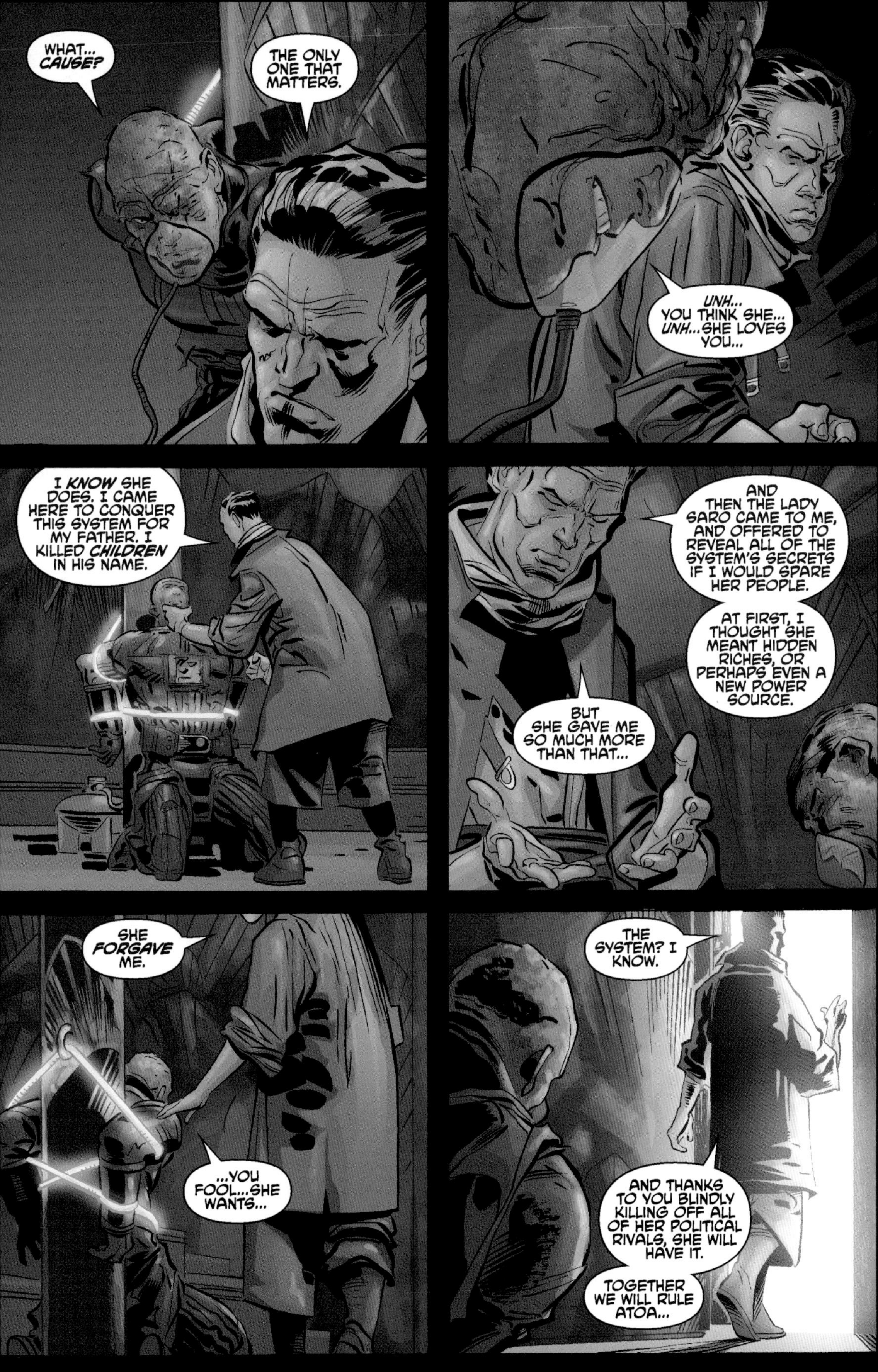
WHAT... CAUSE?
THE ONLY ONE THAT MATTERS.
UNH... YOU THINK SHE... UNH...SHE LOVES YOU...
I KNOW SHE DOES. I CAME HERE TO CONQUER THIS SYSTEM FOR MY FATHER. I KILLED CHILDREN IN HIS NAME.
AND THEN THE LADY SARO CAME TO ME, AND OFFERED TO REVEAL ALL OF THE SYSTEM'S SECRETS IF I WOULD SPARE HER PEOPLE.
AT FIRST, I THOUGHT SHE MEANT HIDDEN RICHES, OR PERHAPS EVEN A NEW POWER SOURCE.
BUT SHE GAVE ME SO MUCH MORE THAN THAT...
SHE FORGAVE ME.
...YOU FOOL...SHE WANTS...
THE SYSTEM? I KNOW.
AND THANKS TO YOU BLINDLY KILLING OFF ALL OF HER POLITICAL RIVALS, SHE WILL HAVE IT.
TOGETHER WE WILL RULE ATOA...

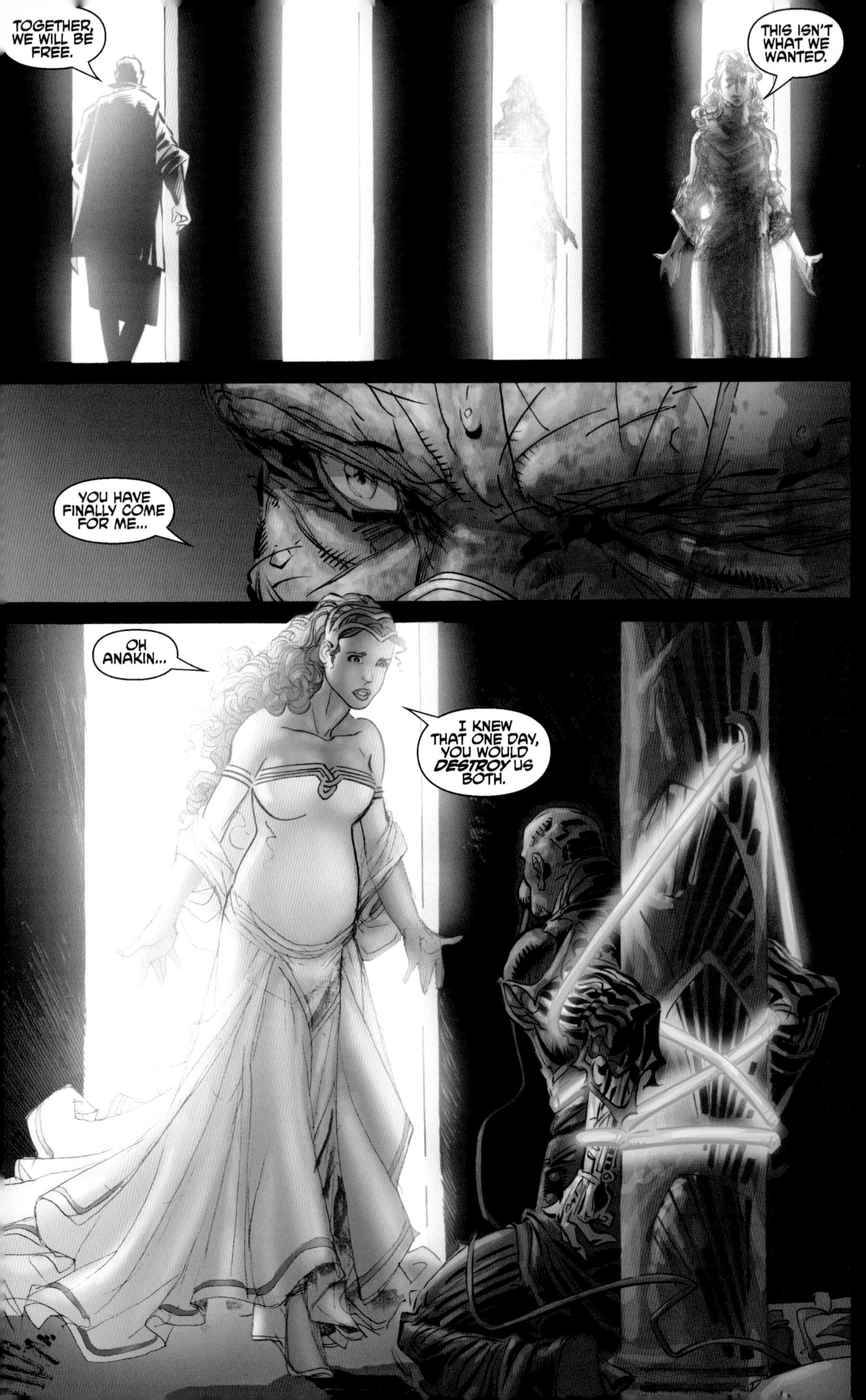
TOGETHER, WE WILL BE FREE.
THIS ISN'T WHAT WE WANTED.
YOU HAVE FINALLY COME FOR ME...
OH ANAKIN...
I KNEW THAT ONE DAY, YOU WOULD *DESTROY* US BOTH.

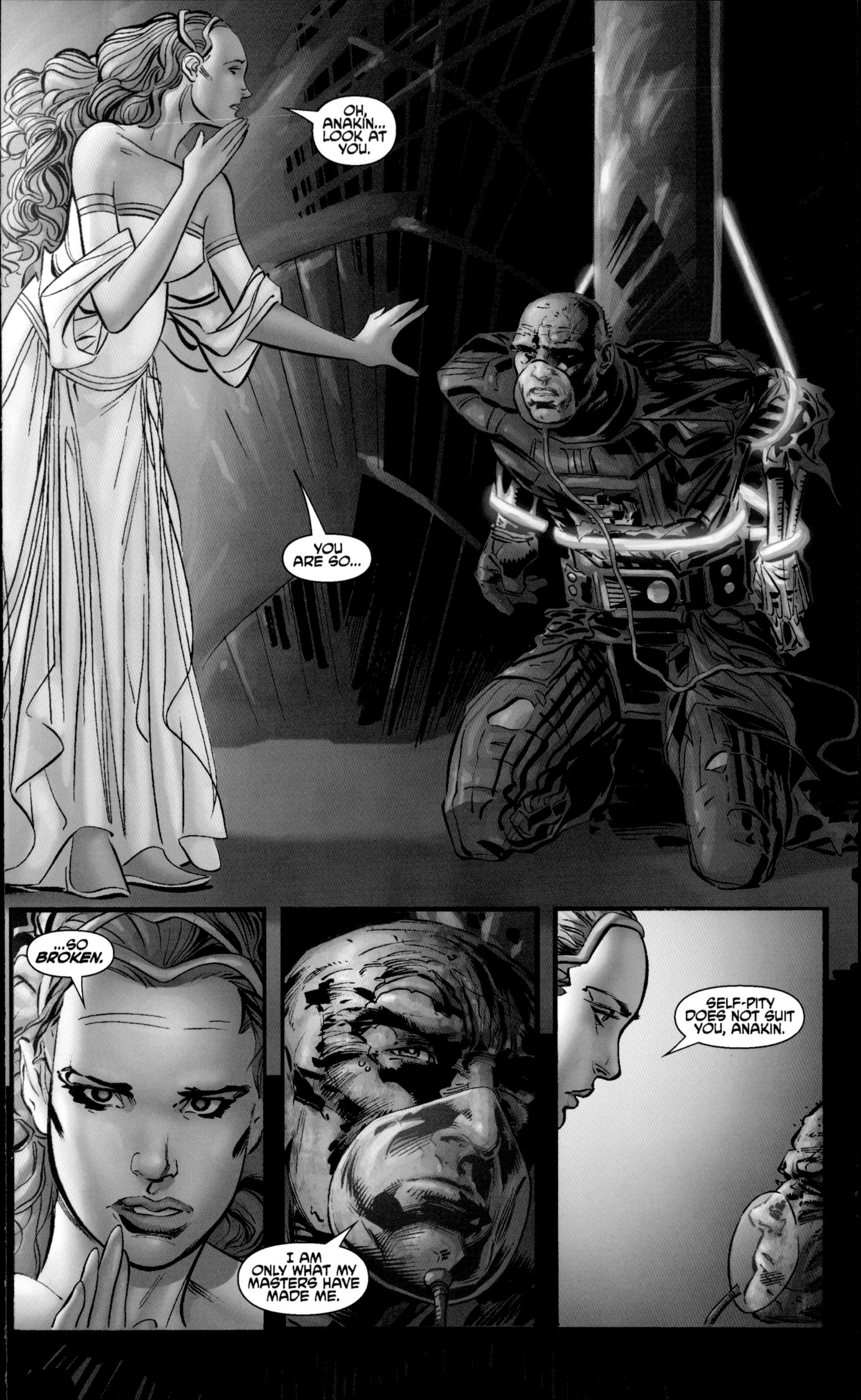
OH, ANAKIN... LOOK AT YOU.
YOU ARE SO...
...SO BROKEN.
I AM ONLY WHAT MY MASTERS HAVE MADE ME.
SELF-PITY DOES NOT SUIT YOU, ANAKIN.

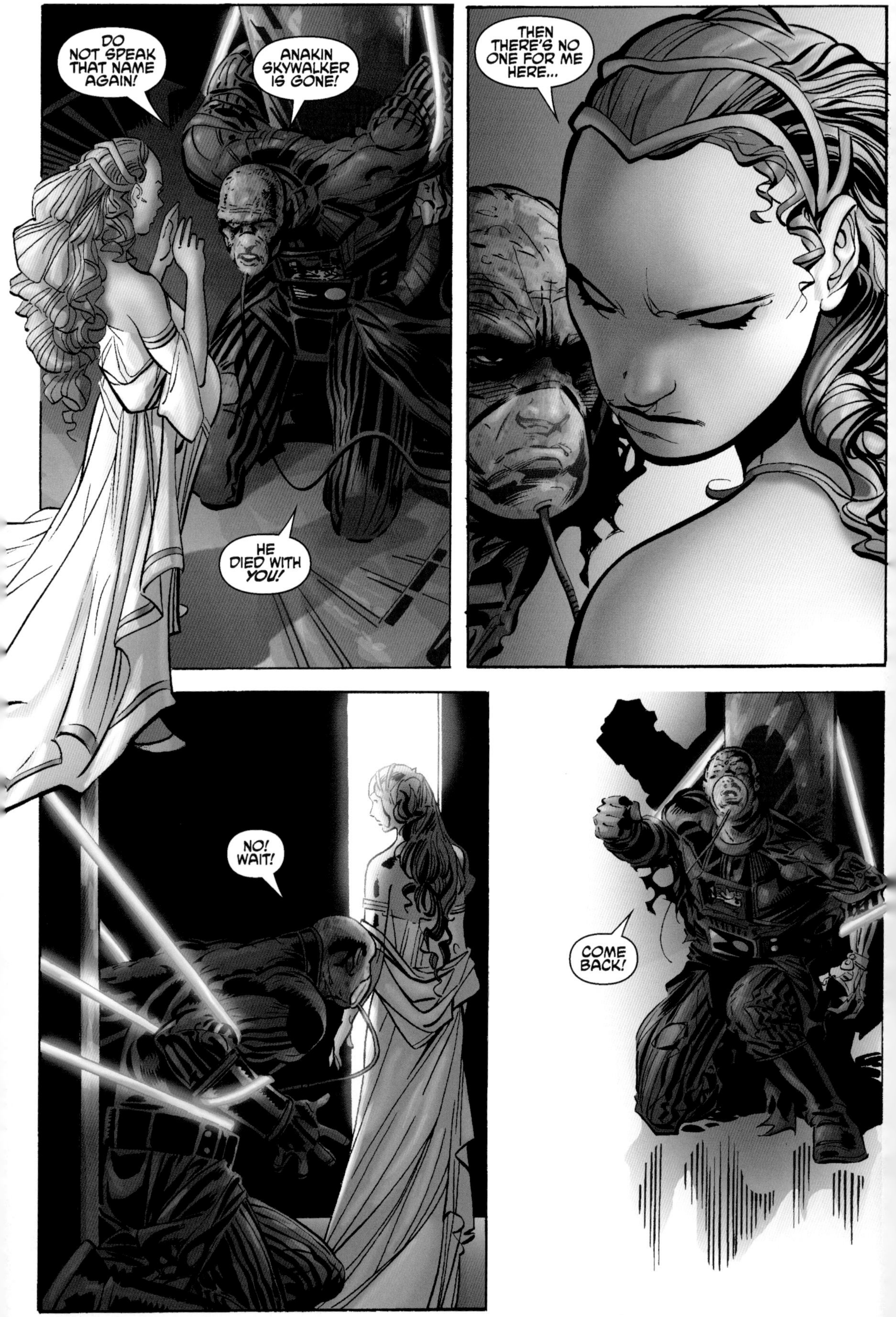

DO NOT SPEAK THAT NAME AGAIN!
ANAKIN SKYWALKER IS GONE!
HE DIED WITH YOU!
THEN THERE'S NO ONE FOR ME HERE...
NO! WAIT!
COME BACK!

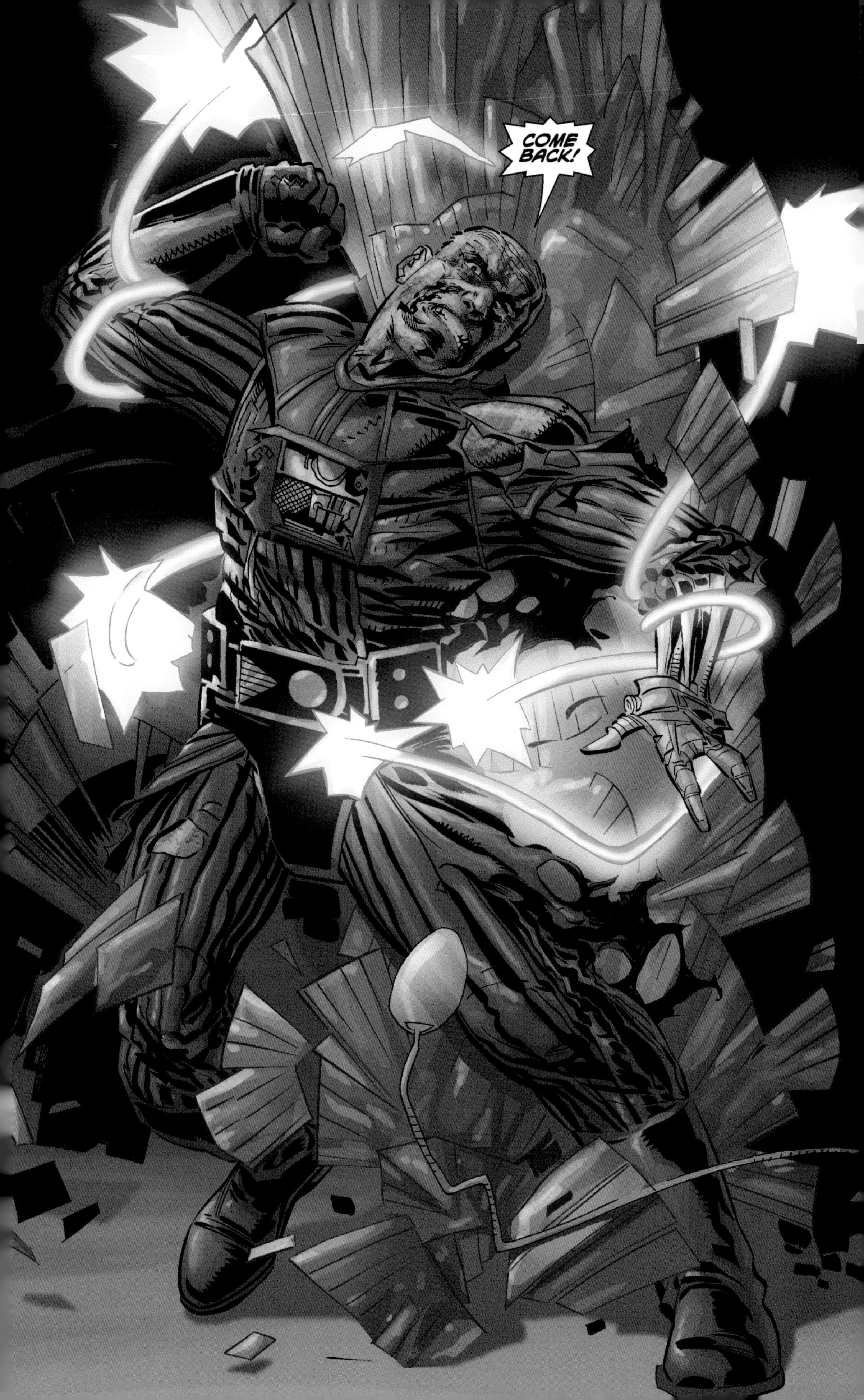
COME BACK!

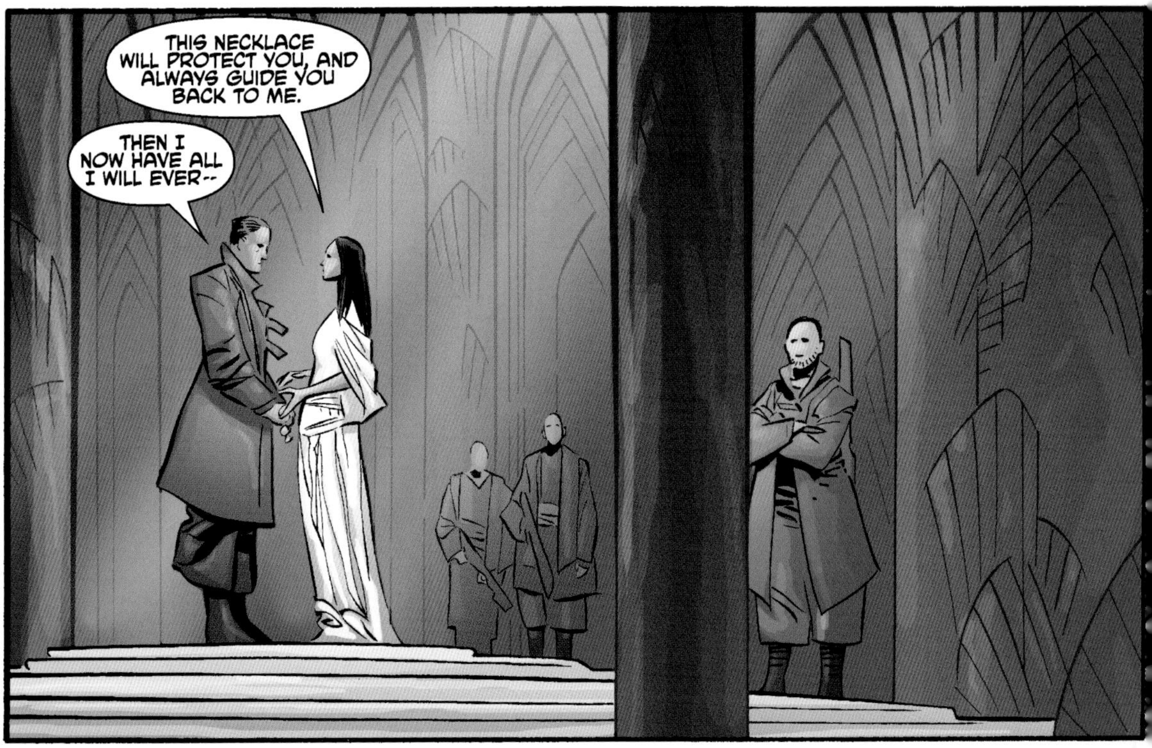
THIS NECKLACE WILL PROTECT YOU, AND ALWAYS GUIDE YOU BACK TO ME.
THEN I NOW HAVE ALL I WILL EVER--

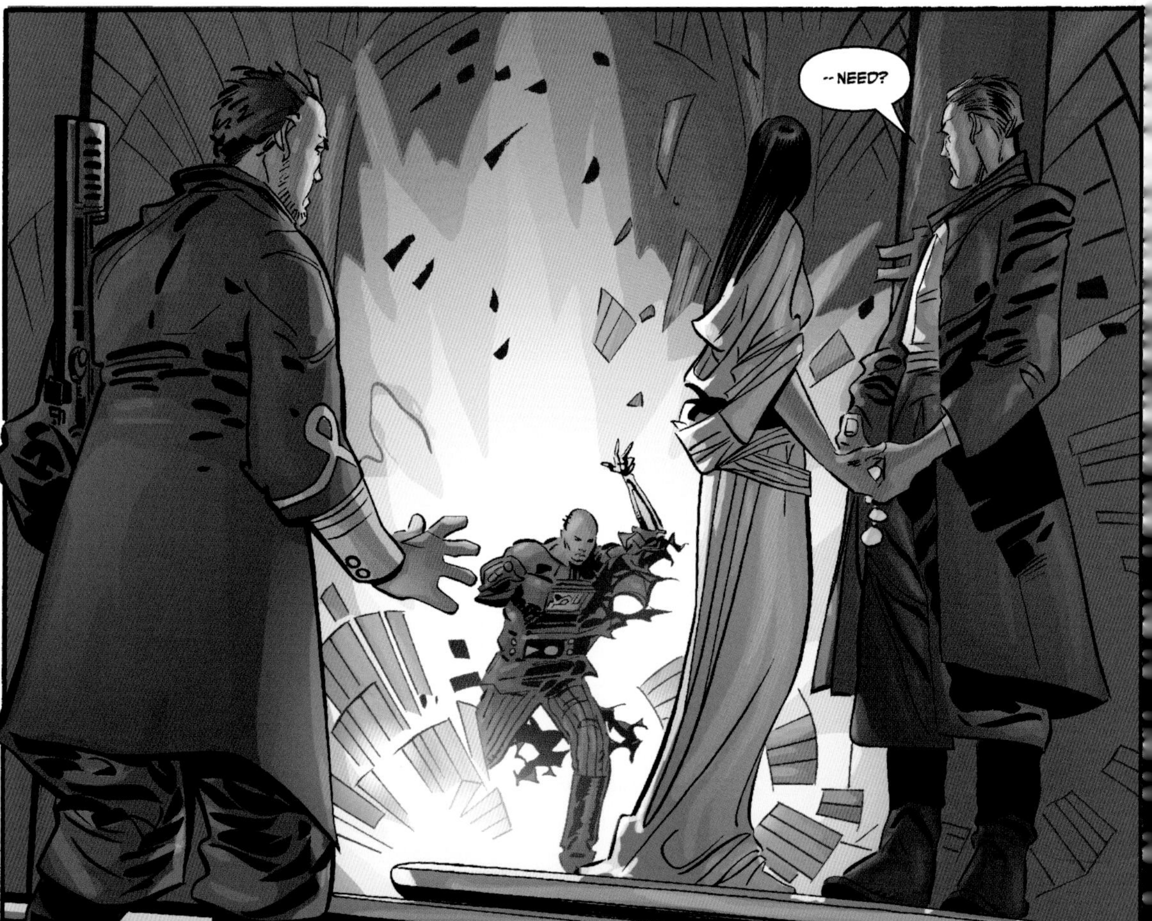
--NEED?

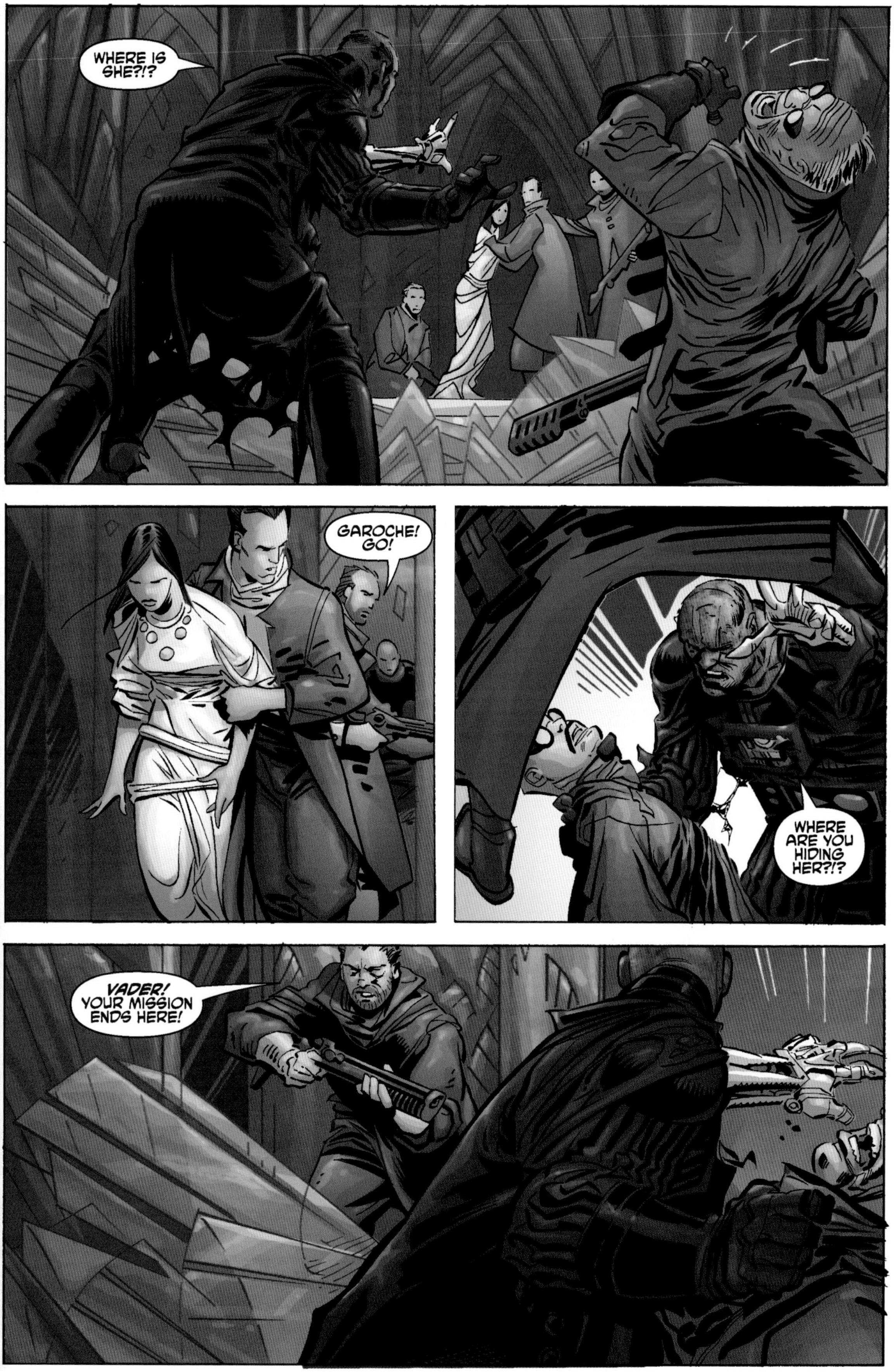
WHERE IS SHE?!?
GAROCHE! GO!
WHERE ARE YOU HIDING HER?!?
VADER! YOUR MISSION ENDS HERE!

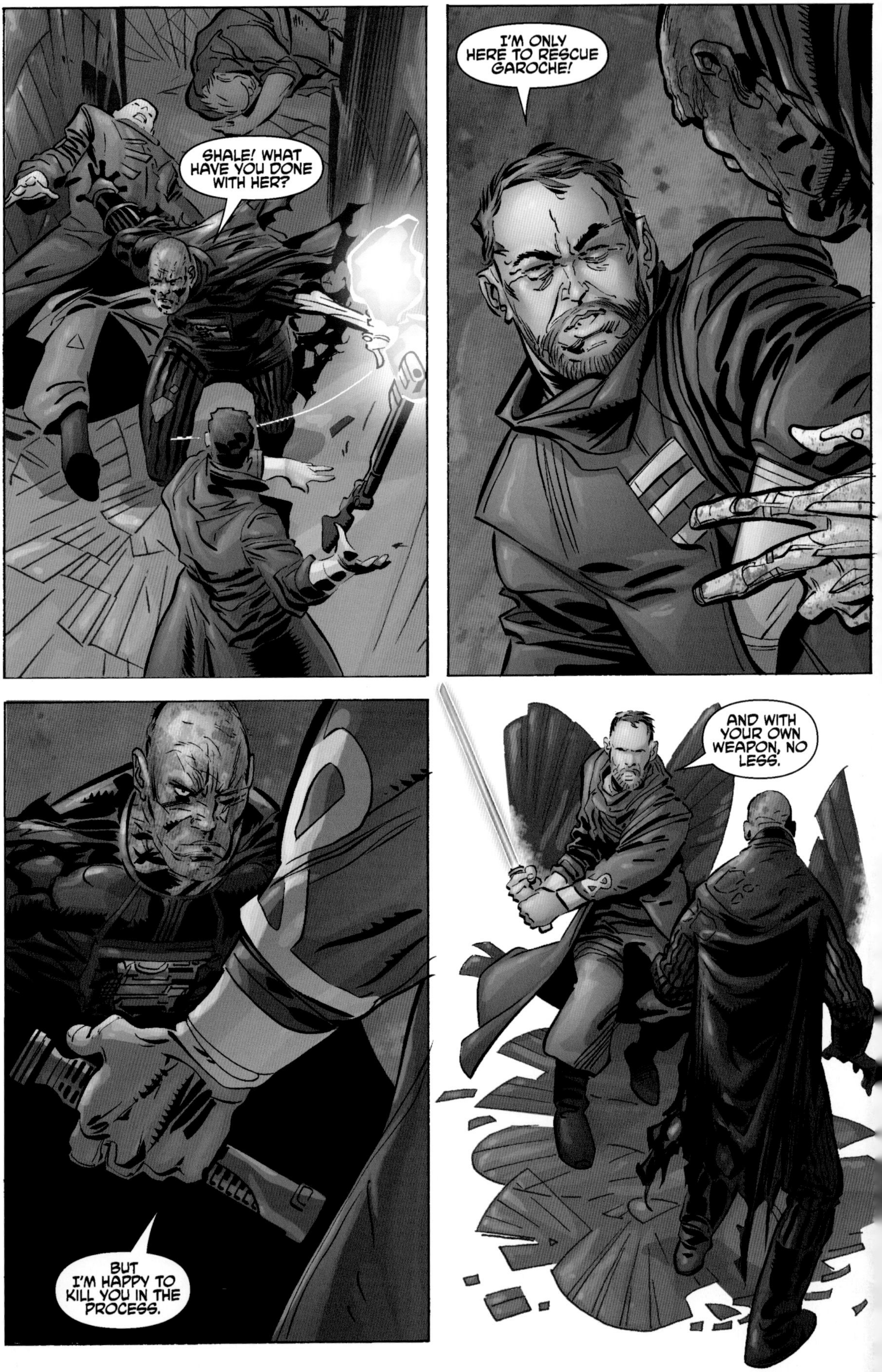
SHALE! WHAT HAVE YOU DONE WITH HER?
I'M ONLY HERE TO RESCUE GAROCHE!
BUT I'M HAPPY TO KILL YOU IN THE PROCESS.
AND WITH YOUR OWN WEAPON, NO LESS.

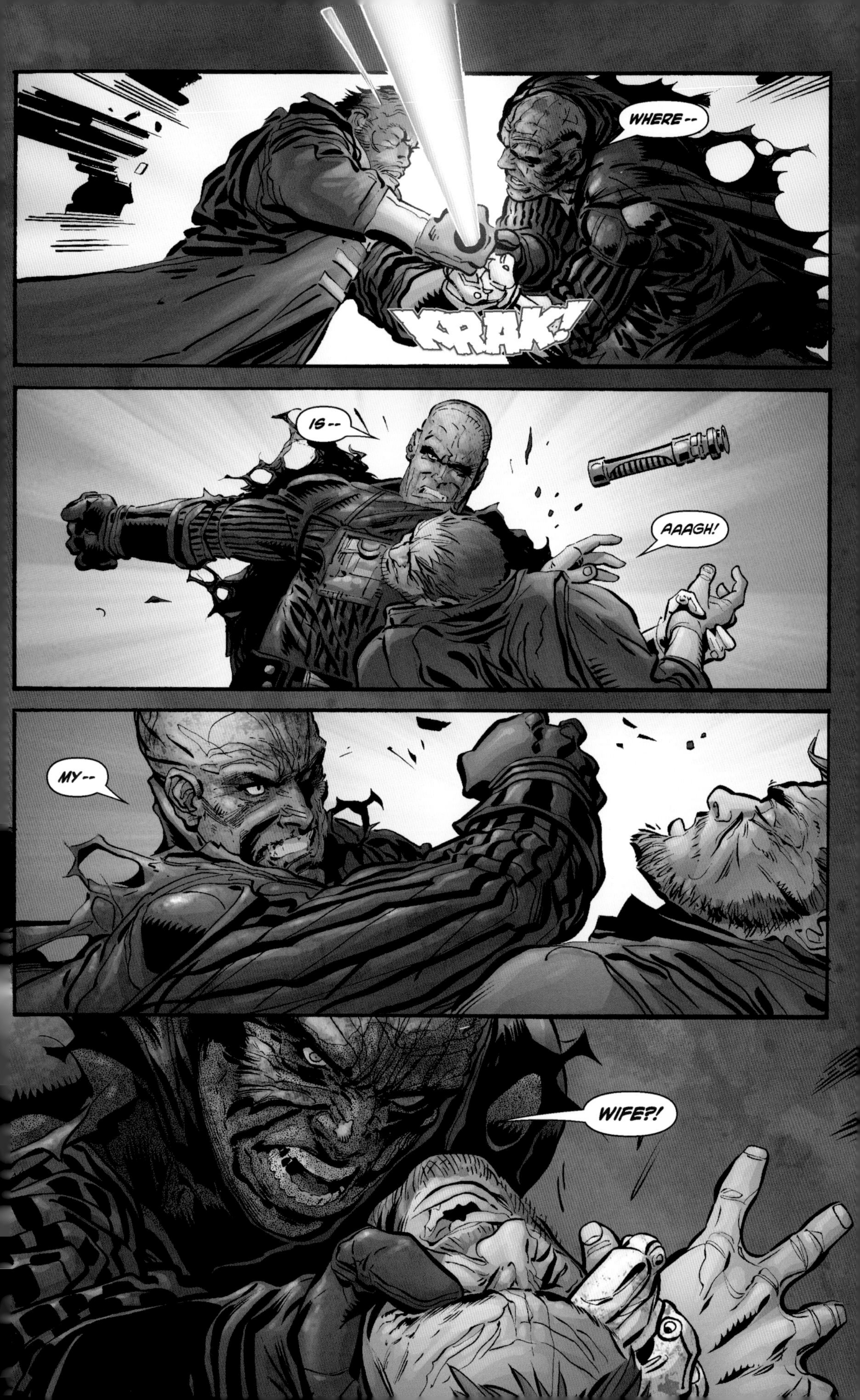
WHERE --
KRAK!
IS --
AAAGH!
MY --
WIFE?!

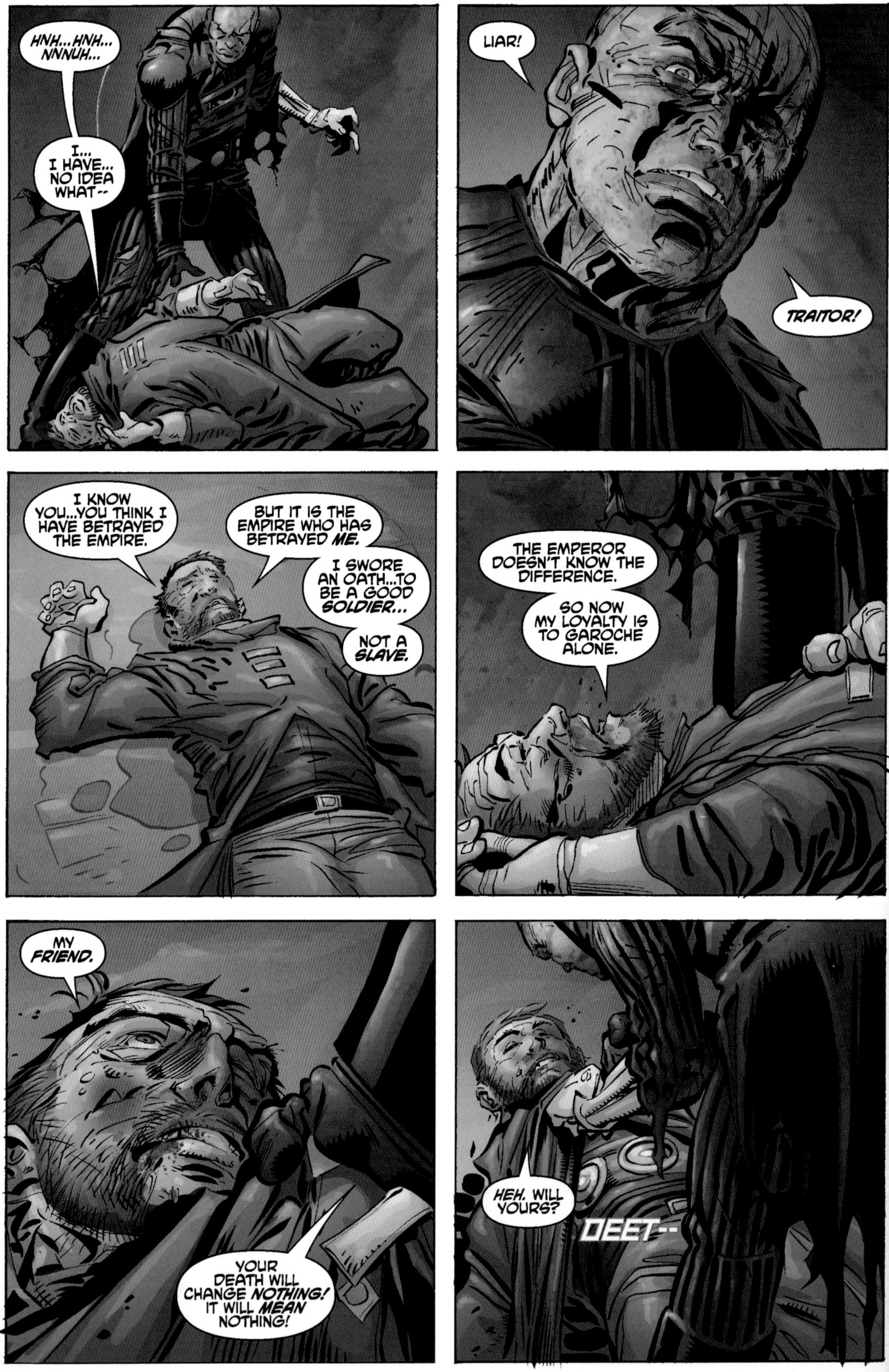
HNH...HNH... NNNUH...
I... I HAVE... NO IDEA WHAT--
LIAR!
TRAITOR!
I KNOW YOU...YOU THINK I HAVE BETRAYED THE EMPIRE.
BUT IT IS THE EMPIRE WHO HAS BETRAYED ME.
I SWORE AN OATH...TO BE A GOOD SOLDIER...
NOT A SLAVE.
THE EMPEROR DOESN'T KNOW THE DIFFERENCE.
SO NOW MY LOYALTY IS TO GAROCHE ALONE.
MY FRIEND.
YOUR DEATH WILL CHANGE NOTHING! IT WILL MEAN NOTHING!
HEH. WILL YOURS?
DEET--

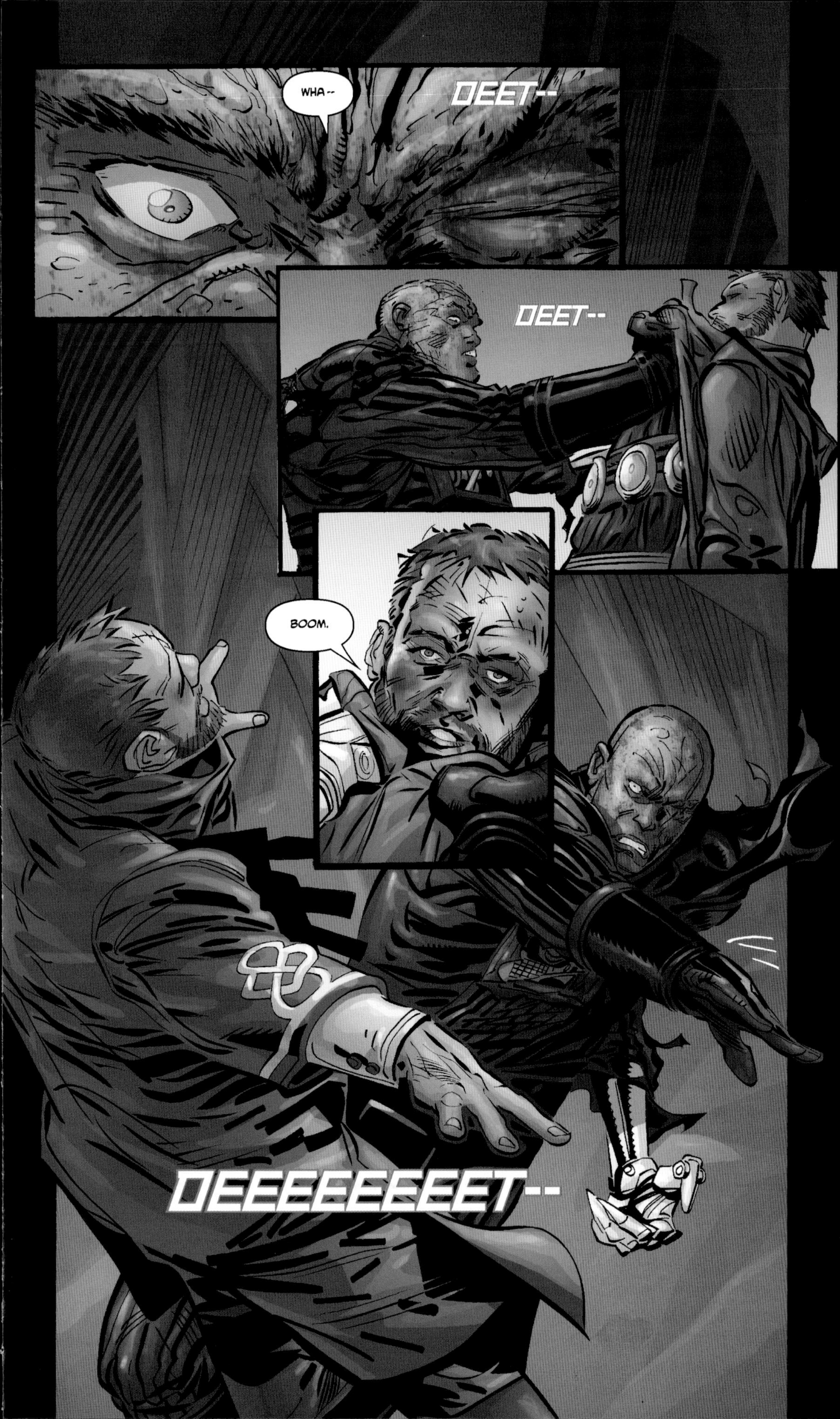
WHA--
DEET--
DEET--
BOOM.
DEEEEEEEEET--

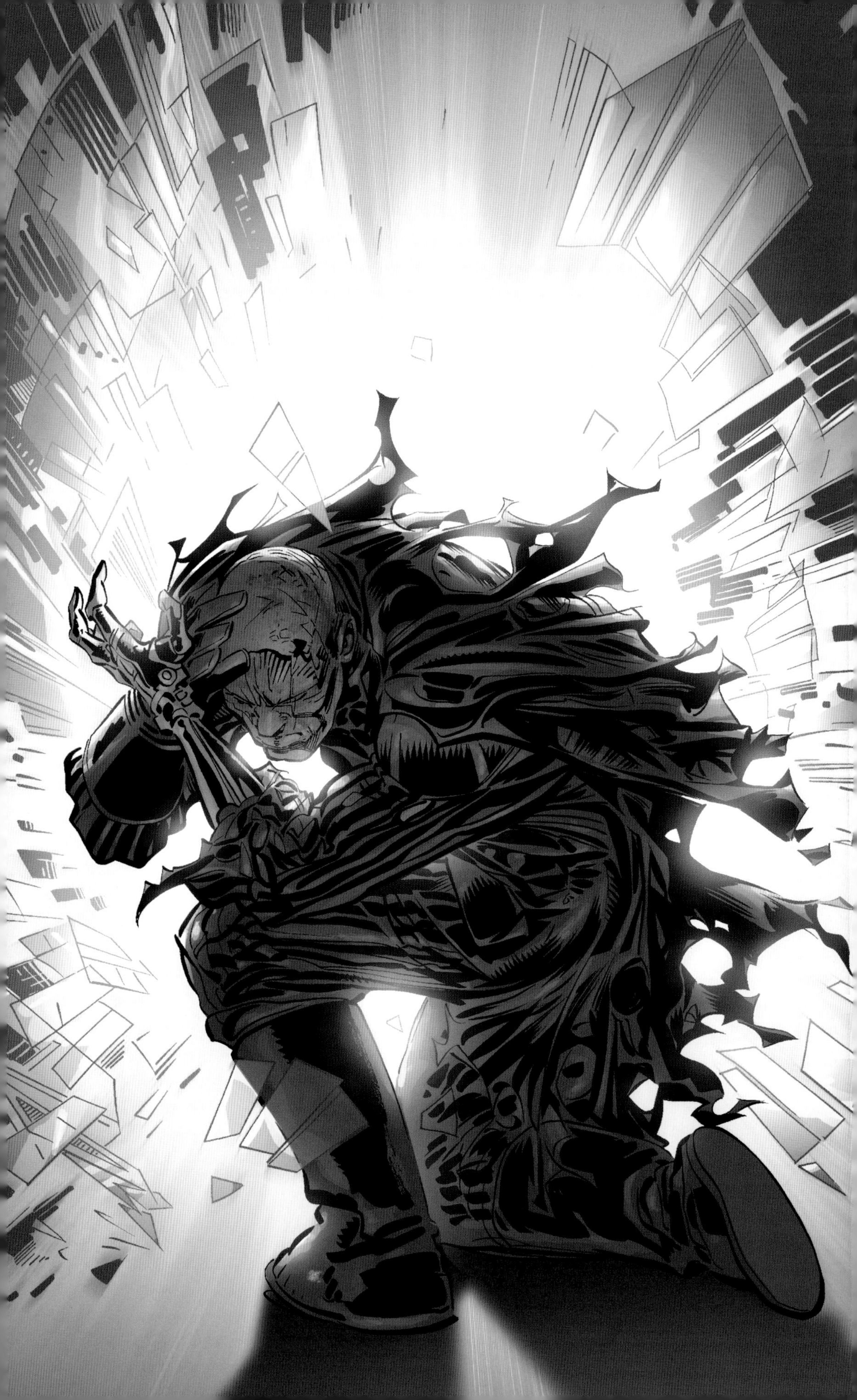

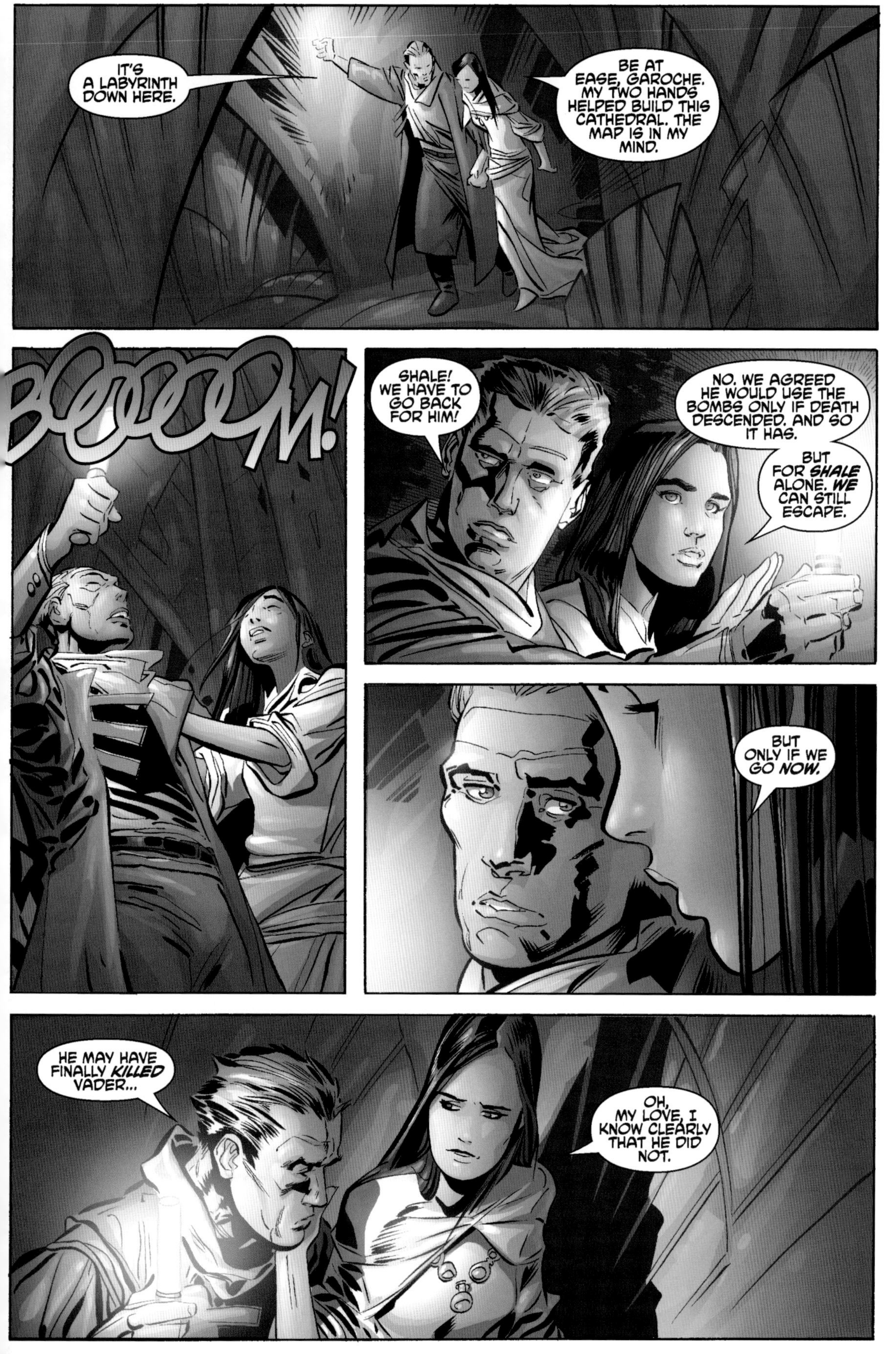
IT'S A LABYRINTH DOWN HERE.
BE AT EASE, GAROCHE. MY TWO HANDS HELPED BUILD THIS CATHEDRAL. THE MAP IS IN MY MIND.
BOOOOOM!
SHALE! WE HAVE TO GO BACK FOR HIM!
NO. WE AGREED HE WOULD USE THE BOMBS ONLY IF DEATH DESCENDED. AND SO IT HAS.
BUT FOR SHALE ALONE. WE CAN STILL ESCAPE.
BUT ONLY IF WE GO NOW.
HE MAY HAVE FINALLY KILLED VADER...
OH, MY LOVE, I KNOW CLEARLY THAT HE DID NOT.

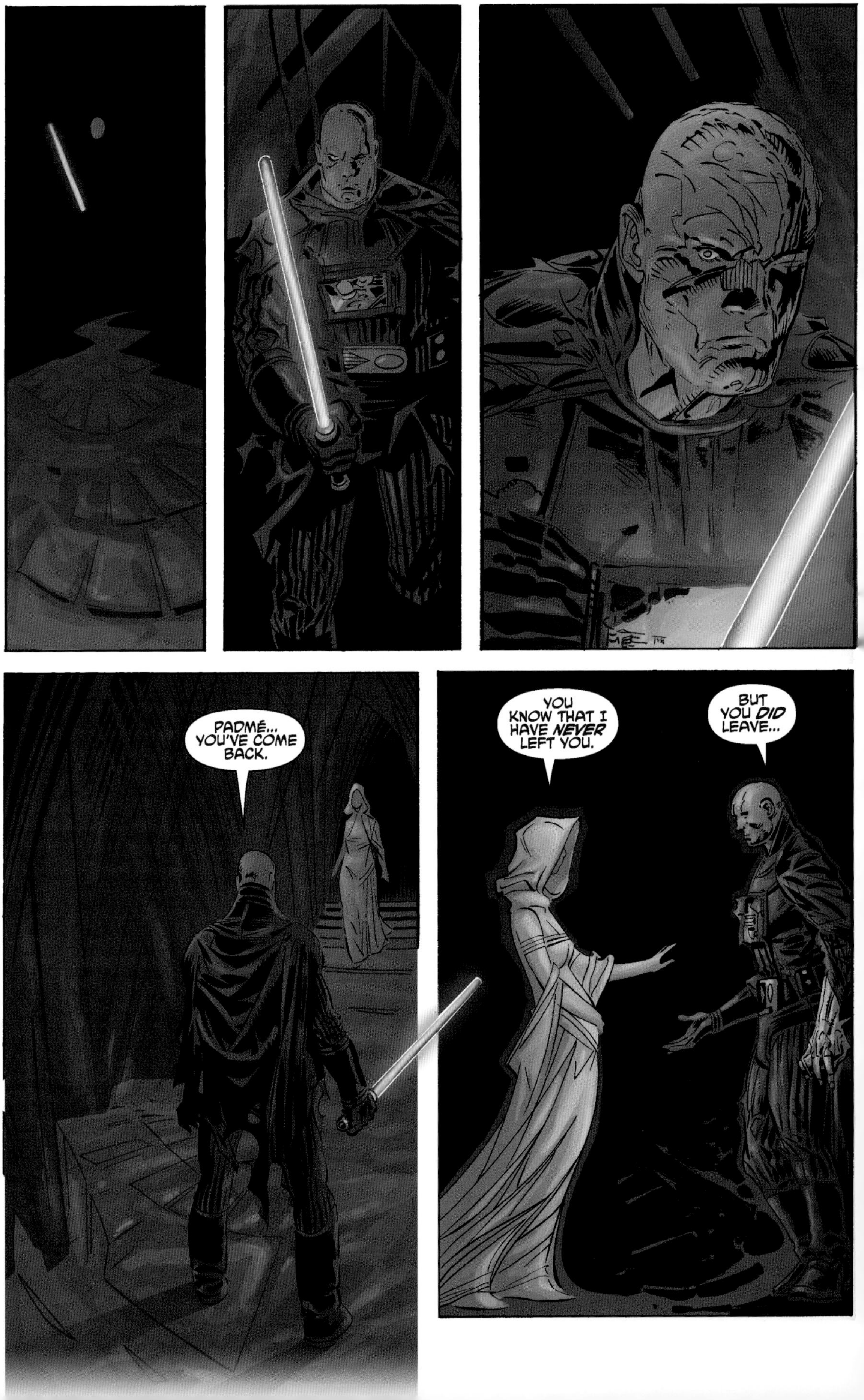
PADMÉ... YOU'VE COME BACK.
YOU KNOW THAT I HAVE NEVER LEFT YOU.
BUT YOU DID LEAVE...

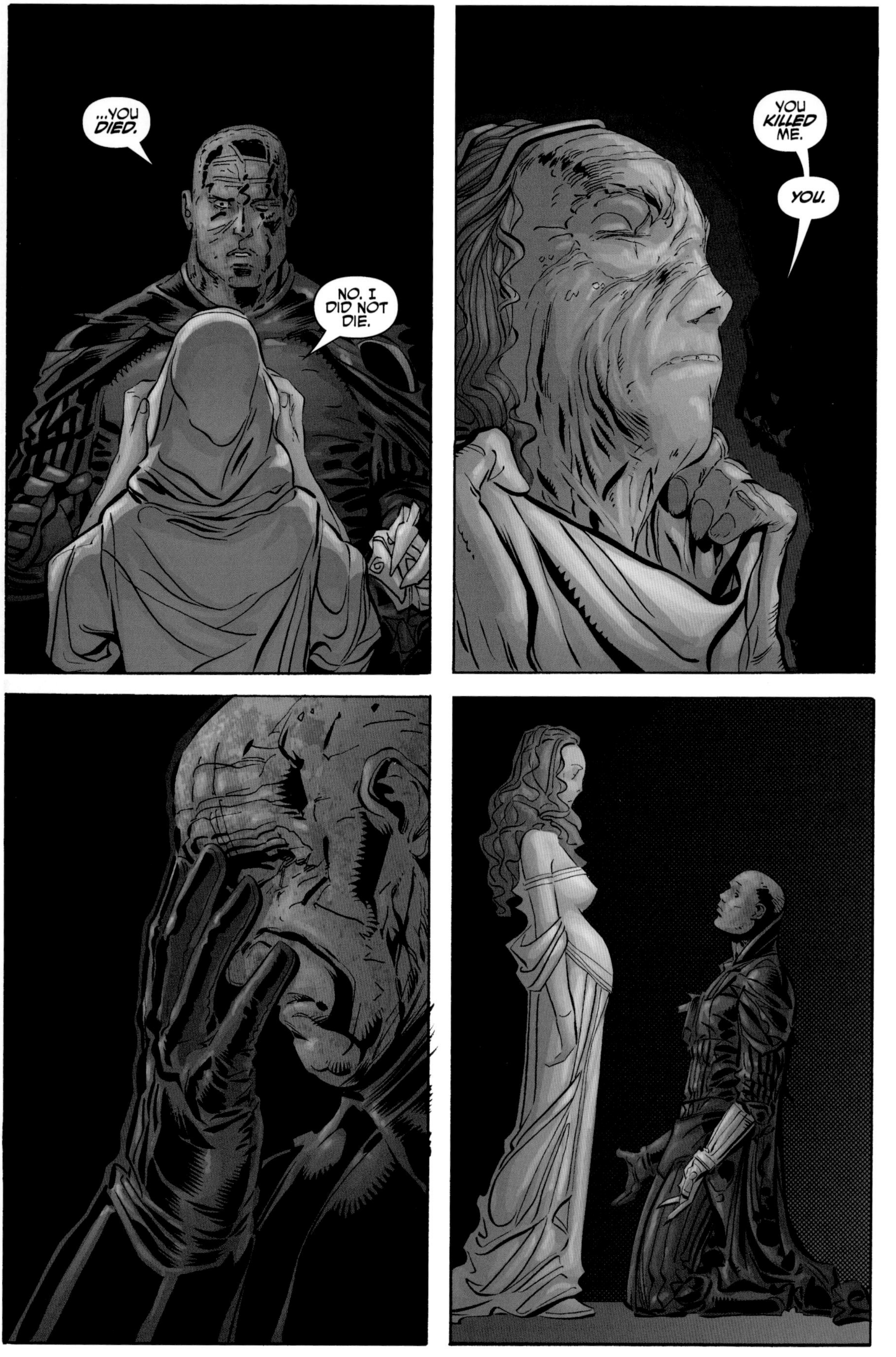
...YOU DIED.
NO. I DID NOT DIE.
YOU KILLED ME.
YOU.

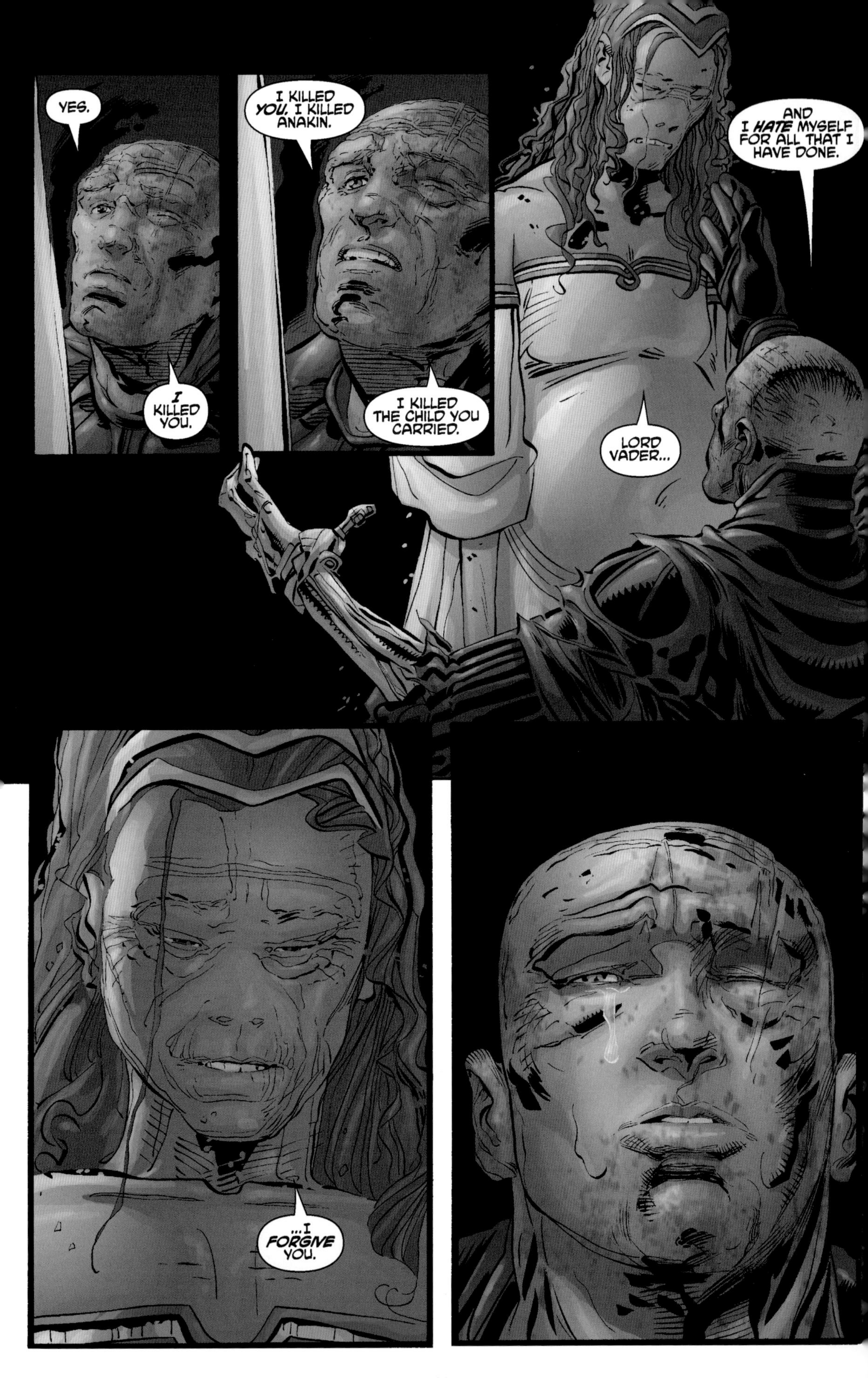
YES.
I KILLED YOU.
I KILLED YOU. I KILLED ANAKIN.
I KILLED THE CHILD YOU CARRIED.
AND I HATE MYSELF FOR ALL THAT I HAVE DONE.
LORD VADER...
...I FORGIVE YOU.

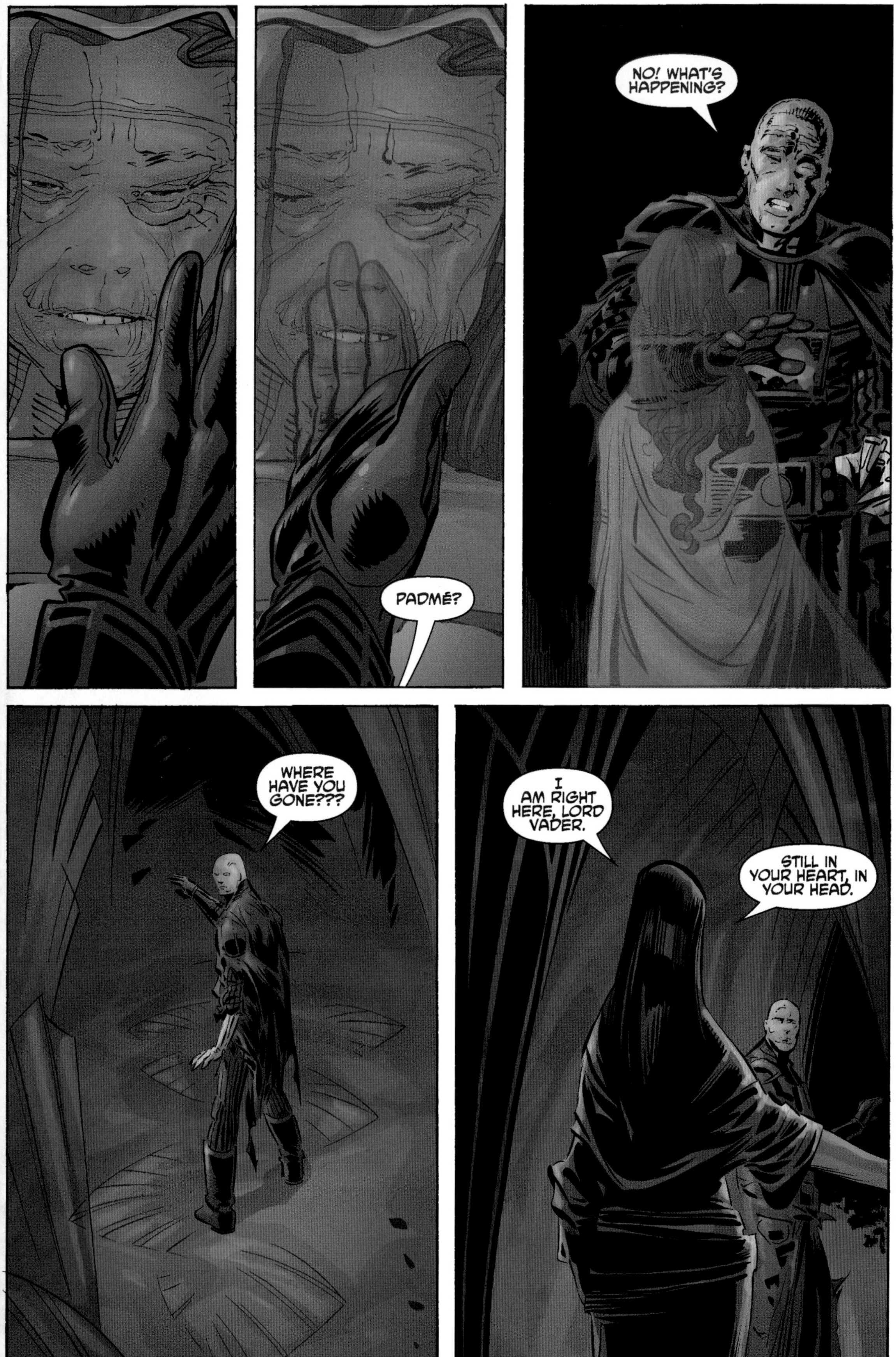
PADMÉ?
NO! WHAT'S HAPPENING?
WHERE HAVE YOU GONE???
I AM RIGHT HERE, LORD VADER.
STILL IN YOUR HEART, IN YOUR HEAD.

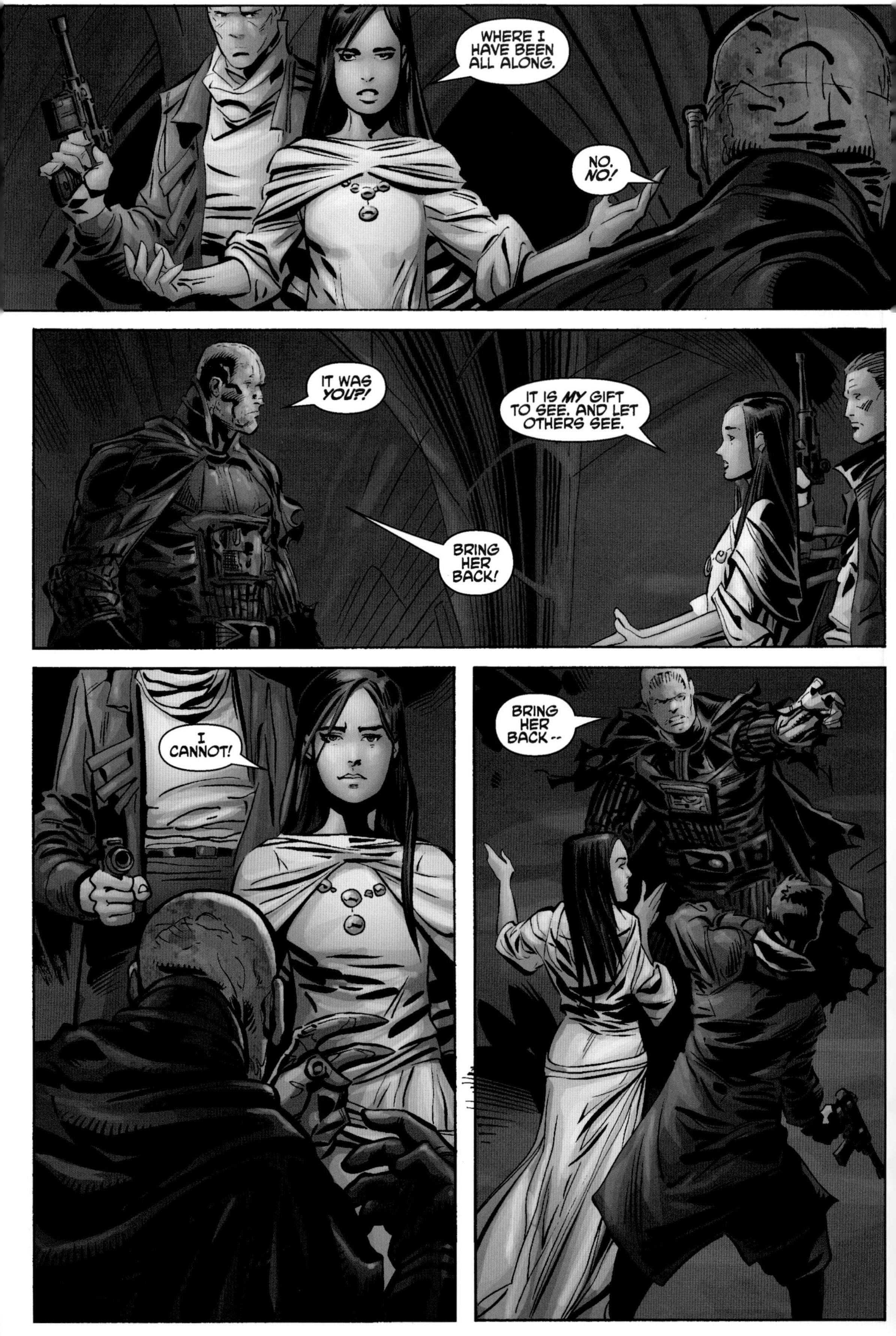
WHERE I HAVE BEEN ALL ALONG.
NO. NO!
IT WAS YOU?!
IT IS MY GIFT TO SEE. AND LET OTHERS SEE.
BRING HER BACK!
I CANNOT!
BRING HER BACK--

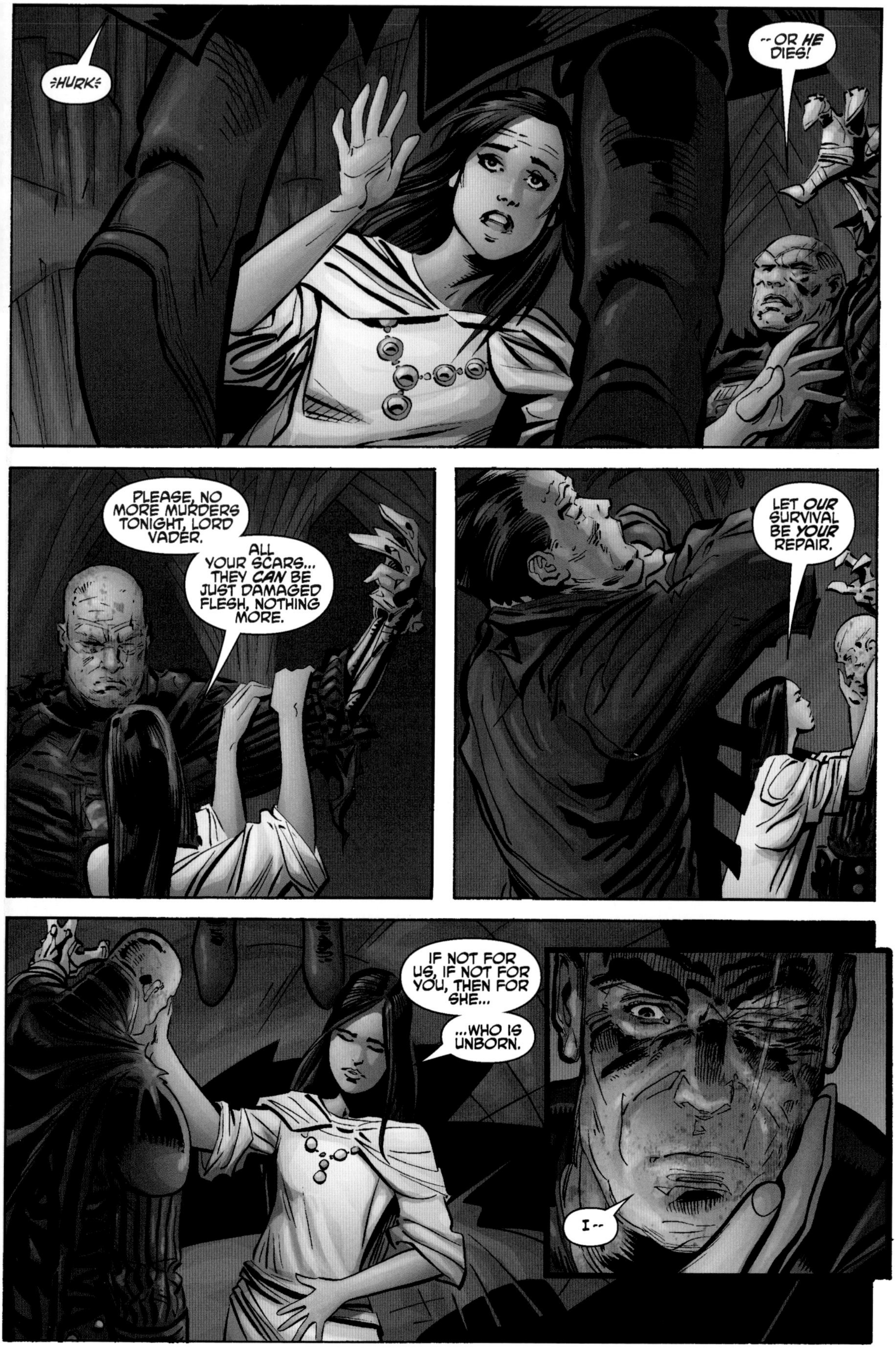

HURK
--OR HE DIES!
PLEASE, NO MORE MURDERS TONIGHT, LORD VADER.
ALL YOUR SCARS... THEY CAN BE JUST DAMAGED FLESH, NOTHING MORE.
LET OUR SURVIVAL BE YOUR REPAIR.
IF NOT FOR US, IF NOT FOR YOU, THEN FOR SHE...
...WHO IS UNBORN.
I --

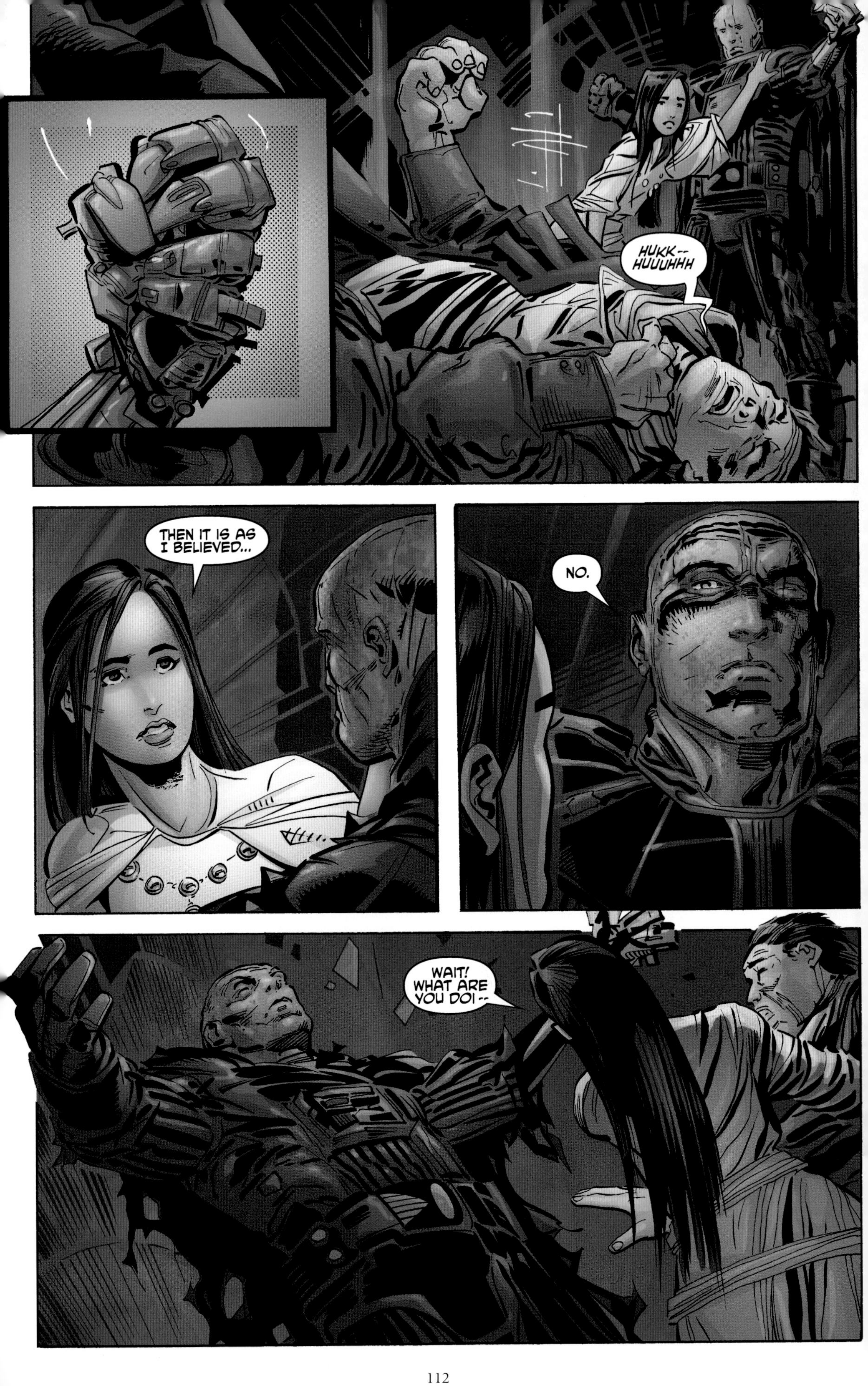
HUKK--
HUUUHHH
THEN IT IS AS
I BELIEVED...
NO.
WAIT!
WHAT ARE
YOU DOI--

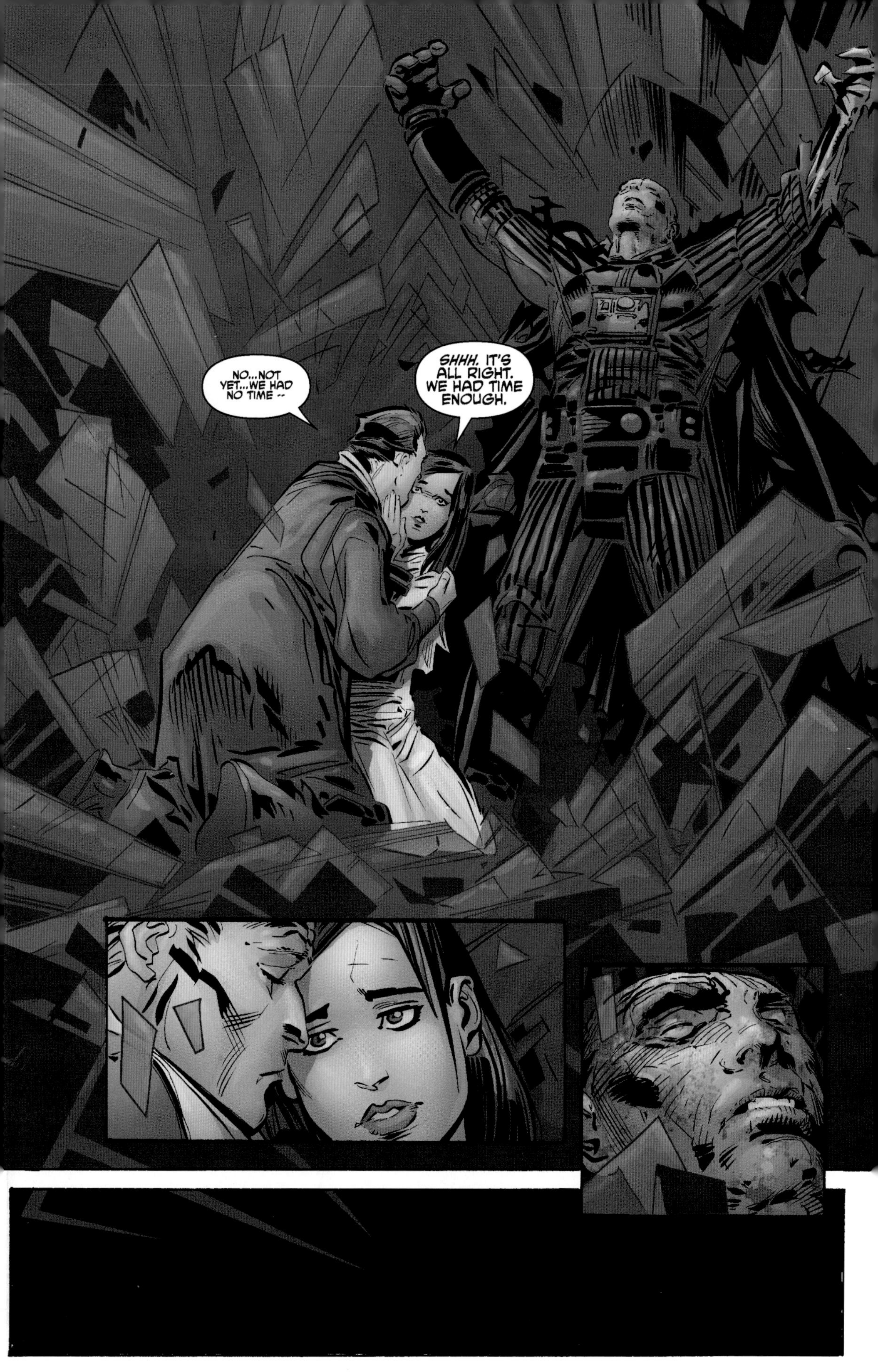
NO...NOT YET...WE HAD NO TIME --
SHHH. IT'S ALL RIGHT. WE HAD TIME ENOUGH.

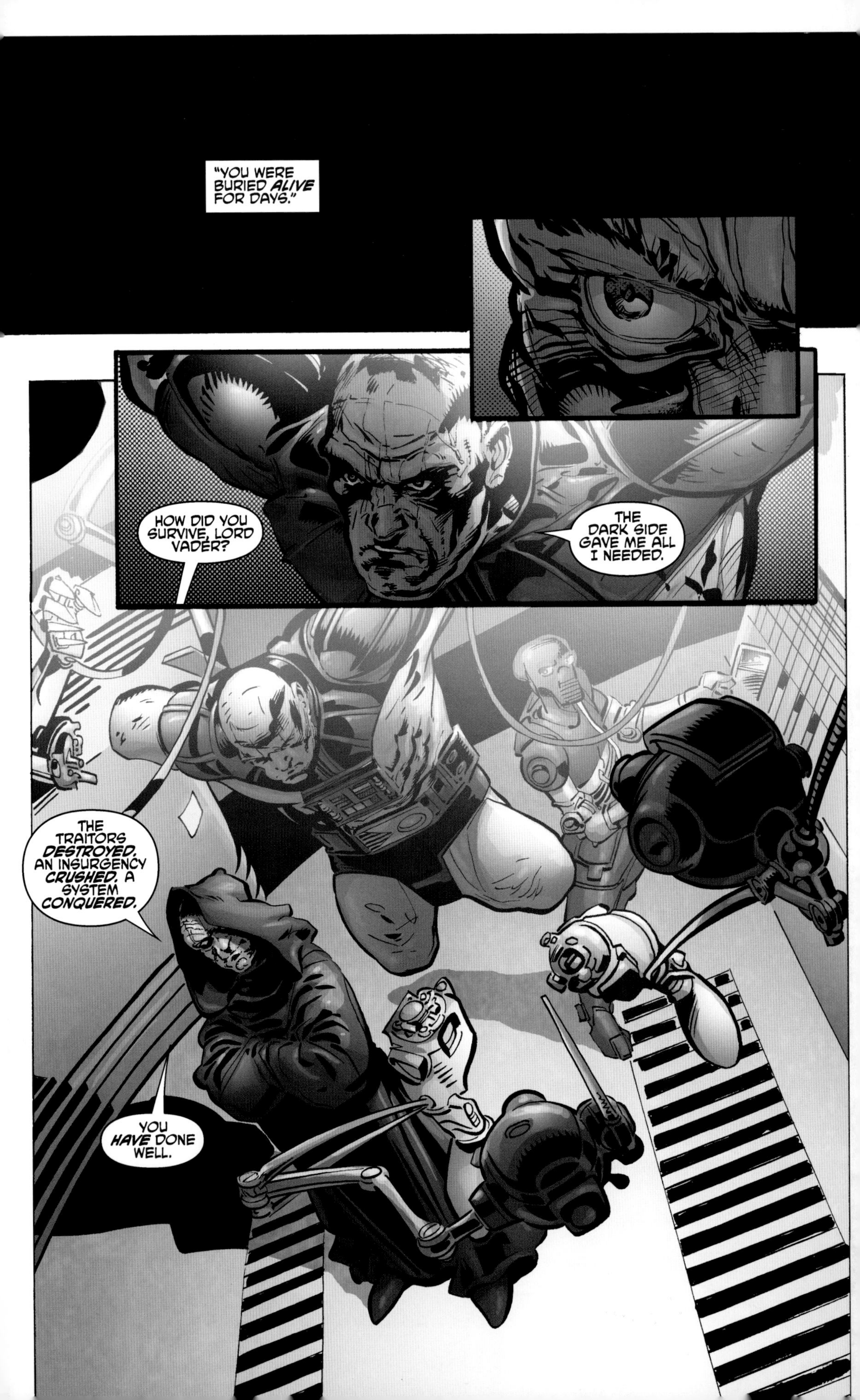
"YOU WERE BURIED ALIVE FOR DAYS."
HOW DID YOU SURVIVE, LORD VADER?
THE DARK SIDE GAVE ME ALL I NEEDED.
THE TRAITORS DESTROYED. AN INSURGENCY CRUSHED. A SYSTEM CONQUERED.
YOU HAVE DONE WELL.

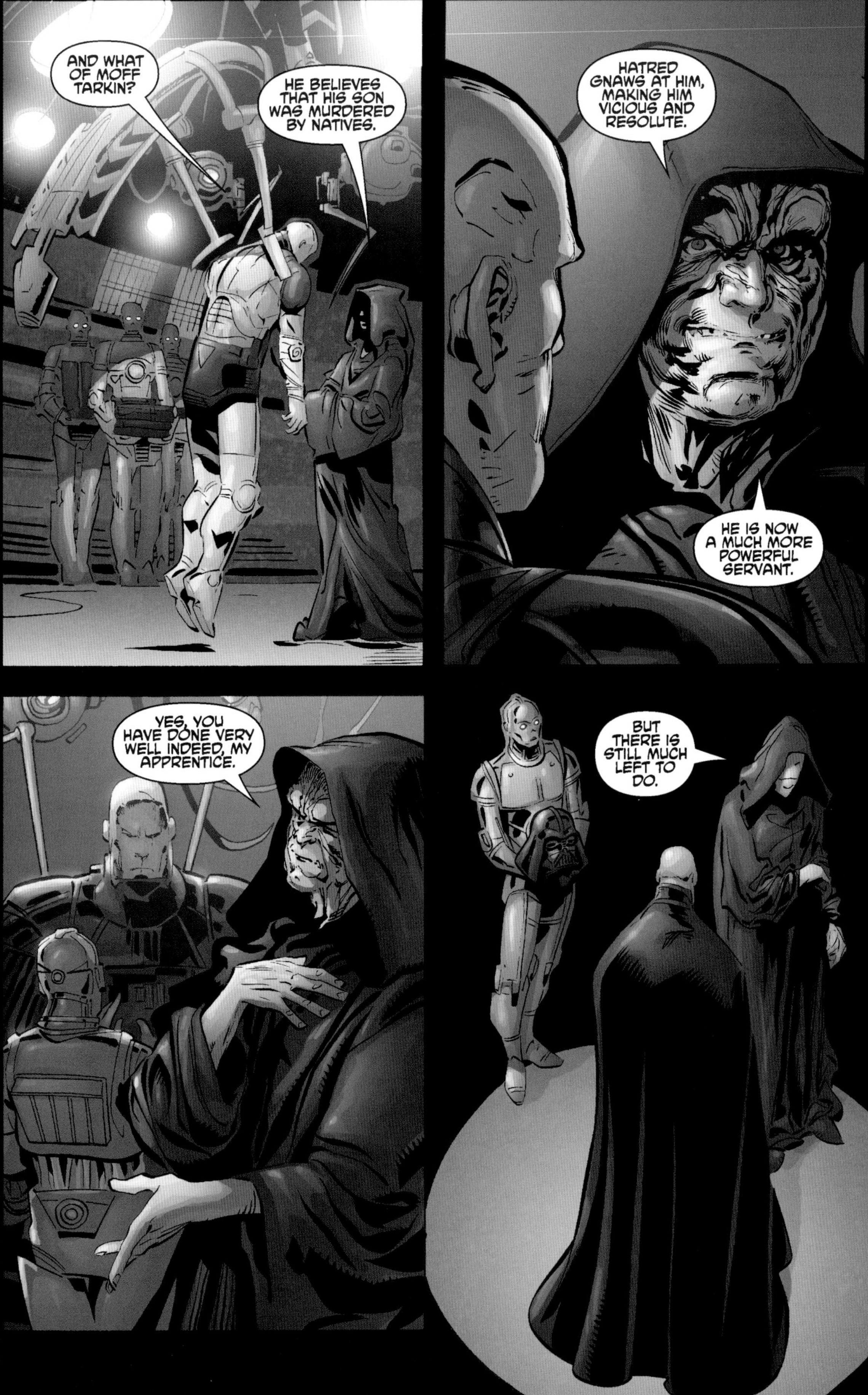
AND WHAT OF MOFF TARKIN?
HE BELIEVES THAT HIS SON WAS MURDERED BY NATIVES.
HATRED GNAWS AT HIM, MAKING HIM VICIOUS AND RESOLUTE.
HE IS NOW A MUCH MORE POWERFUL SERVANT.
YES, YOU HAVE DONE VERY WELL INDEED, MY APPRENTICE.
BUT THERE IS STILL MUCH LEFT TO DO.

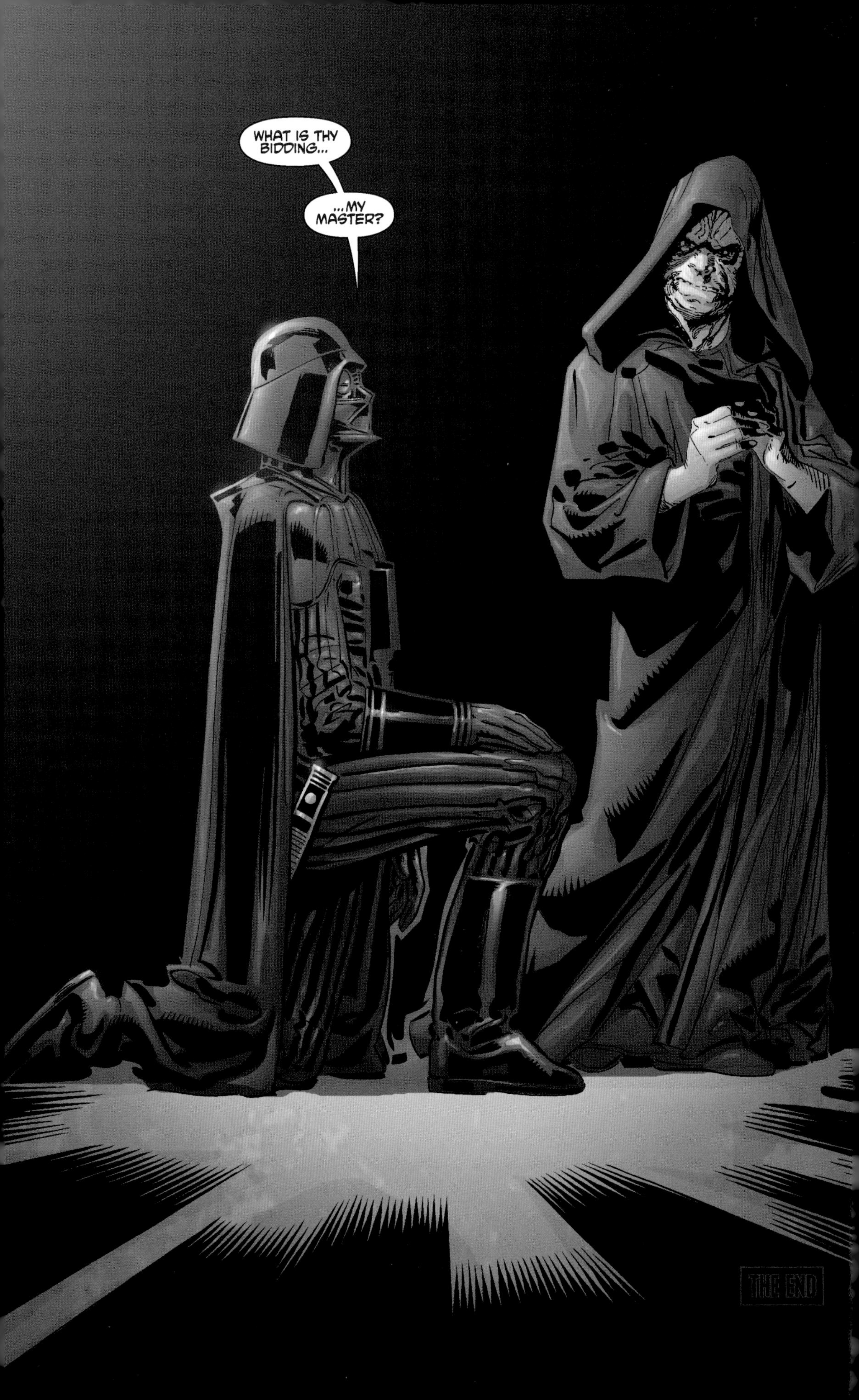
WHAT IS THY BIDDING...
...MY MASTER?
THE END